BELOW
THE
SURFACE

BOOK THREE OF THE GEOPOLITICAL TECHNO-THRILLER SERIES

ANDREW B. LOUIS

A terrorist group threatens world peace.
The Shadow Experts join forces with *Mossad* and the CIA.

For information regarding permission, please write to:
info@barringerpublishing.com
Barringer Publishing, Naples, Florida
www.barringerpublishing.com

Cover, graphics, and layout by Linda S. Duider
Cape Coral, Florida

ISBN: 978-1-954396-20-3
Library of Congress Cataloging-in-Publication Data
Below the Surface / Andrew B. Louis

Printed in U.S.A.

DEDICATION

To those friends and family members who have kept pushing me to write and helped me get better. They know who they are, and I thank them from the bottom of my heart.

OTHER BOOKS BY THE AUTHOR

Other novels by Andrew B. Louis include:

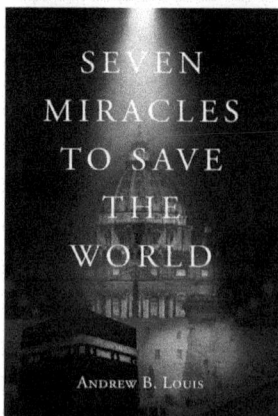

A Crooked Few, The Shadow Experts, Operation Kovesh
and *Seven Miracles To Save The World* available at
Amazon.com.

www.AndrewBLouis.com

ACKNOWLEDGMENTS

Though all the writing and errors are solely my own doing, a number of people contributed to the creation of the text. I would like to thank the numerous friends and family members who were kind enough to comment on various drafts and led me to make material changes for the better. A special mention is reserved for my wife who labored through so many versions that I am sure she has lost count.

SYNOPSIS

Mossad accidentally finds an unknown weapon, ostensibly placed by Palestinian terrorists. More troubling, upon inspection, the weapon bears Chinese markings and is equipped with two Iranian missiles. How did that happen? *Mossad*'s investigations imply that the origin of the weapon is a U.S. discovery dating back a couple of years, and which was principally intended for peaceful purposes, civil aviation for instance. *Mossad* was aware of the discovery, but both they and the U.S. authorities believed that it had been kept secret, precisely because they understood its potential military applications.

With the help of "The Shadow Experts," the group headed by Countess Renate, *Mossad* and the CIA uncover a plot that first took the discovery to China, through post-graduate students; then, China exploited it in its own weapon development. China used the discovery to gain influence in the Middle East, chiefly through Iran, which in turn used it to support regional terrorist organizations. *Mossad* and the CIA must neutralize the new weapon, shadowing the Palestinian ship which brings it from the Gulf of Aden to Southern Lebanon. In the process, *Mossad* uncovers an unexpected source of Palestinian financing.

The mission of the *Mossad* hero, Simon Rabinowitz, is made more complicated by internal political issues which eventually force him to make a very difficult choice. Will he be able to give his full attention to the secret weapon problem? Will the alliance between the CIA, *Mossad* and The Shadow Experts succeed in preventing a broader dispersion of the new weapon? Is there a way to counter it?

Preface: All the parties to this story are totally fictitious and if there was some resemblance to individuals or institutions, it would be purely coincidental.

PROLOGUE

TEL AVIV AND HAIFA, ISRAEL AND LANGLEY, USA

"Jack?"

"Simon? What an unexpected pleasure?"

Jack Turnbull had recognized the voice at the other end of the secure phone line. Jack was the Director of Operations within the CIA; his group was thus responsible for collecting foreign intelligence and for covert action. Speaking to him, Colonel Simon Rabinowitz worked for *Mossad,* reporting directly to the Head of the agency. Simon's group was responsible for the most secretive actions within the Israeli Secret Service. Internally, it was known as disruption, though it did not appear on any organization chart that anyone could procure. The group was in charge of activities which many would consider bordering on the illegal: assassination of foreign leaders, sabotage of certain installations of which Israel did not approve, internet warfare, and the like. But, for Israel, these were not luxury activities, they directly affected its survival ability.

Both Jack and Simon were the ultimate professionals. Both had had impressive careers which had been helped by total dedication, superior technical skills, and solid instincts. Both were happily married and viewed their careers as crucial, though, in a crisis, one's career might need to take second place to family, however briefly. Fortunately, neither had been tested on that front; at least not yet. Where they differed was that Jack was a keen sports fan, who followed his teams, all the way back to when he graduated from university. As such, he had his favorite college teams, both football and basketball, as well as his favorite professional teams, football, basketball, baseball, and ice hockey. He was in solid physical shape, but did not practice any sport with any assiduity, other than the occasional round of golf. Simon, on the other hand, was not a keen sports fan, but he was dedicated to martial arts and tennis. Martial arts were a part of his training, but also his way of keeping his mind in "the right place" as he said. Tennis was another way of getting physical exercise and he was not happier than when he could play a game with Jennifer, his wife, who was just about his equal and always gave him a tough match.

Simon knew that, with Jack, he needed to dive directly into the topic. He described a puzzling set of recent events:

"Hold your rejoicing my friend. You won't believe what we just stumbled upon."

"Pray, tell."

"Bottom line: Hezbollah seems to have access to a new underwater drone which uses a top-secret communication technology developed in Boston a few years ago. And that drone is equipped with a couple of Iranian missiles."

Jack took in a deep breath and with a voice betraying first incredulity and then serious alarm:

"Just a minute! Seriously? What the hell are you talking about Simon?"

Though Jack was generally aware of the various programs which the U.S. government was developing, he had not been briefed on what Simon was talking about. He did not know of any top-secret communication technology developed in Boston, though he was not surprised to hear of it. Boston, with the Massachusetts Institute of Technology in the lead, was certainly one of the two main poles of technological innovation in the country, with Silicon Valley being the, better known, other. He asked:

"What communication technology is that Simon?"

Simon went into further detail, as there had been a relationship between the Boston scientists and Israel. *Mossad*, in particular, had found out about the technology, through a combination of overt and covert sources, and contacted the team directly. They offered some funding in exchange for being able to exploit the technology when it was ready for prime time.

Simon explained to Jack that scientists at Boston Advanced Communication Laboratories (BACL for short) developed a system called translational acoustic-RF communication (TARF for short) which allows underwater sources to communicate with receptors above the water. Hitherto, direct radio communications between underwater and airborne devices had been a major challenge. Underwater sensors cannot share data with those on land and vice versa. Both use different wireless signals that only work in their respective environments. Radio signals that travel through the air die very rapidly in water. At the same time, acoustic signals, or sonar, sent by underwater devices mostly reflect off the surface of the water without ever breaking through and getting in the air. The system which BACL developed, and which was then still in its infancy but had been substantially enhanced since the earliest development, took care of the problem. It used microscopic waves at the surface of the water to permit data transmission.

The technology had crucial uses, both peaceful and military. Locating commercial aircraft black boxes or allowing underwater exploration drones to transmit data to the surface would be two obvious peaceful ones. From a military standpoint, allowing direct communications between submarines and aircraft would clearly be a vital benefit to the submarines that would not have to surface and reveal their location to transmit data. The use which concerned Jack and Simon at this point was the ability to control underwater drones from above the water, as opposed to via sonar from boats or submarines located sufficiently close-by.

Jack whistled his admiration and asked:

"So, what did you really find Simon?"

"Well, brace yourself. We just found an underwater drone, complete with a discreet underwater radio transmitter tethered electronically to the drone. The drone and the transmitters had Chinese markings on them. Even more worrisome, the drone carried two missiles, with Iranian markings . . ."

"Hold it. Can't believe it. China and Iran in the loop?

"Guess so."

"Where did you find it?"

"Assume you mean the drone and missiles; about twenty miles off the coast of Haifa."

■ ■ ■ ■ ■

A week earlier, an Israel patrol ship from the Haifa naval base had noticed a Lebanese-flagged vessel, the *Sea Crescent*, sailing from the south toward Tyre, Lebanon, to the northeast. The ship was beyond Israeli territorial waters (12 nautical miles from shore), but well within its economic exclusion zone (two hundred nautical miles from shore). The Israeli navy is well aware that arms are supplied to terrorists in Lebanon via both land and sea. Yet, it typically will only intercept ships within twenty-four miles from shore (which represents both territorial waters and the so-called contiguous zone) when Israel has some specific early intelligence or when the ships are large enough to warrant attention. Though it would be helpful to catch more of that coastal arms smuggling activity, Israel's navy capabilities would be swamped if they did not pick their targets carefully. However, occasionally and to keep the terrorists on their toes, Israel would launch a massive "catch, inspect and release" operation that involved intercepting for a day or a short week all or at least most possible terrorist ships.

In this case, they did not have specific intelligence and did not view the ship as large enough to matter. Yet, following his intuition and since there was no more urgent priority, the captain had decided to shadow the ship from a distance and set his various detection systems onto maximum precision. Maybe, he would find out something important.

He did not have to wait very long. Shortly before coming abeam Haifa, still about twenty miles from shore, the *Sea Crescent* slowed down and then crawled to a halt. From the Israeli ship, Captain Ehud Lachlan could not see the full action—it was occurring on the port side (the left side of the ship looking forward) of the ship, while the Israeli ship was on her starboard side (the right side of the ship looking forward). Yet, anticipating the potential problem when he had decided to shadow the ship discreetly, Captain Lachlan had immediately ordered an Eitan drone that always patrolled the area some forty-thousand feet up in the sky to focus on the *Sea Crescent*. Loaded with extremely powerful sensing and photographic equipment, and given the exact location provided by Captain Lachlan, the operators of the Eitan had no difficulty finding the *Sea Crescent*. Once they had her in their visors, they filmed everything she was doing, using two cameras which allowed them to see what was happening on the ship and in the sea off her port side.

The first thing the drone picked up was a crane lifting something which looked like a small submarine out of the hold below deck. The Eitan also saw a sailor bring with him an elongated box, probably no more than three cubic feet, if that, which he ostensibly brought from inside the main bridge. The first operator who looked at the film thought:

Must be important to be stored separately from the rest.

Then, after a few manipulations which they could see but not understand, the cameras saw the crane rotate so that the submarine was over the water. It was carefully dropped it into the sea. That done, the crane picked up the elongated box which the sailor had brought, swung over the sea again and delicately positioned it in the water. It seemed to be floating there for a short while and then the Eitan lost sight of it.

Once the drop was made, the *Sea Crescent* resumed its course while, a few minutes later, a helicopter arrived and briefly hovered in the same general area. The pictures of the helicopter confirmed that it was of Lebanese origin, but no one could make any sense of what it had been doing. He did not stay in the area longer than a couple of minutes. Interestingly, analysts noticed a cone hanging from the helicopter being lowered closer to the surface of the water when it arrived on the scene and raised back up when it left.

A ship-to-shore communication was quickly set up and it bubbled up in no time to the office of Simon Rabinowitz. If anything was going to be done, it would have to be a covert operation, thus clearly a part of Simon's world. Simon, who had been aware of the TARF developments, felt right away that there could be a connection, however improbable it would have seemed. He ordered a covert operation to try and retrieve the underwater drone together with whatever other material was with it.

■ ■ ■ ■ ■

It took a couple of days before the deep-sea rescue operation could be organized, in large measure because Israel only had one deep-sea rescue vehicle, thankfully based in Haifa. In order for the operation to be carried out in total secrecy, the vehicle was tethered to a submarine while at the base, in Haifa, and the two were then sent to the general area where Captain Lachlan had seen the "drop." The whole operation would thus be carried out under water, and could not be seen from above, even with the most sophisticated equipment, which Simon, by the way, suspected strongly that Hezbollah did not have. Further, the work was carried out at night, as light hardly matters once one is beyond the first few hundred feet underwater.

The rescue vessel, with full underwater lights on, eventually was able to locate the submarine drone. It sent a signal to the submarine, which went to look for the box which the pictures had shown being lowered into the sea. Predictably, it was harder to locate; it was quite small in a vast sea and was floating underwater but at an unknown depth. Yet, using sophisticated equipment and some not inconsiderable luck, they were able to find it, three feet below the surface. The waters were quite clear and calm at that time. Once the box was located, the submarine started hovering under it and sent a couple of divers to retrieve it. They exited the submarine through the airlock and brought the box back in less than ten minutes. One of the divers was filming the operation so that, should something happen, for instance a motion-triggered explosion, the next mission would know what to expect.

The box was in fact a radio transmitter that floated just below sea level. It was just a bit more than two and a half cubic feet in volume. The top section was about one cubic foot square, and it was about two and a half feet tall. Four compressed air storage units were located at the four corners of the contraption, while its bottom half also seemed designed to contain air. The team eventually theorized that the compressed air mini cylinders were meant to release air into the main compartment, to control the depth at which the transmitter floated, though at the time nobody really knew what the point of any part of the transmitter it was.

Meanwhile, the rescue vehicle recovered the underwater drone that was about twenty feet in length and was lying on the ocean floor about 2,500 feet down. The rescue vessel was secured to the submarine anew and both vessels returned to port in Haifa, running at a sufficient depth that they could not be picked up from overhead. Once at the naval base, they went straight to a covered dock where the submarine surfaced, together with the rescue vessel and the drone it had captured.

CHAPTER.01

TEL AVIV, ISRAEL AND LANGLEY, USA

Still on the phone with Jack, Simon deadpanned:

"Well, I don't know about you, Jack, but I get the feeling that your wish to meet Countess Renate is about to be fulfilled."

■ ■ ■ ■ ■

Princess Alexandra was no ordinary member of the old European aristocracy. After she inherited her parents' financial fortune following their untimely accidental death, she lived a variant on the classical life of a rich aristocrat, but that was only a cover.

Below the surface, Princess Alexandra, a.k.a. Countess Renate, was the head of a global network, which she called The Shadow Experts. That network was as secret as its leader. It consisted of specialists across a wide variety of disciplines who cooperated with and were directed by Countess Renate to defend "good causes." They ranged from micro-biologists to advanced material engineers, to art experts, to cyber engineers, to electronics experts and to many other specialties, each as esoteric as the others. All members knew they were members of the network, but most did not know who the others were. They all knew Renate; most, if not all, had seen her in person or on some video conference call. Yet, no one could claim that he or she had met with her regularly. First, the specialists were all "part time associates" who came into a team to solve a problem and returned to the shadows when they were not needed. Further, Renate had no board of directors. Her only employees were a handful of individuals who worked for her at the Castle, her residence in the Austrian alps. They were the only ones who knew of her twin identities, except for her husband, Prince Karl, who also morphed into Captain Frederik, her pilot and all-around aide when she became Countess Renate.

Whenever a "problem" was brought to her attention, usually through a contact she had helped earlier, she recruited a team among her members according to the disciplines and specific areas of knowledge she would need for that "project."

■ ■ ■ ■ ■

Jack was surprised that Simon knew of his desire to meet Countess Renate. He asked:

"What do you mean? How do you know?"

"You don't remember? In one of our last conversations, you had told me you wished you could meet her?"

"So, that's where this comes from. Now, I do remember . . . The bomb and virus thing, right?"

"Yep!"

"But why now?"

"Don't you think that she could be of great help here?"

"Why can't we take care of that ourselves?"

"Well, it's not intuitively obvious nor simple. Let me explain . . ."

Simon proceeded to argue that he saw the problem they jointly faced as having several dimensions, a few of which were not easy to handle "officially":

"Sure, there are bits that fall straight down our alley Jack. Think of understanding the various relationships between China, Iran and

Hezbollah, to name the three main suspects. That's got to be within the purview of our respective agencies."

"That's pretty clear to me too, my friend."

"Check. But, on the other hand, I'm not sure how we can handle things like how the information about the technology leaked out of Boston."

"Not sure why you'd say that Simon. That's classic CIA work, isn't?"

"In a sense, yes. But look at it from a different angle. We have virtually no hard facts. The only thing we know is that there is an underwater drone, an undersea transmitter and a couple of Iranian missiles. We think we understand how the drone and the transmitter work together. Yet, we can't disclose any of this to anyone if we want to be able to learn more. Say one word about having found the drone and all parties will go on mute: that's good to eliminate the immediate danger, but it leaves all of us open to future problems."

He paused and added:

"In fact, come to think of it, we don't really know how much of the danger is eliminated. Is this the only such contraption they've installed or are there others and, if yes, how many and where?"

"Can see that. And you're right. Add to that the fact that U.S. courts will not allow us to conduct the surveillance we need without some serious proof; they call it "probable cause." And whatever that proof would be . . . that's something we won't want to disclose and thus cannot produce."

"See?"

"Yep. Add to that the current environment."

"What do you mean?"

"Well, the burden of providing some probable cause is always challenging but it remains a needed safeguard. The risk of a leak has always existed, but we used to be able to manage that. But, in the current climate in Washington, it is even more true. Now, more things leak than are kept secret. So sad that people have lost a sense of loyalty to the home country and of the National Interest whatever it is."

"Couldn't have said it better myself. It makes me think of something which Ariel once said to me:

"I want you all to be adventurous, but I do not want to hear about any arrogance. Arrogance is like a line in the sand. I'm not sure where it is, but don't ever cross it . . ."

■ ■ ■ ■ ■

Simon was referring to General Ariel Landau, the almost legendary head of *Mossad*. He was in his mid- to late fifties and relatively short in stature. His hairline had receded virtually all the way, leaving but a small crown of black and grey hair arranged in a semi-circle, going from one ear to the other around the back of his head. He wore black-rimmed, round glasses. He almost always dressed in civilian clothing, though with style, despite the fact that many Israeli officials tend to dump their ties in the summer because of the heat. People said that he had one of the most piercing minds and was noticed almost immediately by his superiors in whatever capacity he was employed. He had an informal nickname within the Cabinet: "Steel Trap." This referred to his mind being like a steel trap—nothing escaped.

■ ■ ■ ■ ■

Simon had one more thought on the challenges any official investigation might face:

"One more thing, Jack. How do we get to understand the roles played by the various parties? We suspect that China and Iran play a role, but we're not sure whether it's official and undercover or rogue. I've got my own views with respect to Iran, but I am a lot less sure when it comes to China."

"Makes two of us."

"Good, then there's the link to Hezbollah. But, what if it's not limited to them? What if Fatah or even Hamas are also involved? We all have views of the Hezbollah-Iran link, but who really knows the full scope?"

He continued without giving Jack the time to reply. Summarizing his point, he argued that someone needed to figure out how such sensitive information had made it from the U.S. to China. Yet, he was not sure either of them would find anything valuable if they proceeded via official channels, adding:

"Would you disagree?"

"Well, you know, Simon, just between you and me and the lamppost . . . As I said earlier, I'm no longer even sure that my colleagues here know how to keep anything secret."

"You must be exaggerating, my friend."

"Maybe some, but only up to a point. In fact, and off the record, I have created a special confidential category, a list of the people I really trust. I call it 'do not share with anyone except the people on the special list.' It's a very short list of people I have known for a long while. The list has four names on it . . ."

"I think I ought to thank you as I seem to be one of them . . ."

"You are. But, in Washington, particularly in the junior ranks or within the political appointees, there are very few people I really trust."

"Sad. Really sad. I have plenty of petty complaints about some of the politics here in Israel. Yet, I have complete trust in Ariel, and that is obvious. But, also, I truly trust most of my peers and direct reports, and I know that Ariel trusts the PM."

Jack could sadly only reply:

"I wish I could say the same. But, I guess, people in your country still believe that *Mossad* is a key element of survival. Here, I don't know if people see the CIA as friends or enemies And to be totally honest, both the CIA and the FBI have at times abused their authority;

so, we're paying for that in a way. But, in the end, I'm afraid that diplomacy and security are two of those areas where not all things should be said, certainly not in public."

They paused and Simon brought the conversation back to the topic that had started it:

"Back to Countess Renate. Should I contact her, or do you want to do it?"

Jack thought for a short period while and replied:

"Let me first make sure I understand: So, you feel that her group should be doing the digging on anything involving the technology and how it may have gone from Boston to other places. And you feel that way because you don't believe the CIA can do that. Correct?"

"Correct. And, by the way, I would add *Mossad* alongside the CIA. Also, I think that she can find ways to dig into things which are not accessible to us. I remember another case where she was able to get some information through a businessman in China, which I had not been able to find out through the regular channels."

"Then, I can't say I disagree with any of it. So, we agree we need to contact her. Now, should it be you or me?"

Jack paused for a couple of seconds in his short monologue and concluded:

"I think you should. So far, you have the evidence, and you were the ones who found it. Further, you know her, and she knows you. I'm sure you have a capital of trust that I wouldn't have. Let's regroup after you talk to her."

Simon nodded and simply said:

"Deal."

CHAPTER.02

TEL AVIV AND HAIFA NAVAL BASE, ISRAEL, TYRE, LEBANON, AND THE AUSTRIAN ALPS

"Countess Renate?"

"Simon. Surely did not expect a call from you. How are you, my friend? Anything interesting?"

"Well, I'd say it's beyond interesting. It's exciting and we might even be speaking of another assignment, my dear Countess, if you will take it."

"For the Shadow Experts?"

"Affirmative. We have just come across something quite odd and with possibly very serious geopolitical implications."

"Can you say anything now?"

"Well, a short summary. How about some top-secret U.S.-developed communication technology with associated hardware which appears on the sea floor not far from Haifa with Chinese and Iranian markings on it and probably under the control of Hezbollah? How's that for an appetizer?"

"A whole meal you mean . . . Can hardly wait for more detail. What the next step?"

"Let me even add that the contraption, whatever it is, has two missiles, with clear Iranian markings."

"Indeed. Urgency?"

"Very, because we don't know whether what we found is the first or the last in a series of drops in the sea around Israel. So, I'd like to organize a conference call with you and Jack Turnbull, from the CIA. Remember him?"

"Sure do. Didn't he help in the case of the bomb and virus combination?"

"Absolutely. Great memory."

"Tell me. He's involved in the thing you were just discussing?"

"Got to be. He's CIA. The technology is American."

"Understood. No problem then. You set up a zoom in the next few minutes?"

"Will do?"

Less than ten minutes later, the three of them were introducing one another and discussing the outline of what their work together was going to entail.

■ ■ ■ ■ ■

Upon hearing of the retrieval of the drone and the related communication device, Simon had immediately instructed *Mossad* agents, "in a word," to "place a tail on the boat that dropped the submarine, the missiles and the transmitter offshore Haifa." The Eitan drone which had filmed the drop-off kept a close watch on the so-called fishing boat, which they actually thought looked more like a supply boat with a small crane.

The Eitan—which means "steadfast" in Hebrew—is a mid-altitude, long endurance, drone aircraft, which can operate at altitudes above commercial air traffic. It is a high-wing monoplane with a pusher propeller at the aft tip of the fuselage, but ahead of the rear stabilizer. It carries a wide array of electronic equipment and its main mission revolves around intelligence, surveillance and target acquisition. It can stay aloft for an extended period of time and has a range which extends as far as four thousand six hundred miles

Both drone and patrol boat followed the *Sea Crescent* all the way to Tyre, Lebanon, one of the oldest, continually inhabited cities in the world. It is known to be under Hezbollah control, with, in fact, a majority of the population supporting the terrorist group. This is not true of the whole of Lebanon where a small half of the population is of Christian descent and would likely prefer a more center of the road approach to regional relations. Tyre originally had two harbors, but now used only one. The one to the South had silted over and was no longer operational, except for very small craft. The one to the North still operates and is used mainly by fishing boats.

Flotilla 13 – Shayetet 13 – the naval commando unit, equivalent to the US Navy SEALs or British Special Boat Service, was charged with approaching the harbor in a three-man submarine. Principally made of carbon composite fibers, the submarine was typically able to evade detection except in circumstances where the enemy had been specifically warned and all detection devices trained on it. Two of the men exited from the submarine through its airlock and swam under water until they approached the boat which had dropped the drone, and which was now docked. The exact coordinates of the boat had been entered on a watch-like device which they wore on their arms. It started vibrating when they were next to it, allowing them to work on the boat without having to surface to check its name. Truth be known, they could have surfaced any time they wanted as the boat, surprisingly, was not on any sort of special protection or heavy guard. As it was daylight, the divers were very careful not to be seen and therefore swam very close to and below the target boat.

Their jobs were to place four sensors. Two of them, were to be placed on either side of the bow section of the boat, below the waterline so that they would not be seen; these needed to be affixed quite strongly as the bow of the boat is one of the highest-pressure areas on a ship. The main concern was to minimize the risk that the sensors might be peeled off as the boat sailed.

Though the bow-sensors were below the water line and thus hard to see when the boat was docked or moving at a low wake speed, they would emerge from the water as the boat picked up speed. Indeed, as a boat's speed increases, first the bow and then the whole boat rise as she reaches the point where she is "on plane." This attitude shift would allow the bow-sensors to emerge above the water surface and thus to be able to send radio signals which Israeli installations could pick up. These sensors were quite small and Shayetet 13 expected that they might go undetected for quite some time. The men carefully scratched the surface of the bow that was made of metal; they wanted to clean off as much of the paint as possible to ensure the best possible adherence. At the same time, they could not allow themselves to be too noisy and thus be detected by anyone who had remained on board. They used a two-part formula marine epoxy which is a sort of permanent, waterproof adhesive which can be applied and will cure underwater. Looking at the sensors from a few feet away, the divers mentally congratulated their colleagues who had painted the sensors the same color as the boat—they were black. This really made them hard to locate, even if one knew where they were.

They placed the two other sensors deeper underwater near the bottom of the boat, on either side of the quill. These did not communicate by radio, but emitted sonar signals which Israel expected to be able to pick up through underwater equipment, such as submarines or submerged buoys. With these sensors, Israel would now be able to follow the boat along its various trips.

■ ■ ■ ■ ■

Jack, Simon and Countess Renate travelled by helicopter from Palmachim Airforce Base where her jet had just landed to the Israeli Navy Base at Haifa. Having flown in from Washington overnight,

Jack Turnbull was with Simon when Countess Renate arrived. They had agreed that they should go and inspect together the drone and the radio transmitting equipment which had been fished out of the sea with it. Simon had invited Marvin Goldstein, a veteran of the service, to join them; he would help with all the technical details. Marvin had an encyclopedic knowledge of the capabilities of each of the branches of the Israeli Defense Forces and of all that was planned. He had a well-documented weakness for technobabble, which people tolerated simply because he was Marvin. You could not do without him, and he did not come without his technobabble. In the present circumstances, his love for technology and innovation would be crucial as he knew as much as anyone in *Mossad* about all the work which had been carried out in the U.S. and, in the more recent past, in Israel on TARF, the communication breakthrough.

"Countess Renate and Jack, please meet Marvin Goldstein. There is very little in the field of modern technology that he does not know about."

"Simon, you're flattering me. However, Countess and Jack, I will confess that I have had a particular interest in this new technology. It could really make a big difference in many ways. We all know of the peaceful applications that are discussed, but I can think of many intelligence tools that we could develop based on it."

As they spoke, they entered the hangar that had been dedicated to their effort on the naval base. Quiet and discretion were assured. That would allow a detailed inspection of the drone and related equipment, with minimal if any risk of leaks. It was right at the back of the covered dock where Israeli submarines would be mooring when the work that was being done on them was supposed to be secret. The harbor was deep enough that they could approach fully submerged and enter the dock still underwater. They would only surface when the giant doors at the front of the hangar had been closed.

The submarine drone itself did not look particularly special, certainly at least from the outside. It was an elongated, cylindrical, blue-greenish tube, with a partially flattened bow. Most of the space in the aft back portion comprised the propulsion mechanism: water jets, with horizontal stabilizers and a vertical rudder. The flattened bow housed the two missile launchers. Those launchers were articulated and could be raised at a nearly vertical angle before a missile was fired. On the drone, above the middle of the tube, where a submarine tower would be, there was an oval-section box which had already been disassembled, though its shell remained intact. It contained a complex guidance and communication mechanism. Marvin jumped in at that point:

"I do not know how much you all know of the TARF communication technology, but you need to understand it to appreciate what this drone can do and why we are concerned about it."

"Marvin, is there a short version of that explanation?"

Marvin smiled. He very well understood that Simon was aware of his tendency to expand too much on details that, though potentially interesting to an engineer, were only of parenthetical interest to people like Simon, and, in this instance, Countess Renate or Jack Turnbull. He replied:

"Sure, Simon. In a word, the system creates mini waves meant to represent either a "1" or a "0" (the digital codes) on the surface of the sea. These waves can then be "read" and decoded by a radar above the water."

"Could it be the role of the cone lowered from the helicopter after the Lebanese boat had placed the submarine in the water?"

"Most likely. At this point, and until someone proves to me otherwise, I am pretty sure it is, Simon. At the same time, honestly, who knows, really? We'd need to see the cone and, but I know that's asking too much, to get our hands on it to be sure."

"Can't disagree with you here. Did you see the Eitan pictures?"

"I did and, as I said, it sure looks like it could well be the interface.

My guess is that the helicopter used it both to read the signals sent by the transmitter and to emit its own instructions to the transmitter which would then communicate them to the drone."

"Thanks, very helpful, Marvin."

"You're welcome, Simon. Now, back to my short history of the system. The first version could only operate in very calm water with a swell of less than a foot, in fact less than half a foot. The system had to understand and distinguish between the waves created by the swell and those created by the transmitter . . ."

Countess Renate interrupted:

"Can see why this should be tricky. What's the solution?"

"Well, Countess, this newer version improved upon the original. It creates a field of vibrations on the surface which can follow the swell. Then, the wavelets representing the "1s" and "0s" are superimposed on that field. The thing that is quite surprising is that we did not believe that anyone outside of the Americans and ourselves knew about these latest wrinkles . . ."

Marvin chuckled and added:

"Wrinkles. . . . No pun intended."

Jack returned to the business issue, ignoring the pun:

"How did Israel know about that?"

"Well, we studied the original published papers and put a team to work on the issue. We were helped when we were able to intercept a message from two of the partners of BACL. We got our hands on their attachment, which send us directly to the solution."

"Is that legal?"

Marvin cleared his throat and said:

"Well, you know that legality is a moving feat within the espionage community. Yet, what I can say is that Israel understands quite well the distinction between espionage, which we need to protect our state, and business. So, we would never have sought a patent on the invention. We knew who should have it. . . . The original inventors.

We were just taking a relatively free ride, though they quickly knew where we were, and we started sharing our findings. Even gave them some development money on the quiet."

Simon came into the conversation to make the point that the key issue was not in the legality of the maneuver. Israel and the U.S. should always be on the same side. The key here was that there had been a leak that was picked up and used to build a prototype. Jack Turnbull could not resist offering his view:

"Add that the system is not really fully operational yet. I'm told they need to improve on the surface vibration field to allow the communication to work in virtually all conditions. Question: what are the chances that the Chinese, if they're the ones behind this, picked the information up the same way you guys did?"

Simon asked:

"You mean from the intercepts of internal transmissions that Marvin discussed?"

Jack nodded his agreement. Simon opined:

"Everything is possible, but in our view it's unlikely."

Marvin did not leave Jack the time to ask why Simon had reached this conclusion. He interjected:

"Simon, I would add remotely possible. Unless the Chinese were working on the topic, and I'm pretty sure we would have found out in other ways, I can't imagine how they would go from the first cut to this version. Somebody somewhere must have helped them dot the 'Is' and cross the 'Ts.'"

"Thank you, Marvin."

Returning to Jack's initial point, Simon added:

"You're totally correct, Jack. We must find out more. When you boil it down, at this point, we know virtually nothing. The only indication we have is in the form of the markings on the drone. These clearly are Chinese characters. So, we have to assume that, somehow, the secrets or at least a number of them have made it to China."

Jack could not stop himself and added with a clear, cynical tone to his voice:

"Terrific."

Simon interrupted:

"Before we go too far, let me add that someone could have placed fake Chinese markings to implicate China, even if they had nothing to do with it."

He paused to let the others absorb his latest point and added:

"This is something where Countess Renate and her Shadow Experts can play a major role, as we discussed earlier on the phone. You have a contact within Boston Advanced Communication Laboratories, don't you Countess?"

"Simon, my friend, you know that I would not reveal anything like this."

"Sorry, Countess, I should know better."

Countess Renate continued:

"Let me simply say that I am sure I can find a way of getting inside information there. But I am not telling you that we have an associate, as you know we call the members of our network, who is an employee . . ."

Turning to Marvin in mid-sentence, she asked:

"Marvin, can you please tell us more about the other piece of equipment, the dark blue one, there?"

"I was getting there, Countess. It is indeed a crucial part of the whole set up. Think of it as an electronically tethered buoy."

Marvin could not help himself. He had to explain the past as well as the present. He therefore added:

"In the past, engineers have tried to address the communication difficulties between submarines and above sea receivers through floating buoys. The submarine would send sonar signals to the buoy, and the buoy would convert them and broadcast them as classical radio signals. The challenge always was that these buoys tended to drift with currents, as they floated and were not attached to the sea floor."

"I see. How did the guys in Boston solve that?"

"Well, Countess, they made the buoys capable of movement, with very small water jets. So, the buoy is in sonar contact with the submarine or the underseas emitter and it keeps adjusting its position relative to where the emitter is located. We assume that they save on energy consumption by maintaining a loose relative position rather than an absolutely fixed one. Actually, one thing that we have not checked yet is whether there is any retractable solar antenna on the system. That could easily solve for them the issue of energy consumption."

He paused and then could not resist adding:

"And if they have not, we could very easily engineer that into our own version of the transmitters."

Thinking aloud and captivated by his own technobabble, he suggested:

"I'm sure we can dispense with one of the four compressed air cylinders and locate a solar antenna at that corner . . ."

Simon interrupted:

"Quite smart, Marvin, quite smart. But I don't think that now is the time to discuss this."`

A bit chagrinned, Marvin returned to the explanation he was providing Countess Renate when he veered off into his dream world:

"Now, this buoy which you see there additionally does not float on the surface where it could be seen. It is normally a few feet below the surface. Actually, it sits low enough that there is considerably less water movement there. In fact, at depths greater than half the wavelength, which is the distance between two adjacent wave crests, the water motion is less than four percent of its value at the water surface."

"But then, Marvin, how does it communicate with the outside?"

"Well, Simon, that's the ingenious trick. The buoy is always able to receive a signal from both underwater and above water. The first line of the signal simply tells it to rise closer to the surface and the last line of the transmission sends it back to its resting place. They do that by varying the amount of air in an air pocket that sits below the rest of the equipment. The signal is broadcast louder and with a lot less complexity. Even if there are interferences, it is simple enough for the buoy to understand."

"Interesting, Marvin. But then how is the communication transmitted?"

"Simple, Jack. The system is "warned" by a radar receiver nearby that some transmission is about to take place, ingoing as well as outgoing."

Marvin continued:

"As we said earlier, we assume that the helicopter came in to guide the drone down to its resting position. The helicopter must have broadcast whatever signal was necessary to get the drone to dive and take up position. You can see a digital camera at the front end of the submarine tube, here, between the two launchers and just below the light projector" he added as it was pointing to the equipment. He went on:

"So, we assume that the submarine drone was broadcasting pictures of where it was so that the operators above would not bring it too hard down onto rocks. And all that was taking place with the transmitter serving as a sort of interpreter—receiving sonar signals from the drone and broadcasting radio signals to the helicopter via its cone."

Simon thanked Marvin and offered a final comment:

"We have to believe that some other aircraft, maybe a helicopter, maybe something else, even possibly a flying drone would come back near enough the site to give firing instructions when the operators wanted to launch their missile or missiles. They could do that under the cover of darkness, and it would be very hard to pick it up."

He added:

"Now, for us, it is not the end of the world, because our Iron Dome would have ample time to intercept the incoming missile."

■ ■ ■ ■ ■

Simon was referring to Israel's all-weather, air defense system, which was designed, with the help of the U.S., to protect the country against incoming rockets or artillery shells. It had proven its worth in recent times, when it managed to intercept a large number of rockets fired from Gaza or even from Lebanon. Unfortunately, though it might arguably be the world's most advanced missile defense system, it had only been ninety percent accurate.

■ ■ ■ ■ ■

Simon continued his explanation:

"Yet, we have to fear at least a couple of possible developments. First, imagine what would happen if instead of having a couple of missiles fired at us, we had many more. Remember, we intercept about ninety percent of all missiles. We would not want to have one get through. Second, and still worse, imagine that the missile is tipped with some nuclear contraption, even if it is only a dirty bomb."

Countess Renate asked Simon to summarize for her benefit. Her particular interest was to understand who did what to whom. How much of the material they found on the sea floor was engineered in China, how much came from Boston. She added:

"Same questions with respect to the transmitter. I think we can safely assume that the Chinese manufactured the missile launchers and Iran the missiles."

"Quite probable, Countess, though, as I said earlier, I would not immediately assume that China is in the loop. For all I know, Iran could be doing it and using Chinese markings to retain some measure of plausible deniability."

"How do we get some determination on that?"

"Let me suggest that, at this point, we don't, though we keep trying. So, we continue to assume it is China, but we still keep an open mind should we develop better information."

"OK, Simon. Makes sense. So, continue."

"In fact, the Boston group had nothing to do with the submarine drone. We've agreed to assume it is entirely a Chinese contraption. But, for all we know, it could have been made elsewhere. The technology is pretty basic. Moving a submarine up or down, forward or backward is not rocket science, whether the submarine is manned or a drone."

Simon paused for effect and then continued:

"The only part of the drone which comes from Boston, literally, is the communication equipment in the cavity at the place of the submarine tower. Somehow, whoever made this was able to connect the motion technology they already had with the new transmission technology."

"That's great. Thanks, Simon. Now, what about the transmitter?"

"This one was ostensibly manufactured somewhere other than Boston. But the blueprints came from Boston and all its technology, including its electronic tethering, is part of the contract which BACL has with the Pentagon. . . . Correct, Jack?"

"Absolutely, Simon. And that's the real worry. The use of these transmitters, tethered to some specific position markers, was supposed to remain secret. I'm pretty sure that our friends at the Pentagon will not be delighted if they ever find out. And, by the way, eventually, they will have to know."

"Totally agree, Jack, but let's make sure that they find out as far into our research as possible; we don't need any panic. And you know there will be panic then, particularly if it leaks out to the press, which it most likely would."

CHAPTER.03

A group of scientists was meeting in the offices of Charles Parker, a well-known venture capitalist on the Boston financial scene. In fact, Charles specialized in the earliest stage of the financing of new enterprises, usually known as "angel financing." Angels typically came into very new ventures that had too little information that they could share with classical venture capital financiers to get access to the funds they needed to keep their activity going. Angels usually come immediately after "friends and family," and frequently at the same time.

■ ■ ■ ■ ■

Frank Lord, Xi Shi Tsu and Michael Lennon had met a few years earlier. The three of them were from the Massachusetts Institute of Technology, where Dr. Frank Lord was a co-chair of the fluid mechanics department with Dr. Xi. Michael Lennon was also a tenured professor, though, having earned his tenure recently. After receiving his PhD in Singapore, he first taught at National University of Singapore, as an assistant professor. He then returned to Australia, the country of his birth; he taught and conducted research at The

University of Notre Dame, Australia, initially in Broome and then at the main campus in Fremantle, his hometown.

The three scientists were recently joined by Ng Ho Lim, a PhD from Tsinghua University, recognized by many as the best engineering school in China. Ho Lim had arrived at MIT on the strong recommendation of Adrian Lee Yeo Min, PhD, who had served as research assistant to the three professors. He had just returned to Tsinghua, in the northwest of Beijing, Haidian Qu. Before leaving, he had thought that Ho Lim's recent work at Tsinghua would be very useful. Ho Lim had indeed been working on fluid mechanics, a discipline which combines the study of fluids in a static state—fluid statics—as well as when in movement: fluid kinematics and fluid dynamics.

All four were attracted by the challenge associated with enabling communication across the air-water barrier. The first three had formulated a theory that used what was seen as the major challenge, the water surface layer, as the element of the solution. The idea was to transform sonar signals into micro-waves on the surface of the water; waves which could then be read by a radar and broadcasted through regular radio channels. There were numerous issues that still needed addressing before any prototype could be constructed. Yet, they kept pushing themselves to overcome all the various challenges. The three professors were fascinated by the theoretical challenge and the potential for substantial financial rewards, though it would be fair to say that Xi Shi Tsu was probably less focused on financial gains and more on public scientific recognition. Their research confrere, Ng Ho Lim, had been attracted by the opportunity to collaborate with a team which had proposed the first theoretical solution to the problem. While the group had kept all the detail of their works to themselves, a few of their ideas had been expressed in papers. Ho Lim was fascinated when Yeo Min had shared them with him.

A year later, their joint efforts, undertaken under the umbrella of

MIT, were clearly starting to bear fruit. They decided to take their work with them to create a company to exploit its financial potential. They agreed right away that some equity in that new company would have to be given to MIT. The university was not particularly keen on letting them go or on providing them additional finance. Yet, there came a point where the scientist trio had more trump cards in their hand. A neutral observer would conclude that the leadership of the university could see the potential implications of the idea to the Pentagon, a substantial source of funds for the university as a whole, while the researchers were chiefly interested, on the surface at least, with commercial applications. Similarly, one could speculate that MIT's leadership saw in their discovery the potential for a Nobel Prize which, though it would be awarded to the team and not to the university, would surely bring a share of its glory to MIT.

In the end, the trio reached an unwritten agreement with the university. The worldwide patent which they secured on the results of their work so far would be the joint property of the three professors and MIT. MIT would then contribute their share of patent ownership, as would the professors, as the base intellectual property of a new company, for which MIT would receive twenty five percent of the company. The balance of the ownership of the company they created would be shared among the three professors with a small allocation reserved for Ho Lim. Additionally, MIT agreed to keep each of the three professors in their day job, with full pay, even though they would only teach one class per semester. They would also be able to continue to use the MIT lab for experiments.

The trio had kept aside ten percent of the company as unallocated capital, which they intended to use to attract some outside financing. This brought the three professors and their research associate to the offices of Charles Parker. Would he agree to provide some angel financing?

■ ■ ■ ■ ■

"So gentlemen, let's recapitulate where we are. You feel you need at least $5 million to operate and get to the prototype stage of your idea. Is that correct?"

Frank Lord, the self-appointed de-facto leader of the group, agreed. Shi Tsu could just as easily pretend to the title of leader of the group, but he was by nature more retiring and understated. In fact, if truth be known, Shi Tsu probably was the sharpest engineer in the lot. But he had little time for office politics. He was thus quite happy to leave that role to Frank who, by contrast, seemed to enjoy the honor. Charles next asked where they expected to get the money. Frank replied:

"So far, we expect a research grant of $1.5 million or so from MIT, with the potential for it to be extended in the same amount next year. We hope to raise about $2.5 million in angel financing for about ten percent share of the equity."

Charles immediately interrupted:

"Those are not very kind terms for your external financiers. How do you arrive at the ten percent? You're effectively valuing the company at twenty-five million dollars. Isn't that a bit rich?"

"Well, to be fair, we did not start with that number; we worked our way toward it."

"Not sure I understand, but please go ahead and explain."

"Thank you, Charles. First, we decided that the patent, which was transferred to the company, was well worth fifty percent of the value of the company. I'd think this is reasonable; that's the guarantee of the intellectual property which is totally vested in the company. Don't you agree?"

"I'll grant you it's reasonable, Frank. But continue, how was the rest allocated?"

"Well, the exchange of the patent gave MIT twenty-five percent, and to each of the three of us a third of the other 25%. We gave Ho Lim a five percent share in exchange for him accepting a more modest compensation level than he could get outside. We wanted the three of us to have exactly the same share, and we settled on twenty percent each. That left ten percent."

"Gentlemen, I do not want to go into more detail than necessary. However, I have to tell you that I see a problem. We cannot use your logic as stated."

"Why?"

"Well, Jack, if I follow you, the 50% in exchange of the patent would give the three of you the other 25% after MIT had gotten its own 25%. That left 50% of the company up for grabs . . ."

Frank interrupted:

"I can anticipate where you are going, Charles. But the three of us are still going to work at the company and, just like Ho Lim, we are not being paid market rates. We need sweat equity, isn't that reasonable?"

"Gentlemen don't get we wrong. I would surely not expect any of you to work for nothing. Yet, your investors would not want to provide funds for peanuts either."

Michael intervened, with his discernable Australian drawl and little time for formalities:

"OK, Charles, so what does that mean?"

"Would you be willing to give up some of your own equity if it was needed?"

Frank replied:

"We might consider it, but there are clear limits, Charles. We will not dilute either MIT or Ho Lim. That's our agreement."

"Is that documented in writing?"

"Not in a legal document per se, but certainly through a chain of emails and in our oral conversations. Call it a gentleman's agreement which we are not prepared to go back on."

"Well, I'm not sure how to react to that Frank. I want to help, but I've also got to fight for our investors."

"Understood, Charles. But we've given our word. So, I'm afraid that there is very little wiggle room there. . . . We have not talked about it yet, but looking at my two professor partners, we might be willing to shave a couple of percent of each of our equity allocation, but it would surely have to be worth our while. Correct my friends?"

Both Shi Tsu and Michael nodded their agreement. Charles asked:

"You're still short $1 million, correct?"

"Yes. But we have a couple of ideas. One involves going directly to the Pentagon."

"Would they want equity?"

"I sure as hell don't know, but they might impose market limitations. My guess though is that they'd probably see it as a research grant; that would give them greater control over the intellectual property."

"I see . . . I see . . . Well, I cannot commit to anything at this point. Too many moving pieces. Could you start your work with half that money?"

"We surely could. MIT has offered us the use of certain facilities. So, our initial capital requirements are limited. Three of us are still salaried professors so we don't need too much extra. But we need our friend Ho Lim, and we have no budget for him."

"Tell you what. Do contact the Pentagon. I'll talk to our usual potential investors and will be back to you in under a week."

Thanking Charles, they all left his office.

■ ■ ■ ■

Sitting in the cafeteria at Next House on the MIT campus, the four researchers were plotting their next move. They were disappointed by Charles's initial reaction. Part of them understood that Charles had to have a negotiating position. Shi Tsu went even further, arguing that the way they reached their current equity shares probably was "egocentric" as he said. At the same time, he made the point that, even if they agreed to drop their own shares to 15% each. . . . Frank interrupted:

"How do you get to that number, Shi Tsu?"

"Easy, Frank, that number is simple, and it is the simplest one that is such that any two of the three of us can outvote MIT, provided the third abstains. If the three of us want something and we can convince Ho Lim to come with us. Nobody can force us to do anything."

"I see. Makes sense. Well, that would free up 15% of the capital, which would allow Charles and his investors to have as much as 25% of the firm."

They were at the point where the three senior scientists were negotiating with one another when Ho Lim offered a possible solution:

"I have a good contact with a Chinese venture capital fund: Tsin Hua Ventures—it is a joint venture between the government and my university. I could talk to them if you want."

Frank's interest was piqued:

"What do they do?"

"They're located in what foreigners used to call Canton and we now call Guangzhou. They finance innovation throughout the province."

"Any government link?"

"Sure! More than a link. They're government majority owned. But it is the provincial government, not the folks in Beijing."

"Is that real independence?"

"Well, up to a point, but still . . ."

"Do you know much about them?"

"I assume you're talking of the venture fund. No, not off the bat, but I'm sure we can find a lot about them on the Internet."

"What do you all think?"

Xi Shi Tsu was the first to reply. He mentioned his worry with bringing the Chinese government into a project which might also include the Pentagon. Michael Lennon agreed but wondered whether some clause could protect the secrecy of the work. Ho Lim suggested that the best thing to do would be to have a very general conversation without any specific discussion of the project, adding:

"A sort of hypothetical discussion."

Frank agreed. He asked whether Shi Tsu could be on the call as well so that the two of them could take notes and compare them afterwards. Shi Tsu still had some reservations, but he took comfort in the fact that he had been told by their lawyers that the patent they had was quite broad. Their intellectual property was unlikely to be taken from them. And then he thought: *Unless they steal it.*

Ten days later, the four partners were back in Charles Parker's office.

■ ■ ■ ■ ■

Since their last meeting with Charles, Ho Lim and Shi Tsu had talked to Ho Lim's venture capitalist contact. Though he could see that the questions that were asked were reasonable and covered the right topics, Shi Tsu was quite surprised that someone like Ho Lim, who at thirty-five, was junior in Chinese circles, could get such a rapid agreement from Jen Shao Wah, his contact. In short, Shao Wah was willing to contribute up to $3 million, only requesting a 10% share of the equity. More importantly, he agreed to a clause that there would be a clear wall, which the friends had a funny feeling calling a "Chinese Wall," between the detail of operational and technical activities and financial information. The Chinese partner would receive full access to the financial information but would not get anything on the technical and operational front. Thus, the secrecy which they expected the Pentagon to request would be protected.

Shi Tsu remained cynical when Ho Lim and he presented the draft agreement and term sheet for the deal to the whole group. He said that it would be up to them, the partners, to ensure that these secrets were protected. In particular, and ominously, he mentioned that one would need to be very careful with any individual the fund might want to second into the new company for a short while or for longer-term employment. They saw a particularly careful hiring discipline and an industrial-strength cyber security protocol as absolute prerequisites. Frank suggested that he and Shi Tsu might want to consult with the Pentagon to see if they could help them with both elements of security.

The group had decided not to discuss the Chinese offer with Charles until he had made known where he stood. Indeed, now, with the Chinese help, the commitment from MIT and a $1 million research grant from the Pentagon, they could afford to be choosy. As Frank explained:

"I would not mind building up a stronger cash cushion; it can't hurt us. But we certainly do not want to give up more equity than needed. Here, we are at our target and would retain sixty five percent of the equity among ourselves, twenty percent for the three senior partners and five percent for Ho Lim. Come to think of it guys, we may need to think of some mechanism to allow Ho Lim to buy more equity over time as his role and performance permits. He's definitely earned brownie points with this contact."

Ho Lim smiled all the while signaling with his hands that the issue did not keep him awake at night. They all thanked him for his dedication.

■ ■ ■ ■ ■

Back in Charles' offices, Frank asked directly where he was in his discussions with his potential investors. Charles was not pessimistic, but yet seemed to argue that the deal looked somewhat challenging. He turned around and asked how the fund raising was progressing. Charles was stunned when Frank replied with a smile:

"We've got all we need, though we would not mind getting a bit more . . ."

"Wait. Wait a minute. You got your $5 million?"

Frank was matter of fact as he replied:

"Yep. I can't give you any detail at this point, though I can say that we only had to give up thirty-five percent of the equity, including MIT's share."

"Well, based on our earlier conversation, you mean you got around $3.5 million for only 10% of the equity. I can't believe that."

"In fact, it's closer to $4 million, because MIT has not finalized their investment yet."

"OK. OK."

Charles was visibly trying to calm himself. He was going from a position where he thought he held all the trump cards to one where he was on the verge of being out of the deal. His mind was racing as he was wondering what it was that he was missing. He asked:

"Can you tell me if that includes the Pentagon?"

Frank replied with a smile:

"Sure can. They gave us a research grant."

"How much?"

"A million to start. They have some control over who can buy into the technology."

"OK. OK. So someone else gave you three million dollars for 10% of the equity."

Frank was now enjoying the cat and mouse game, though his partners, all of whom had some Chinese ethnic connection, kept signaling that there is never any mileage humiliating anyone. In Asia, one must always allow the other party to "keep face." He was calmer as he replied:

"That's about right."

"So, if I offered you say $1.5 million, how much equity would you be prepared to give me or more precisely my investors?"

Frank did not miss a beat. He replied:

"Not more than 5%. The last contributor set a new price, I'm afraid. In fact, as whatever we would offer to you would have to be divisible into three,"

Seeing that Charles did not follow, Frank explained:

"Those shares would have to come from Shi Tsu, Michael and me. So whatever number it has to be divisible into three. So, we might only offer 4.5%, effectively taking 1.5% from each of the three of us . . ."

"Have you showed this outside investor anything you have not shared with us?"

"No. They've seen the value proposition and loved it. Note that they do not know the technical details."

"What's in it for them?"

"They view it as a great invention."

Charles took a deep breath and looking straight at Frank he said:

"Frank, Gentlemen, I may be missing something big. Yet I have to tell you that something in there simply does not compute. There is something very wrong."

He paused for effect, and to confirm in his own mind that his position was the correct one. He added:

"I would have loved to be a part of your venture. Yet, I think I'm going to pass. I have little doubt that you're onto something with this invention. But it's hard for me to value the company at something like $30 million with no prototype, no final technical specification and by your own admission still a number of hurdles before you have real practical applications. In a word, to me, it makes no sense. Please, don't take this personally. I'll be happy to "eat my hat" if you all succeed."

For once beating Frank to the post, Shi Tsu replied:

"Trust us, Charles, no one will insist on you doing that."

Boston Advanced Communication Laboratories (BACL for short) thus started operating with a $5 million cash cushion.

CHAPTER.04

BOSTON, MA, USA

Countess Renate organized to meet with her associate Xi Shi Tsu in Boston. Xi had indeed become a member of the Shadow Expert group long before he and his three partners had formed Boston Advanced Communication Laboratories. Countess Renate had been subjugated by Shi Tsu's knowledge, reputation and apparent character. She knew that his specialty was not in the greatest of demand within her current clientele, but who knew what she would need in the future? Shi Tsu, on his end, loved the idea of the challenge. Plus, the relationship with people whom he humbly thought were all smarter than he was a major intellectual motivator. In fact, it was joining Countess Renate's network that led him to make the decision that he was not willing to fulfill the full responsibilities of Department Head at MIT. That is when he agreed to share the duty with Frank Lord.

Frank Lord may not have known it, but the position of sole Department Head had been offered to Shi Tsu before it had been decided that the two of them should be co-chair of the department. While Frank was a good professor and actually a great fundraiser, Shi Tsu was indeed a "pure" researcher. His interest was in finding new ways of doing things or simply ways of achieving things that hitherto had been impossible. The first paper written on the issues created by the air-water boundary in data communication was his work, and it had inspired a number of followers; it was one of the papers that led to the recommendation that he should join the Shadow Experts.

Countess Renate had booked herself in the Four Seasons Hotel on Boylston Street, opposite the Boston Public Garden, which serves as a prolongation of the famous Boston Common. She had organized to meet Shi Tsu at the 'Aujourd'hui Lounge' on the second floor, overlooking the Public Garden.

"Shi Tsu, it's good to see you. The Shadow Experts may have an assignment which might require your participation. In fact, the situation into which we've been brought involves your invention . . ."

Shi Tsu was taken aback. His mouth remained open for a few seconds, and he seemed at a loss for words. Recovering his composure, he only asked:

"What are you talking about, Countess?"

■ ■ ■ ■ ■

Renate had previously, exceptionally in her mind, cleared her next steps with Simon. She had not included Jack Turnbull because she simply did not know him as well. She just said to Simon that she would need to disclose some of the information he had given her. Simon did not know that this would involve disclosing the information to a BACL insider, but he probably would not have objected if she had told him. Clients of the Shadow Experts knew how Countess Renate operated and trusted her. Simon was no exception.

■ ■ ■ ■ ■

Renate went on to describe to Shi Tsu the full suite of events which had unfolded in the Mediterranean Sea off the coast of Haifa. His immediate reaction was total disbelief:

"Wait a minute. Can't believe it. How is that possible?"

"That's what we need to find out my dear friend. . . . Any clue?"

"Honestly, at this point, absolutely none."

He paused for a few seconds, caught his breath and continued:

"Let me think . . . leak, leak. Must have been a leak. But where did it come from?"

Answering his own question, he went on:

"Could only be from us, from MIT or from the Pentagon. Who could benefit? Certainly not any one of us. MIT? Same thing. The Pentagon? Well, there you never know, but it would have to be a spy. Can't imagine someone leaking this to the press to gain notoriety; however, who knows?"

He pause again and added:

"So, to me, again, Countess, it makes no sense unless there is a spy in the Pentagon."

■ ■ ■ ■ ■

Once the company was formed, the four researchers had immediately taken to their work, though they initially did not even need to move from their offices. MIT had allowed them both to keep their campus offices and to continue using MIT's facilities and equipment. The money which they had raised only served, initially, to pay Ho Lim who as not on MIT's payroll and to acquire the materials they needed to build the prototype. They indeed felt that their latest enhancement was such that they should pause, build a prototype and evaluate it thoroughly. Given the requirements imposed by the research grants given by both MIT and the Pentagon, they needed a solid proof of concept if their backers were going to invest more, as research grants or seeking equity. And a proof of concept had to start with a prototype.

The initial effort was dedicated to build a working scaled-down prototype that they could test first in a small body of water. Their next step after that would be to move from a deep bathtub to a swimming pool. Testing required them to identify the distance that they could afford to maintain between the underwater transmitter that created the mini waves and the water surface as well as between the radar "reading" them and the water surface as well. Any system would need to offer the opportunity to read the waves from a far enough distance to be truly operational in practice.

It was at that point that they encountered the first obstacle: differentiation between the waves created by the system and those that occur naturally on the surface of water whether they were caused by normal tidal movements or by the wind. They had figured out that the challenge would be less acute if the only waves were tidal, or wind induced. Where the problem begins to be more severe is when these waves, wind waves, tidal waves or both, interfere with one another. This is broadly similar to the classical experiments parents or science teachers use to teach their children about magnetic fields. Place two magnets under a sheet of paper and drop some iron dust onto it. Then move the magnets closer or further from each other. If they are far enough, each magnet will have its own field, defined by some pattern of iron dust above it. Then move them closer and one begins to see that where the magnetic fields overlap, the iron dust pattern becomes quite different.

Similarly, as the drivers of waves begin to interfere with one another, there can be a multitude of smaller, at times quite small, waves created at the surface of the ocean. At some critical point, the smaller waves could "compete" with the waves created by the transmitter created by BACL. Nothing would be "readable."

The great discovery involved the idea of creating a calm water surface over a small enough patch of water so that the contrast between that and the mini waves would be clear. In fact, this was the first patent that they obtained in the name of the company: prior protection had been granted under the partner's names and MIT and exchanged for equity with BACL. Their invention allowed that calm patch to be created even if there was significant swell in the sea. The critical idea was to allow that "calm surface" to "ride" on the larger waves. It required the ability to have a sharp focus on the radar that would read the mini waves. They solved the problem with a clear shock in the middle of their desired calm patch. Its disturbance would be picked up by the radar. The waves created to "calm" the surface in a radius of less than three feet would simply involve reading the natural disturbances at the surface, adding the impact of the shock and sending those together within that circle thus neutralizing any motion other than the mini waves with the signal. To some extent, this is conceptually the same principle as that used by noise-cancelling headphones, for instance.

The Pentagon had been delighted to hear of that major breakthrough. It had required, as the research grant contract allowed them to do, that secrecy be maintained around the whole effort. The team would be allowed to investigate applications, whether eventually usable in the civilian or military fields. But they would need approval from the Pentagon before anything was said to anyone outside. The Pentagon had even placed an embargo on any research paper that the team would have wanted to publish. Ostensibly, Shi Tsu, as the most academically bent member of the team, was not happy at that constraint, but he understood it. He obtained the right for the paper to be written and notarized as having been written at some particular date. Thus, any eventual publication could cite an unpublished document that clearly proved that they were the first with the invention, together with the fact that they, as partners in BACL, held the worldwide patent. Ho Lim was instrumental in writing quite a bit of the paper, helped by Michael Lennon. Frank and Shi Tsu would appear as authors as well, though their written contributions were more modest. Their main contributions resided in their conceptual breakthrough.

■ ■ ■ ■ ■

Jack Turnbull and Simon were discussing the discovery, and more importantly, the required next steps, while they knew that Countess Renate was working on the source of the informational leak. Recalling a prior affair which needed resolution, Simon suggested that they should replace the drone in the water, as near as possible to where they had found it. They had indeed assured themselves that the drone did not seem to be programmed to send regular signals that it was operational; they had assumed that the terrorists wanted it to remain as secret and unobtrusive as possible while waiting for the order to strike. Yet, Simon recalled an instance where terrorists could remotely trigger communication with bombs to verify that they were still where they were supposed to be. Simon indeed felt that playing, as they had in an earlier case, with geolocation would be too complex in the current environment, if only because of the problem of transmitting data from an underwater source. The transmitter would help but there would have to be regular and frequent helicopter overflights to read the transmission. That would create too great a risk of attracting attention. Jack agreed right away with the analysis. They discussed a small number of modifications which would ensure that the drone would be inoffensive and decided to go ahead with the plan.

Looking carefully at the missile launchers, they were surprised to find that the coordinates of the targets for each missile to be "hard coded" into the drone systems. They assumed that this reflected a low degree of confidence in their ability to communicate with the drone and send the instructions to fire. It confirmed their earlier assumption that automatic geolocation probably made little sense. They concluded that the terrorists were quite sure they could trigger a launch, but less convinced that they could communicate the precise coordinates of targets in a remote manner. This offered the team the opportunity to change the targets. First, they made sure that there was sufficient fuel in the missiles to reach the new targets they picked. Then, they simply instructed the missiles, when fired, to go after two areas in southern Lebanon which were known to have Hezbollah training camps. They were sorry that there might be civilian casualties but wanted to make sure that the missiles would at least serve some useful purpose. At the very least, the camps were some distance away from the Christian Lebanese population. They had discussed the alternative of simply removing the explosives but wanted to be certain that the terrorists would feel some pain, other than the sheer disappointment that their attack had failed.

The major challenge which the joint CIA-*Mossad* team had to face related to the fact that they had not been able to capture the radar that the Lebanese helicopter used to provide instructions to the drone after having dropped it. This made it impossible for them at present to decode any message sent by the drone. Surely, both the CIA and *Mossad* had developed their own version of the system. However, these versions did not yet provide communication capabilities with what seemed like an early version of the BACL system—the terrorists were not using the latest system. Marvin was asked to add a feature that would allow Simon and the team to monitor any movement of the drone and capture any communication it received or emitted in real time. To enable it to communicate with the team, they placed a floating buoy which would relay any signal it received. The buoy was tethered electronically to the drone, using the same system as its own communication system.

■ ■ ■ ■ ■

The next step for Simon was to ensure that *Mossad* could integrate its own work into the system developed by BACL, which he naturally assumed was powering the transmitter recovered off the coast of Haifa. Simon asked Countess Renate whether there was anything she could do to help. She replied:

"Simon, I can and will help. But I must swear you to total secrecy."

"That shouldn't be an issue, Countess, but I don't understand."

"I see. Let me jog your memory. . . . Do you remember asking me if I had a contact in BACL?"

"Sure do, and you replied you could not tell me. Ah. Got it. You do and to help us you would need to reveal his or her name."

"You're very smart, Simon. And I like your sense of humor. Indeed, we do have a contact. More to the point, one of the partners is an associate of ours."

"Really? Which one?"

"You know . . ."

She paused. Her first reaction was to express what almost looked like repressed anger. Yet she swallowed hard and added:

"I know I have to tell, but that has to remain secret . . . forever, Simon."

"No problem here."

"Fine. It's Xi Shi Tsu. But listen, he was an associate of ours long before they formed BACL. In fact, he once told me that his decision to join our effort was behind his decision not to take the sole chairmanship of his department at MIT."

"Too much work or a conflict of interest?"

"The former. But, in my humble opinion, he also prefers to work behind the scenes. He was introduced to me as the best engineer in his field. But you would not guess it from his demeanor: simple and easy-going. A real gentleman."

"Would he be willing to travel to Israel to help us?"

"I am sure he would if that is a part of a Shadow Expert assignment."

"Well, that's settled then. Let me do a quick check . . ."

He paused for a minute or so as he was checking whether El Al flies non-stop from Boston. Simon went on:

"Well, luck is not on our side. We'll have to send a jet for him.

There is no non-stop flight. He'd have to stop somewhere, in New York, in Europe or in the Middle East."

"Shi Tsu would never ask for a private jet. But, if you're willing to provide one, I'm sure he won't turn it down."

"No problem, other than reminding you that military private jets do not always incorporate the amenities found in other private jets. Never seen the inside of yours, but I bet you it's more sophisticated than a military jet."

"You're probably right, Simon. But whatever it is, it's got to be more comfortable than flying, even business class, on a scheduled airline."

■ ■ ■ ■ ■

Simon had Shi Tsu fly into Palmachim Air Base and organized a car to bring him to the office. He had a chance to sleep on the plane and to use an arrival lounge at the base to shower and change clothes.

"Dr. Xi, it's wonderful to meet you."

"Unless you want me to keep calling you Colonel Rabinowitz, Simon, may I suggest we dispense with "Doctor" and you just call me Shi Tsu."

"So much easier. I know that Countess Renate has fully briefed you already, but let me ask you: is there anything more you require?"

"Frankly, not really at this point. Well, maybe, you could tell me exactly what you need, in your own words."

"Well, it's deceptively simple, though I believe it might be quite complex in reality. As you know, we have been conducting our own research into your work and based, with your agreement, on your patent. What I would dearly like is to allow any advances which were not yet public, yours or ours, to be incorporated into the current set-up."

"Set-up?"

"Yes, the transmitter we retrieved . . ."

"Oh. Yes. Sure. I thought Countess Renate told me you replaced the two contraptions where you found them."

"We did. We did. But we know where they are and could retrieve them anew and make required changes if it came to that. One point is that we would like to ensure that the terrorists could do nothing that was not picked up by the CIA-*Mossad* team."

"Understood. Will that be OK with the Pentagon?"

"Yes. Jack Turnbull, our CIA counterpart, has cleared the request with the Pentagon. They were only too happy to oblige. I don't need to tell you how distressed they are that a technology which was supposed to be secret ostensibly had leaked. Although, I should add that they only know there has been a leak; they do not know the details. . . . Wanted to avoid any form of panic on their side."

Shi Tsu could not hide his own real disappointment:

"Sensible. Sensible. I should add that we too are disappointed. Quite disappointed. Well, let's get to work then. What version have they got?"

Simon took Shi Tsu to the laboratory where all the information was located, together with every picture they had taken.

■ ■ ■ ■ ■

Simon and Jack agreed with Countess Renate that their effort was going to try and answer three key questions. First, they needed to figure out how the secrets had leaked and to plug that leak as quickly as possible. Second, they had to find how the Chinese "discovery" had made its way to Iran, and what was the current state of play between China and Iran; they viewed the relationship as a potential geopolitical gamechanger. Simon was particularly worried that Iran may have now been able to gain the ability to manufacture both the drones and the communication system. Even, hypothetically and optimistically, if they still needed the Chinese for the receiving radars, that window would probably close within a short time. Third, they had to find a way to disturb and, if possible, disable these manufacturing facilities. Failing this, Israel's future would be jeopardized and so would stability in the region and possibly the world.

Following extensive consultations with the higher-ups at the CIA and Ariel Landau, they also agreed that it was not within their purview to do anything with respect to China, other than unearthing the evidence of spying. They were to close that avenue and let the U.S. government decide what to do about it. Israel might provide some assistance, but it was clear to all that it was not to get involved into retaliations unless something threatened or directly hit its territory.

■ ■ ■ ■ ■

As expected, Shi Tsu had no difficulty identifying the various answers which Simon and others sought. Yet, he quickly came to the conclusion that he would need the transmitter to be able to work on it and make whatever changes he could. Simon asked:

"Do you need it here, or is this something you could do aboard a submarine?"

"At this point, I believe we're talking code rather than equipment. So, I could probably do it from a submarine, though I've got to tell you . . . I've never been in one."

"There's always time for a first."

Shi Tsu smiled, though a careful observer might have discerned a hint of apprehension.

■ ■ ■ ■ ■

Simon emerged from his last meeting with Ariel with a face that displayed some serious degree of discomfort or at the very least surprise and puzzlement. A couple of his lieutenants observed him as he was returning to his office. Yet, when, independently, they asked him if everything was fine, he assured them that there was not a trace of worry on his mind. David Heller, one of his closest direct reports, remained incredulous, and shared his concerns with Mark Levi who had come back to Israel after a posting abroad the purpose of which was to allow time to pass following a case he had very successfully led. At that time, about a year earlier, Simon and Ariel had agreed that Mark and his wife needed to be away from the country for some while. This was to make sure that terrorists could not make him pay the ultimate price for the cost imposed on them when he solved a prior crisis. A year had passed since then, and Simon now felt that Mark and Minoo, his wife, could return to Tel Aviv, with their newborn son, David Cyrus Levi.

Neither David nor Mark could conceive that Ariel had announced to Simon his intention to retire from his post and that he wanted to recommend that Simon be appointed to succeed him. Had they, they would surely have been able to imagine the many confusing feelings that were gyrating within Simon's head. What an honor? Would he want to do the job? Could he do the job? Would he like a move further away from operations? And many others. To say that Simon found himself internally conflicted may be the understatement of the century.

CHAPTER.05

"Ariel? You wanted to see me?"

"Indeed, Simon. Come in, come in."

Motioning to the sofa in the corner of his office, he added:

"Sit down, make yourself comfortable. Coffee, or should I offer you a scotch?"

"No thanks to the scotch, sir. A bit too early in the day, don't you think? Coffee, please. That would be nice."

"Hannah, two coffees please."

Ariel sat down in a wing chair opposite the sofa on which Simon was seated and smiled. Then he asked Simon:

"So, how's that new project going? What is it?"

"Well, as you may have seen in a confidential email, it's a pretty routine matter."

He smiled and Ariel suddenly looked quite quizzical. He did not say a word, but his face betrayed the fact that he did not understand. Simon ignored Ariel's body language and continued:

"Some supposedly secret U.S. communication technology shows up on the sea floor about three thousand feet down and about twenty miles off the coast of Haifa. Upon closer inspection, it carries Chinese markings and is equipped with two Iranian missiles . . . nothing but the everyday stuff, General."

At that point, he broke out into laughter. Ariel's facial expression immediately changed. He understood that Simon was joking, and he laughed as well. With great seriousness he replied:

"You know, Simon, that I do not joke about these matters . . ."

Now, it was Simon's face to betray his surprise. Ariel added:

"Got you back."

And he laughed heartily again. He then tilted his head slightly to the right and asked Simon:

"I assume all is in the right hands, correct?"

"Absolutely. Multiple dimensions. I brought Countess Renate in to help us with the source of the leak at least. She may be able to do more, but at this point she is best for that role. Jack Turnbull and I have liaised quite closely. In fact, he was in Haifa when Marvin Goldstein gave us a rundown of what they had found. Clearly quite a surprise. But we also need to find how Hezbollah sources these missiles and drones and stop them."

"But, we have the Iron Dome."

"Sure. We do. We certainly do. But they could use it within the broader Palestinian political universe to unite the current three groups under their own command. Would make our job quite a bit more difficult. And, as you know, neither Fatah nor Hamas have anything like the Iron Dome."

"I see. This could indeed change things quite a bit. Anything else?"

"Well, yes, we placed the submarine drone back into the sea and made sure that it would be in constant communication with us. Also, we reprogrammed the targets for their missiles away from Tel Aviv and Jerusalem to the two main Hezbollah training camps in southern Lebanon. Oh, and by the way, we have sensors on the boat that delivered the drone; with any luck, it will return to Iran at some point. . . . One last point, a member of Countess Renate's team is here and is working on a few changes to the communication system. We agreed to take him to the underwater location with a submarine, and to have him make whatever change he needs to make, from the submarine. We'll retrieve the equipment, bring it aboard, have him fiddle with it and place it back where we found it. And it's the first time he will have been on a submarine."

"Well done. Well done. As usual, you seem to have everything under control. Please, keep me in the loop as things develop as the PM is definitely interested in this issue. . . . The geopolitical dimensions, particularly. We do not want ever to be caught with our pants down! For us, as you know, it's a question of survival."

"Will do, sir. Will do."

Ariel paused for a minute and shifted in his chair to get more comfortable, placing his right leg across his left thigh. He smiled again and looked Simon straight in the eyes, with an unusual intensity:

"Simon, I'm about to share with you something totally secret. Nobody knows it, not even the Prime Minister."

"I am honored, Ariel. I hope it's not bad news."

"No, not bad news. A change, a big change, but not a bad piece of news. Let me cut to the chase: I've decided to retire, probably next year. No date is set, but the decision is made."

Simon recognized the way his boss's head worked. He had weighted the various alternatives and had come up with his preferred solution. *Typical,* was all he could think. Yet, in his surprise, words came out, but it was not a well-thought-out sentence. Rather a staccato delivery of key words:

"You? Ariel? Retiring? Why?"

"Well, my friend, first of all, I'm not getting any younger. . . ."

Simon was going to interrupt but Ariel motioned him not to with his right hand in front of his right eye. Simon stayed put and Ariel continued:

"I know I could do this a while longer, but, frankly, there's another thing I'd rather do."

Ariel paused again. Simon was surprised to see his boss, who was always so friendly, but also so cool, particularly under pressure, seem almost emotional. Simon decided to stay silent and let events run their course. Ariel inhaled a large breath of air and continued:

"Golda, my wife, had a small stroke last year."

Simon was again very surprised. Though a wonderful boss always seeking news from his associate's family, Ariel was not in a habit of revealing much about his. Simon again elected to stay quiet. He wondered when that could have happened. He had not noticed any change in Ariel's demeanor at any point. Ariel went on:

"Nobody knows it. Frankly it came and was gone in a few days. It happened at night. Thankfully, we were both awake. She noticed something was wrong; she was suddenly losing vision from her left eye. I immediately called an ambulance, and she was treated within five to ten minutes. The fact that we were able to get assistance that quickly was crucial, I'm told. She was almost back to normal the next morning, though she was still in intensive care; she came back home a couple of days later. . . . So, I decided that I did not need to share the development with anyone. Think I should have, Simon?"

"Who am I to know, sir? I recognize your style: privacy and a desire not to impose more pressure on your team than necessary. Plus, talking to the PM . . . frankly, I don't know him well enough to be able to gauge whether he would or would not expect you to share it. . . . Yet, I'm very sorry to hear this, sir. Real sorry. She is OK now, isn't she?"

"She is. She is. I know you mean it, Simon, and it's very important to me. Thank you. You've become one of my closest advisors and I feel at ease telling the story to you. I've got to say that I would not have shared it with anyone else. . . . Don't ask me why."

"Again, Ariel, I am honored. Can I do anything to help?"

"Simon, Simon, exactly the reaction I would have expected from you. You may well be able to help; hold on. But first let me finish the story. The episode made both of us think, and here I mean my wife and I when I say 'us.' We have virtually everything we want, but this job takes me away from home much too much. And, when I am home, sometimes, the stress is such that I am there physically, but not mentally. Not emotionally."

"I can appreciate that."

"I'm sure you can. Must be the same for you. Anyway, we have decided that we do not want this to end with me dying of a heart attack or Golda of another stroke. We have our health, and it would be nice to be able to enjoy ourselves as well as our children and grandchildren."

"What do you plan to do?"

"After retirement, I don't know. Before retirement, I will need to speak to the PM. He will probably announce it to the War cabinet and keep it quiet until he appoints my replacement."

"Any thought on that front?"

Simon immediately looked sorry that he had asked the question. He recognized that it was a natural part of the flow of the conversation, but he was prodding and shouldn't have. He added:

"Sorry, Ariel. I shouldn't have asked that question. Ignore it if you wish."

"Well, since you're asking, I will tell you: I intend to recommend you as my successor."

Simon looked genuinely surprised. More than that, he was totally taken aback. He mumbled:

"Me? Ariel?"

He paused as if he was at a loss for words. In truth, it would be ridiculous to say that he had never considered that eventuality. Yet, with Ariel going strong and himself enjoying his current work, he had sort of placed the issue on the back burner. He mumbled further:

"I'm not sure it's such a good idea."

"Why?"

"Look, I love what I am doing, and I love the agency. So, don't get me wrong. Also, I obviously recognize the honor. I can't believe it in fact."

"Come on Simon. Don't tell me the thought never crossed your mind."

"Sure it has. Sure, it has. But it was not an action item as far as I was concerned. I worked for you and that was it. Let me think out loud."

"Go right ahead."

"But, at the same time, one of the things I really love about the job is that I am close to the action. I can talk to you when I need to, and you effectively remove any form of political interference from me. I'm not sure I could do that part."

"The political stuff?"

"Yes."

"Well, you should know that my working relationship with the PM is very much like the one we have between the two of us. You've told me you trusted me and felt I was around to help you where I could, correct?"

"Absolutely."

"Well, it's the same between the PM and me. I feel he trusts me and believes that his job is to shield me from many political pressures as well."

"Still, what if he disagrees with you?"

"Well, if the disagreement is on an issue of policy, he has the last word, and I will support him. I may ask for more of facts or details, but, in the end, he is the boss. But, and I see your eyes my friend, if the disagreement is on a matter of intelligence, on something where I believe *Mossad* are the experts, I will not yield. I can respectfully disagree. In the end, he would have to force me, and he knows that he cannot go too far, as I would simply step down."

"Wow! Still, got to guess that a lot of your time is spent on administrative matters. Right?"

"Correct. That's an important part of the job. See, our own working together: you tell me what you're going to do, you ask me for the resources you need, but you do not ask me to work alongside you all. In fact, come to think of it, that would be a disaster."

"Why?"

"You cannot ever have more than one general on the field. Imagine I am next to you and that a decision has to be made. How much are you willing to bet that whoever comes to ask for the decision would look to me rather than to you?"

"Good point, Ariel. Excellent point in fact. But now turn this thing around. What if what I really enjoy is the planning and the execution of missions. Would your job meet those needs?"

"Probably not. But you've got to ask yourself: what do you want to do when you grow up?

"Do I need to move up in the ranks? Can't I stay in my role?"

"There are two answers to that. The first is: how would you like someone being parachuted on top of you?"

"I see. Well, I think I could work with someone else . . ."

"I'm sure. But what if you cannot build with that person the relationship we have?"

"You've got a point . . . I don't know."

"The second answer is different: how would you feel your troops would react if it looked as if you're stuck in place?"

"Fair point too. I get it. Looks like I've got a lot of thinking to do."

"Agreed, my friend. Tell you what. We don't have to decide now. I certainly don't have to talk to the PM tomorrow or later this afternoon in fact. So, let's have the two of us do some more thinking."

"Sounds very generous, Ariel. Thanks."

"You're most welcome. Now, let me give you an assignment."

"Shoot."

"I want you to think of my retirement as a given. Don't try to change my mind. At best, I'll delay a few weeks if that helps. With that, I want you to think about what your ideal job would be, in that new environment. You can come back and ask for my job and that's OK. You can come back and say you want to stay where you are and that's OK too. Maybe, you can come up with some hybrid, and that might be OK as well. Give it some thought. I'd suggest, but it's your call obviously, to discuss it with Jennifer."

Ariel was referring to Simon's wife and the mother of his two children, Ari, the boy and Devorah, the girl. He continued:

"Let's regroup in a week or two. Your call if you're ready early. My call if I really need your reply. Deal?"

"Very fair deal, General! And you're right. Jennifer has to be a part of the deliberation; she is quite calm, and she will know what to ask me. At times, I think she knows me better than I know myself."

"Don't take this the wrong way, my friend, but isn't that true of most happily married couples?"

CHAPTER.06

BOSTON, MA, USA

Shi Tsu returned from Tel Aviv and called a meeting of the four partners of Boston Advanced Communication Laboratories right away. He had not originally mentioned to any of them that he was taking the trip. He saw it as a matter for the Shadow Experts, although his earlier meeting with Countess Renate in Boston had clearly told him that BACL was involved in one way or another. On the flight back from Israel, his mind had been focused both on the issues which the visit had raised and on how to explain why he was there without telling his partners about the Shadow Experts. He elected to play it "straight bat" as cricketers say of circumstances when batsmen play defense against a good throw. He would simply claim that a friend from Israel had asked for his help.

He started the meeting with an ominous statement:

"Friends, I am the bearer of bad news; very bad news in fact."

Everyone in the small conference room sat more erect and appeared to be totally focused. He told his tale about his visit to Tel Aviv and proceeded to describe for his partners what had transpired from his trip. Not only was he constrained in terms of explaining the reason for his visit; he also was not supposed to reveal that the drone had actually been taken out of the water and replaced. He had worked with Simon, Jack and Countess Renate and concocted a story that was entirely based on pictures that were taken from a drone. Thus, to anyone in the room with him, the submarine drone had not actually been discovered nor *a fortiori* had it been dissected. He could tell that, as his story progressed, the ambiance in the room was becoming increasingly tense. The only person whose body language was betraying some degree of discomfort was Ho Lim. The other two looked quite concerned, but their demeanor did not suggest that they saw any direct threat to themselves. Shi Tsu concluded:

"In a word, I was shown a number of pictures that are quite worrisome . . ."

Frank, who kept playing the role of leader of the group, interrupted:

"What do you mean, Shi Tsu?"

"Well, Frank, the pictures suggest that someone has a drone which looks like it has our technology in it. . . ."

"How is that possible?"

Without giving Shi Tsu or anyone else the time to reply, Michael added:

"And, by the way, how do we know their communication method from the pictures you saw?"

"Two great questions, Michael. The pictures show that the drone has Chinese characters on its body. I read the characters and they said Bohai Shipyard and also China Shipbuilding Industry Corporation. I happen to know that the shipyard, located in the Bohai Sea, opposite the coast of North Korea is a major military shipyard, though they also build civilian ships."

Frank interrupted:

"Why would they have their names on a drone like that one?"

"Well, that I do not know. And you're right, Frank. On the surface it makes no sense. But assume that the drone was not originally intended for the purpose for which it was used and, all of a sudden, it's a lot more reasonable. For instance, I don't know that the drone got to its eventual destination directly from the shipyard . . . it could easily have been bought by or delivered to the MSS (the Ministry of State Security). It's the only publicly known official intelligence agency in China, though we all know there are many others."

Frank conceded:

"Makes sense. But whoever shipped it to the Middle East has to be a complete idiot to have left the markings."

"I wouldn't disagree with that, Frank. Yet, imagine another scenario. A local country, client of China already or where China would like to gain influence, requests Chinese help for its protection against foreign attacks. China identifies the drone as the solution and sells them one or several. Again, what's wrong with that?"

"Up to a point, I guess not. Hmmm. I see."

Frank paused and then added:

"Anyway, how do we know that this drone has our technology?"

"Well, this goes back to Michael's second question. It is true that nobody has seen the drone in reality, other than on the pictures. But the pictures also showed another contraption being lowered into the sea after the drone. The Israelis located it, removed it and were able to look at it, though they eventually replaced it where they found it. It is the unit that transforms the sonar signal from the drone into the surface waves. . . . That's our technology, gentlemen."

Frank exploded:

"Holy shit. That's huge. Do you mean that others now know of our technology?"

"Well, we can be pretty sure that the Chinese, if they really behind the whole thing, know about it, aside from what we have had to show to the Pentagon as per the research contract. We also know that the Pentagon shared these designs with the Israeli Defense Ministry, as per their own joint-research agreements. . . ."

"But they should have told us."

"I saw someone from the CIA there. I asked the same question and he told me that it was in the small print: they are allowed to share it with their research partners. I'm told the line can be read to mean only firms like ourselves, but it can extend to a close geopolitical ally. . . . The one thing that does protect us is that we have the patent. So, any commercial use will have to bring us a fee. But a secret military use. . . . Who knows?"

Frank came back:

"Well, look no further. The leak must have come from the Pentagon or from any other research partner with whom they shared it. By the way, I'm prepared to exclude Israel from the list of suspects for all the obvious reasons"

"You know, Frank, fearing Pentagon leaks is exactly where my mind went. Now, Jack Turnbull, the CIA guy, agreed that it was totally plausible. He did add that he had checked: so far, it appears that the Pentagon has not shared the secret with anyone else officially. So, the leak must come from them or from us. I agree with you that implicating Israel would make little sense. Though, there are people spying on Israel as well. Who knows, there could be a double agent within *Mossad*. . . ."

Shi Tsu let that last thought linger for a while. The faces around the table told various stories, from total disbelief to the concession that even Israel and *Mossad* could be suspect, if not directly, though a mole. He added:

"They tell me that *Mossad* is on it and that Jack, the CIA guy, was going to share the issue with the FBI. The investigation will be totally secret and under the responsibility of the CIA."

"How do we know that they will be able to keep it secret? Washington leaks like a sieve."

Shi Tsu simply replied:

"We don't. We don't have a choice, my friend. Do we?"

■ ■ ■ ■ ■

A couple of days after that meeting had ended, Ng Ho Lim knocked at Shi Tsu's office door. He looked different from his usual happy appearance. He looked terribly serious and quite concerned. He asked, surprisingly in Mandarin:

"Shi Tsu. Do you have a minute?"

"Sure do. What can I do for you?"

Ho Lim came to him and sat on the sofa which Shi Tsu pointed to him. Shi Tsu sat in the armchair set at a right angle vis-à-vis the sofa. Ho Lim noted the few papers and magazines on the coffee table and remained silent for a little while. His seriousness had by now morphed into visible embarrassment:

"Well, I've been thinking real hard over the last couple of days. . . ."

"Troubled by the leak?"

Ho Lim motioned his agreement by a nod of his head. Then he breathed in heavily and blurted out:

"Yep. I need you to know something, but I'd like you to keep it totally secret."

Shi Tsu was surprised by the request. He could not see why Ho Lim would react this way. Though he only recalled the event after the fact as it occurred in his subconscious only, he started to wonder whether Ho Lim was the leaker. With that thought deep within his mind, he replied, shifting back to English:

"Unless you are here to tell me you are the leak, in which case I can't protect you, I can assure you that whatever you say will stay here"

"Thanks. Well, first, be assured that I have nothing to do with the leak."

Shi Tsu breathed a visible sigh of relief. He had indeed been the one senior partner who worked most closely with Ho Lim, possibly early on as he was the only one who spoke Mandarin. He said:

"Well, that's good. So, what's wrong? What's supposed to be so secret?"

"I did not cause the leak, but I could have . . . I was sent here by the Chinese government."

Shi Tsu was completely lost. His mind was racing. Yet, he could not figure out what was going on. He could only ask:

"Sent here by the Chinese government? To do what?"

"To follow on the work that Adrian did before I came."

Shi Tsu recognized the name of the Chinese research assistant that had worked with them while at MIT. He asked, with his voice rising toward the end of the sentence:

"Lee Yeo Min?"

Ho Lim nodded:

"Yes sir. He was a spy and was supposed to report to China whatever you all were doing. They had heard of your line of work. Having a means for submarines to communicate with the surface while remaining deep underwater is one of their major challenges."

"Oh. My God. So they knew?"

"Well, judging by how far your research had taken you when I arrived, the only thing they knew then was that you were making progress in the direction of signal conversion."

"So what did you do?"

"Initially, I did what they asked me. My first mission was to make sure that you did not run out of money. That's why I introduced you to the Venture fund."

"Here we go. Now it's clearer. . . . Not a bad deal, by the way."

"No. It was a good deal. But, for whom? It was meant to be a good deal to allow your group to keep working. . . . Plus, they had a small financial interest . . . the ten percent equity."

"I see. I see. But now, what do you do?"

Ho Lim paused for another few seconds that felt like minutes. Then he said:

"Well, that's the point. I want out of their grasp. I decided that I wanted to stay in the U.S. I don't want to be a spy. I want to work honestly. So, I have not told them anything recently. Been mum on my intentions. And on the project, I've simply reported that there was nothing to report."

"And they believed you?"

"Well, initially yes. They wanted more detail, but I said there weren't any. They left me alone. But, more recently, I have been under a lot of pressure."

"Why were you surprised?"

Looking straight into Shi Tsu's eyes, Ho Lim blurted out:

"Honestly, Shi Tsu, I was more than surprised. I was floored. They seemed to know that progress had been made. Their questions were very pointed. They were based on knowledge that they were not supposed to have."

"Hold it. Hold it, Ho Lim."

Shi Tsu was disturbed, but Ho Lim made it clear he was not finished. Shi Tsu let him continue:

"I know they could not have found that out from me. Yet, they knew, and they were asking me why I was not reporting it. So, I can only conclude that someone else is giving them the information."

"OK. Let me take the two points one at a time. First, what did you tell them?"

"The only thing I could do. I had to give out something but did not provide any useful information. I repeated stuff they already knew but presented it a bit differently."

"And they bought it?"

"Well, so far, yes. But I'm real worried."

"A bit late, my friend, is it not?"

Ho Lim looked really contrite, replying:

"Sure, but the famous line says that it's never too late. Plus, I think I'm bringing some new information."

"To whom?"

"To you and to BACL."

"Tell me."

"Well, to me, the big thing is that they know more than what I've been telling them. There's only one possible explanation."

He paused for a couple of seconds and added:

"They must have another source."

Shi Tsu jumped up figuratively. His face displayed both elation and terror, or rather elation and real deep disappointment. He had finally picked up on the point that he had been missing earlier in the conversation. He was so distressed to know that his protégé and partner was a spy that initially he kept focusing on that. Now, he got the bigger message. Now he realized that Ho Lim was telling him there was a spy somewhere close. . . . He asked:

"Within BACL?"

"That, Shi Tsu, I don't know. The only thing I know is that they know things I haven't told them. So, please, can you help me?"

Ho Lim's voice was unabashedly pleading now as he continued:

"I'd like your help to come clean, to defect and be protected by the U.S."

Shi Tsu, touched deep down, smiled and simply replied:

"I'll see what I can do. But, please, two things."

"Sure, what?"

"First, not a word of this to anyone else."

"You can count on me."

"Second, let me know the minute you sense the pressure is rising. We don't want to let you dangle longer than safe . . ."

Ho Lim was close to tears. He did not break down but looking straight in Shi Tsu's eyes he said, again in Mandarin:

"I knew I could count on you. I'll do whatever you ask me to do."

▮ ▮ ■ ▮ ▮

Shi Tsu called Countess Renate to discuss the development. He had decided not to share any of this with his partners. He was particularly shaken by the possibility that one of his two other partners was a spy. After all, he had to wonder how Adrian Lee Yeo Min had initially known about their work. So, he felt that he should discuss two issues with Countess Renate:

"Countess, we have a couple of issues."

"Already? That's great, Shi Tsu. So, what's up?"

Shi Tsu immediately realized that his initial comment could easily be misinterpreted. So, he elected to rephrase the problem:

"Well, first, I found out that our earlier research assistant was a Chinese spy."

"What! How bad is it? And what did he know?"

"Little. Thankfully little. So, unless he installed bugs into our computers, you'd have to assume he is not the source of the leak. We still must get our computers swept and I may need some discreet help?"

"What was your second issue before we explore this one?"

"Absolutely. Ho Lim, our current junior partner. He told me that the Chinese know more than what he had been leaking to them."

"Leaking to them?"

"Yes, initially he was a spy too."

"You're joking."

"Afraid not. But now he wants to come clean and defect."

"Nothing's simple."

"You said it. Note that he has not made any direct accusation. He did reveal Adrian's role but has not talked of anybody else. Now, Adrian is out of our reach. So, a cynic might even say that he is still a spy and wants to get himself deeper into our activities."

"That's quite true. But where does that leave you, Shi Tsu?"

"Well, combining the two, I think it's leading me to keep everything away from all partners, Ho Lim, but also Frank and Michael. I can't let any of them know that we are sweeping their computers."

Countess Renate paused for a second. Then she said:

"So, we're back to the idea of sweeping your computers. What are you looking for?"

"Truth be told, I'm not sure. That's where I need help."

Shi Tsu paused to take a breath and then rattled off a few ideas:

"I sure would like to see all email communications, both incoming and outgoing."

Countess Renate was not opposed to the idea, though she downplayed it at least initially:

"You wouldn't think that if one of your partners is a spy, he would have been dumb enough to send or accept to receive email from the office?"

Shi Tsu had a short laugh and replied:

"Of course not. But he could not have sent anything without some stuff going from the office server to his home server."

"Good point. So, you'd want to see all downloads and uploads as sell."

"Yes. But, you know, I'm not giving up on correspondence with the office's server. Imagine that the leaker is not a real spy."

Countess Renate appeared surprised but did not want to ask anything specific. She let Shi Tsu continue.

"What if someone is spying on them without them knowing?"

"You should write spy novels, Shi Tsu. How would your idea work?"

"Don't know. But thinking out loud. A wife, for instance, is the real spy. She asks questions. She may even have bugged her husband's computer. He might unwittingly have brought the bug into the office computer environment. By the way, why stop at someone's wife. Someone could be blackmailed for any reason and be forced to do what they're doing."

"Tell you what, Shi Tsu. I'm way beyond my depth."

"Makes two of us, Countess."

Countess Renate told Shi Tsu that she should bring in another Shadow Experts associate. She noted the following:

"We have one guy in Asia who is great. We'll conference him in when we're through with our current conversation."

"Before we get to that, Countess, how do we deal with Ho Lim?"

"Ho Lim?"

"Yes, the junior partner who wants to defect"

Countess Renate was unsure. Remembering an earlier comment from Shi Tsu, she first asked:

"How do you know he's legit?"

"I don't. I don't and that's where I was hoping I could get some help from people you know. We don't want to open even broader the doors to the sheep house."

"What do you mean, Shi Tsu?"

"I'm not making sense, am I? I don't want to allow him deeper into anything if he is a spy. So, one thing we could do is to fire him and send him back to China."

"You serious?"

"Yes. But I know that makes no sense. He would feel betrayed."

"Excuse me?"

"Betrayed if he is not a spy. And if he really wants to defect, we shouldn't miss the opportunity. But doing that means that we broaden the circle of people who know that he was not straight, at least at the outset."

Countess Renate answered quickly. It was obvious to Shi Tsu that this was not the first time she was dealing with an issue such as this. She simply said:

"Leave that one with me. I'll talk to Simon and to Jack. We'll see. Anything else?"

Shi Tsu felt somewhat relieved. He knew he had to be careful. After all, he never harbored any suspicion vis-à-vis Adrian. He had missed the whole thing. He could just as easily be missing Ho Lim's game. Yet, at the human level, he felt that Ho Lim was genuine. He believed his reactions. So, knowing that someone was going to help with the issue was good news. He would not have to fire Ho Lim and they could remain friends unless he was a master comedian.

Switching slightly to another topic, he added:

"Well, there's one point that Frank made when the four of us had our meeting to discuss my censured version of the findings from the Israel visit. Could we say that the leak could have come from the Pentagon?"

"That's fair. What did you reply?"

"I cannot remember my exact words. I must have said that Jack Turnbull was going to bring the FBI in. I think I also said that the investigation would be totally secret."

"Good to know. I'll mention it as well to Jack and Simon. Anything else?"

"Nope."

"Good, Shi Tsu. Now, let me bring in Wong Hai Chock, our cyber security expert. He will surely know what to do. OK with you?"

"Sure. Look forward to meeting him, even if only via video-conference."

CHAPTER.07

Back in Washington, Jack Turnbull knew he needed some help. The basic issue had to do with the leaks. The problem was that the CIA had no jurisdiction to investigate U.S. citizens within the territory. It does conduct and has conducted operations within the U.S., through its National Resources Division. Yet, these typically related to the U.S. activities of foreigners or foreign entities. Further, when revealed they often led to cries that they violated the U.S. Constitution, because some U.S. person might have been caught in a wide net. He therefore needed to bring in his opposite number at the FBI, Clay Mitchell:

"Clay?"

"Yes, Jack. What an unexpected pleasure. Anything I can do for you?"

Clay, just like Jack and Simon, was one of these dedicated, civil servants who are moved by "doing the right thing." He took his job quite seriously, though he would certainly not refrain from criticizing certain instructions he had received, frequently from political appointees. In fact, he had recently had a lengthy conversation with his wife of nearly twenty years to the effect that trends toward the politicization of the civil service was nothing but a poison. That it might be insidious only made it worse. He had his own political opinions and was not jealous about sharing them in private with friends or relatives, to the extent that doing so would not trigger a free-for-all. Yet, he had had no difficulty serving political masters whose views differed from his for as long as they were geared to the principal role of the agency. His main worry was that politics were now tainting the work of people who should be above politics; in his view, the FBI was about law enforcement, not about kowtowing to the fashion of the day. In particular, "wokeness" drove him close to depression.

He knew Jack well and was happy to hear from him.

Jack replied:

"Well, you may possibly help me, my friend but I must first swear you to secrecy."

"OK. We've known each other long enough. Happy to oblige, but, as you know, I will not swear that I'll remain silent if I hear of a federal crime."

"Fair enough."

"So what's up?"

Jack first proceeded to give Clay the general outline of the problem which he had uncovered in Israel:

"We have a case of a nasty security leak. An invention by a private company under a research contract with the Pentagon was just discovered in three thousand feet of water about twenty miles off the coast of Israel. Plus, it has Chinese markings on it and carries two Iranian missiles."

Clay smiled. He recognized the seriousness of the issue. Yet, he could not help himself and deployed his trademark humor:

"Anything more complex?"

"Seriously?"

Clay's initial reaction had surprised Jack. Yet, as both knew each other very well, some adjustment quickly took place. Clay realized virtually instantly that the seriousness of Jack's voice and the revelations he had just heard made it plainly obvious that this had to be a top secret and very important issue. At the same time, Jack knew quite well that Clay had a personality trait which all of his colleagues appreciated; he always tried to defuse any tense atmosphere with a joke or at least with something light. Jack adjusted to Clay's humor, though he did not share that ability to have fun in tense circumstances. He was all about business. Some of his friends would argue that he almost had a twin personality: at the office, he appeared to have no sense of humor but, in private, he often was the first one to tell funny stories. Clay's joke thus appeared to go partially over his head. Clay apologized and rephrased his question:

"Sorry, any lead?"

"Well, I can think of two generic sources for the leak, but would be happy to hear of another."

"Let's first hear those you are considering."

"The first is the obvious one, the company itself."

"Makes sense. On that, what do we know?"

"There are three professors, the senior partners, and they typically have had a senior research assistant. We know that the one they currently have started with them prior to the formation of the company."

"Where were they, then?"

"MIT."

"Ah!"

"We know that one assistant was a Chinese national and we just learned that he was a spy?"

"From whom did you learn it?"

"Well, that's the piece that has to remain totally between you and me, at least for some time."

"I sense a conflict coming. But fire away."

"The source of that info is their current research assistant, a junior partner in the company."

"How does he or she know?"

"Well, it's a "he." He is a Chinese national as well and was sent by the Chinese government as a spy. He confessed in total confidence to one of the senior partners. He said that he was tired of the work he was asked to do. He was being pressured and he had decided to defect and to seek asylum here."

"So simple. . . . Is he credible?"

Jack went on to explain that the issue was complex. Ostensibly, there was a mentor-mentee relationship between the assistant and the professor. The professor was above any form of suspicion. Yet both the source, the professor, and the people through whom he, Jack, got the information, agree that the research assistant cannot be taken off the list of suspects, adding:

"A kind of play: I'll pretend to defect, so that you tell me more and then I'll go back to my old master."

Clay replied:

"Classical. I see the complexity. We'll talk of what we can do about it. You mentioned a second potential source of leak. What is it?"

"Well, we know that the invention was shared with the Pentagon as per the research contract. So, is it possible that the leak came from there? After all, if the guy who was supposed to leak at the company did not, you'd have to believe that it came from outside the company."

"Unless there is another spy at the company. . . ."

"That's what the partner with whom we work worries about."

"How about him as a start?"

"Have you ever heard of Countess Renate and the Shadow Experts?"

"Vaguely, but not really. What about them?"

"Well, it's an international network of specialists whose expertise covers a vast swath of current scientific knowledge. Each of the members of the network is sworn to secrecy and they are brought in by Countess Renate, the Head of the Shadow Experts, to help solve problems which people like the CIA, MI6 or *Mossad* cannot solve by themselves."

"So, what's the point here?"

"The partner in question may be a Shadow Expert."

"What do you mean? He is or he is not."

"That's the point. Countess Renate will not tell anyone who her associates as she calls them are. So, we cannot be sure that the fellow is an associate. Yet, she introduced him to us and he seems to know a lot."

"I see. And you vouch for him."

"Well, I can't personally, but Simon Rabinowitz the head of the Disruption Unit of *Mossad* sure does. Simon backs her up. So, from my point of view, Countess Renate has to deal with that one; so far, she seems adamant the professor is on our side. A wild thought: he may not be a Shadow Expert, but she may be trying to recruit him."

Clay nodded and agreed with that as the basic assumption, though he added:

"I agree, but have to tell you that, to me, he's got to be as suspect as the others. I won't actively investigate him, but I've got to tell you that I would have to do something if I found something fishy."

"Wouldn't have expected anything else."

Jack paused for a second and then asked:

"What do you think you can do?"

"What do you need short of a full-fledged investigation which would never stay secret long enough. . . ."

Jack cleared his throat. He conceded that a full-fledged investigation at this point would be too early, particularly given the international dimensions of the problem, and specially the fact that he had to follow the lead of *Mossad*. Clay immediately asked why and just as quickly realized from Jack's comments that he did not want to go there, or at least go there quite yet. Jack offered a couple of thoughts, prefacing them with the caveat that these were first thoughts. Clay signaled that he understood. Jack suggested that the group had signed a contract with the Pentagon, first when they were at MIT and second in the name of the new company. He added:

"Must have gone through the background of the partners."

"And they missed the one that was a spy."

"True enough, my friend. But it's also possible that they focused on the top three partners? These each own twenty percent of the company, while the junior guy only owns five percent, and I am not even sure he had that equity then."

"They should have looked."

"Can't disagree."

"Anyway, where else should I look?"

"Any chance you can look into who has had access to the reports from the company at the Pentagon?"

"Sure, but that's gonna be harder. Have you considered hackers that might have penetrated their computer systems?"

"We have. The Shadow Experts are on it. I'm told that they can break into anything. In fact, a year ago or so, I worked with Simon and the Shadow Experts on something which remained totally secret. Their cyber security expert was on the team. Quite impressive!"

Clay could not contain himself:

"Didn't hack anything in the U.S. right? That'd be a crime."

Jack quieted him down, saying:

"No, he didn't, but they saved us from some serious harm. Remember Covid-19?"

"Who's forgotten? Still partially with us, right?"

"Well, without them, the Shadow Experts, and him in particular, we would have seen something that would make Covid-19 look like a dress rehearsal.

"Oh my God."

■ ■ ■ ■ ■

Jack's next call was to Simon to bring him in the loop. He summarized the conversation with Clay Mitchell and expressed the hope that he would have a reply some time soon. Simon asked him:

"What about the question of Ho Lim, you know, the spy who wants to defect?"

"I haven't done anything yet. . . . Mentioned him in confidence to my contact at the FBI but said that I wanted it totally secret at this moment."

Simon told him that he had had a couple of nasty thoughts that he wanted to share with him. He started:

"I don't want to take sides yet. But I've been ruminating on a thought. We have two options. First, Ho Lim may not be for real. In other words, he still is a spy; if that's the case, what do we do? How do we flush him out? Second, what if he is for real? What if there is another spy in BACL?"

"I think I've had a similar thought. Still, can you expand a bit more on yours, my friend?"

"Well, how can we trap Ho Lim to make sure that he is not effectively trying to become a double agent? On the other hand, if he is legit, what is the risk that another spy within the company will be charged with liquidating him if we're not terribly careful not to point to him?"

"I see, Simon. I see. Excellent questions. Any suggestion?"

They discussed the nature of a trap as a first move and decided that they would not even bring Shi Tsu into the loop. Simon conceded that not bringing Shi Tsu into the loop certainly did not look like a friendly gesture. He added:

"Can easily be accused of not being a team player. Yet, that's the only way we can be sure. I would not bring Countess Renate either. By the way, I am not entirely sure what the relationship is between her and Shi Tsu. From experience, he could well be an associate of hers; but then again . . ."

Simon did not finish his sentence and let it hang in the air. Jack thought for a minute and quickly questioned Simon with respect to Countess Renate:

"Isn't she going to be mad?"

Simon hesitated for a second. Then, he made the point that not bringing her in was the safest way for everyone. He conceded that the risk of her slipping, given her experience and reputation, was minimal. But adding her to the loop would bring nothing to the solution and had an outside chance of creating an issue. Simon added:

"She's the ultimate professional. She knows the game. She'll understand why we did what we did. In fact, I'd bet that she'd say she would have done the same thing herself."

Jack asked:

"What if it was to create tensions between her and Shi Tsu?"

"Didn't think of that."

Simon paused for a short while. Then he continued:

"In my view, we could use that rationale for not bringing her in the loop. She could never be accused of having tricked one of her own associates. . . ."

Jack congratulated Simon, though he added:

"We'll have to come clean quite quickly if we don't want to jeopardize the whole project."

"Agreed."

Simon paused and then switched to what he called the second leg:

"What about Ho Lim's protection if he passes the first hurdle?"

"I'm thinking that it should follow the first within less than twenty-four hours. He will have to disappear, though he may be somewhere where Shi Tsu knows where he is and where he can be helpful to the project, but safe. . . ."

"What in the world are you thinking of?"

"He might take on residence in Israel for a while. . . ."

"Smart. Very smart. But is that truly practical?"

■ ■ ■ ■ ■

Simon left the office relatively early that evening, as he knew that most of the urgent matters were in hand. He had told Jennifer that there was an item which they needed to discuss in the quiet of the house. He had only given her the headline. She uttered a small shriek and could only add, in an incredulous tone of voice:

"Simon? Is that for real? Gees!"

He confirmed that it was. She agreed that she would feed the children early and have a dinner for the two of them after Ari and Devorah had gone to bed, adding:

"We can start to talk while they watch a movie or something. We'll put them to bed, have dinner and continue our conversation."

Simon agreed. After he got home and spent the required time with the children, Jennifer's "Plan A" was put into action. The children enjoyed their dinner and were delighted to be allowed to watch a movie despite the fact that this was a weeknight. Jennifer and Simon sat down in Simon's office, which offered more privacy and some measure of noise protection:

"So, honey, tell me more."

Simon went on to describe his conversation with Ariel in all the detail he could remember. He spend a bit of time emphasizing the end of the conversation, adding:

"But I do not know what I can and cannot ask for."

Jennifer brought him back, as she always did, to the central question:

"What do you want to do?"

Adding:

"We can always think of how the message is presented . . . later."

Simon smiled and kissed his wife. He rehearsed for himself and for her the key issues. He always felt that verbalizing the issues helped resolve a problem. Thinking of them silently exposed him to skip a logical step; he needed to hear himself say things to make sure he was going the right way. He casually remembered when his first assistant at *Mossad* was surprised to hear him talk to himself in his office. He had simply told her not to worry:

"I need to talk issues out loud to make sure I do not miss anything."

At Jennifer's prodding, he went on with the key points that he could think of at present. He really enjoyed his job; the work and the responsibilities were the main reason for that. Jennifer interrupted:

"Would you say the same thing if Ariel was a complete jerk?"

"Interesting way to put it, dear. I really don't know. In truth, I've never had to work for a jerk. Each and every one of my bosses have been really good."

With a reproachful tone in her voice, Jennifer replied:

"Simon, remember your army days, before you joined *Mossad*. I seem to remember a Captain . . ."

"Captain Loeffer."

"Exactly. Did not seem to like him. And it seemed to be reciprocal."

"OK, that's true. That's true. But I knew it would not last for a long time. So . . . I put up with him"

"I know you did. But would you go as far as to say that you enjoyed that time? I know you didn't. I wouldn't say you kept talking about it, but it certainly was the topic of quite a few conversations. Wasn't it?"

"Again. OK. I'll grant you that. But where does that get you?"

"Well, you have had the experience of a bad boss. The big thing, for me, is that you were able to assume that your time under Captain Loeffer would not last. Your quiet brain was your saving grace. Would you be able to say that of your time under another Head of *Mossad*? And if not, what's the alternative?"

Simon let out a brief whistle. Jennifer was surely not mincing words or beating around the bush. He conceded:

"Can't disagree. You're hitting the nail on the head. And so far, I haven't thought of an alternative. So, what's your thought?"

"Well, let me try to summarize. I think your current happiness with the job and the position are due in part at least to your relationship with Ariel. Make sure you don't forget that."

"I see that. In fact, you won't believe it, but Ariel raised that very point."

"He not only likes you; he knows you. It's great to have a boss like that. Would everyone be like him?"

She paused for a second and added:

"Think about that. The job in question is the top job. So, whoever gets it will not rotate out of it in a few years to take the next step. You may well finish your career under that individual or have to leave *Mossad*."

"Well, that's true, but less true today than in the past."

Jennifer looked surprised. Simon added:

"Years ago, the identity of the Head of *Mossad* was a state secret. The position was the culmination of a career. So you stayed there until you retired. Now, it's a bit different. His name is known. I even heard someone speculate that, someday, Ariel might want to run for the PM office himself."

"OK, love, that's new news to me. So, it might be that you would not be stuck kind of 'forever.' The good news if Ariel were to run for PM is that you could still have him looking over the new boss's shoulders and protect you, somehow. But is that what he wants?"

"Truth is: I don't think so. Ariel shared a secret with me that convinces me that he is really looking forward to retirement."

"I know I shouldn't ask, but I will. His health?"

"No. His wife's."

"Ah! That does it for me. You've got to assume that he will, at best, be in the shadows. He could probably get you moved to a different job, but nothing more. And that job would have to be outside of *Mossad*."

"Unfortunately, I agree."

"So, where does that leave you?"

"Still don't know. Let's agree that I couldn't do my job with the wrong boss."

"Wouldn't phrase it quite that way. I'd say let's agree that you couldn't enjoy your job with the wrong boss."

"Better. I agree. But the question is: how do I know who the other candidates are?"

"If I was Ariel, I wouldn't tell you, unless there is only one person. Couldn't afford for someone to know that someone else knew that he was considered and passed over."

"Good point."

"So. What if you got the job? Could you do the job and maintain your hands-on control over Disruption?"

"I guess that's a question I need to raise with Ariel, among several others. Truth is, I am really stretched quite thin currently."

"How so, honey?"

"You know that I do not like to talk about the office. But I am on a case right now that is about as complex as anything I've ever done. Massive drama."

"Can you tell me anything?"

"Unfortunately, not much. Yet, let's say that there are international spying issues, regional geopolitical issues and the future of Israel in the balance."

"Par for the course, Simon."

She giggled and hugged him, telling him that she knew he would come out on top.

CHAPTER.08

As soon as Frank Lord received the email, he immediately called his three BACL partners to an ad hoc meeting in the conference room. He looked flustered and quite unhappy. He dispensed with any form of nicety and just announced:

"Guys, I just received this crazy email from the Pentagon. They are telling us that there is a major bug in our invention."

Shi Tsu was the first to react, probably because he had been focused on the issue of the transmitter because of the *Mossad* discovery.

"A bug?"

"Yes, Shi Tsu. They actually call it a bug. They tell me that they have found an easy way to circumvent the communications which we claim to enable."

Shi Tsu, as the most academically oriented in the group, interrupted again. He needed them to make sure they used the correct words:

"Circumvent?"

"Yes, they're saying that the underwater transmission systems can be more easily detected than we anticipated."

"I'm still unsure what that means. Sorry to be a pain, Frank."

"Understood. They claim that, once they know where the transmitter is, they can actually take it over and instruct the drone to perform virtually any maneuver."

Shi Tsu was increasingly confused. What Frank had just described, other than the piece about external detection of the transmitter, was exactly what they had designed. He exclaimed:

"Well, hold the phone here, Frank. Isn't that exactly what the system should do? It's not a bug, it's a feature."

"Well, it is. The connection between the transmitter and the drone is working just fine, I guess, though they don't say it."

Shi Tsu was becoming agitated.

"So, what's wrong?"

Frank added:

"Sorry, I'm not being clear enough. The real issue is not here. They claim that they can give instructions even if they are not the "owner" of the device."

Shi Tsu had finally figured it out. He was mad at himself for not having sufficiently focused on Frank's initial words: "take over the system." He realized that what Frank described was the ability for a third party to take control, very much like the hacker who penetrates the defenses of a server or a laptop. He then uses a virus or a worm to "make" it do things that the owner of the server or the laptop does not want and does not know about. That was very serious. He summarized:

"Oh! I see what you mean. A third party can come in, locate the device, and effectively take over the drone. Just like a virus takes over a computer."

Frank smiled a polite but unhappy smile. He offered a positive element:

"Well, in some ways, that's right, Shi Tsu. But truth is we did not really protect against that."

Shi Tsu conceded that they had not anticipated any sort of

intrusion. In his mind, hacking would not be, should not be an initial issue, if only because the system and its technology were supposed to stay secret. Yet, internally, he was fuming and blaming himself, arguing to his partners:

"We should have anticipated that. The best defense is always the offense. Hacking into the transmitter is the weakest link of our system."

Frank interrupted Shi Tsu's train of thought:

"We can find a solution. Can't we? Shouldn't be too hard."

Shi Tsu agreed. But he shifted the topic marginally:

"One piece I do not understand is how they can locate the underwater transmitters. We always thought they were small enough that no one could find them unless they knew where they were."

He stopped, slapped his head with the palm of his right hand and continued:

"Just had a thought. What if you had been able to intercept one transmission? Then you'd be able to locate the source. From that point on, you know where it is."

Frank was not buying it:

"Hold it here. There's no transmission from the underwater transmitter, other than whatever it takes to create the mini waves. That can't be detected, can it?"

"Well, there are two possibilities. The first is that they've been able to detect that mini signal; like you, I doubt it. The other is that they're detecting the sonar signal from the drone to the underwater transmitter."

Frank beamed:

"Shi Tsu, that's brilliant. That's got to be the explanation. The detection of the sonar signal. But, what to do about it?"

"I don't know off the top of my head. Yet, I can think, in theory at least, of quite a few potential solutions. Let me give it some more thought. By the way, while we're at it, let's us all give it some thought."

They all left the conference room with faces that showed some serious disappointment and worry. One of them was visibly less concerned than the others. Could he be the leaker?

■ ■ ■ ■ ■

Countess Renate and Shi Tsu had finished discussing the problem of the leak. They still did not know whether it came from within BACL or from outside, but it seemed to them that an initial approach toward the solution had to be for someone to sweep BACL's server and all the office's computers. Countess Renate dialed her go-to cyber expert in Singapore:

"Hai Chock?"

"Yes, Countess Renate. Didn't expect your call. . . ."

"By the way, I'm not alone on this call, Hai Chock. Meet Dr. Xi Shi Tsu, one of our associates. He is a founding partner of Boston Advance Communication Laboratories and a full professor at MIT."

"Wonderful to meet you Shi Tsu. An honor in fact. Your specialty is in the air/water barrier in transmissions, right?"

"Very impressive. Glad to meet you too. By the way, I thought we are all associates with no pecking order."

Countess Renate stopped the self-congratulatory exchange and added:

"Hai Chock, we have a problem and I think you can help us."

"Shoot. I'm all ears."

Shi Tsu went on to describe the issue to Hai Chock. Countess Renate had told him that there was no need to discuss the whole of the mission. Hai Chock just needed to have enough facts to understand its urgency. So, Shi Tsu only focused on the point that a communication technology which was supposed to be top-secret had been found in a place where it should not have been. He conceded that the group had received at least two global patents, but assured Hai Chock that it would be practically impossible to reverse engineer the whole thing just on the basis of what was in the patents. Shi Tsu then turned to the part of the problem that dealt directly with Hai Chock's specialty: cybersecurity. Hai Chock could not help but interrupt Shi Tsu when the latter explained the issue of the leak and the consequences associated with it. Listening to the end of the story, he asked:

"How much do you know about your own computer set up, Shi Tsu?"

"I assume you mean the set up at the office."

"Correct. You've got to have your own server, yes?"

"Well, we do now, ever since we formed the company. But, at the outset, we were using MIT's network. They're pretty good, I'm told."

"If they're not, I don't know who is . . . though I've got to tell you that I've never tried to hack into it. So, I've not failed to penetrate it either."

Shi Tsu smiled and continued:

"But, in short, our set up is quite simple now. We have a single server which provides email services as well as file storage for all of us. One interesting trick which we put in is that there is an audit trail that tells us whenever anyone using the system, including any one of us, uploads something from the server onto their personal server. The upload can be direct, via e-mail, for instance, or through thumb drives or other external devices."

Shi Tsu was referring to a protection which MIT's cybersecurity department had recommended. Tracking any file movement from the host server to the outside is a simple way of identifying any leakage of intellectual property. The consultant engineer had explained that all uploads are not necessarily criminal, but any criminal activity would involve at least one upload. Hai Chock needed to know more to understand the problem. He asked:

"Can you be a bit more specific please?"

"Sure. Say that I download a file from the server onto a

thumb drive."

Hai Chock interrupted. He had figured it out. He expanded:

"Quite smart. Nobody can take a file from the system without it being seen. If you send it to your own private email, it will be listed as a "sent message" and if you just upload it, it will be seen as an upload. Quite smart indeed."

"Right. Right. Thank you. Now, what I'd like is to do is to check all sent messages and all uploads from anyone. That should allow us to discover whether the leak was from here."

"Well, it should help. But you cannot assume that someone has leaked a file just because they moved it to their home server."

"True enough. Our consulting engineer had warned us on that issue. But we have a policy that we must work on all business files from our business computers. So, even if I am working from home, I must use my office laptop or connect to the office network. So, anyone that sends a file from our server to the outside is suspect."

"Good to know. So, by the way, that means you do not use the Cloud, correct?"

"True. Again, our consultant suggested that a well-protected server is more secure than the Cloud."

"Debatable, but that's not the point here. So, now, there are two ways to proceed from here. Option A is you give me the credentials needed to get into your system as an administrator. Option B is you allow me to send a virus to you."

Shi Tsu thought for a minute. Computer engineering was not his specialty, but he was still a first-class engineer. He replied:

"Option A won't work. The system would record that someone has received the relevant credentials. It would quickly be flagged."

"Check. So, it's got to be option B."

"To tell you the truth, that one is not too appealing either."

"Why?"

"Wouldn't someone see the virus?"

"Not necessarily, my friend. In fact, most likely not unless your virus detector flags it. I have developed viruses that currently cannot be spotted."

Shi Tsu was warming up to the idea and asked:

"Is that legal?"

Hai Chock laughed and replied:

"No. I'm looking into their files without a warrant. But who will find out? And, by the way, I'm always doing it for a good cause; nothing to gain personally."

Shi Tsu smiled and added:

"Right. The good cause. . . . Now how would your virus option work?"

"Quite simply. I would send you the virus as an attachment to an email. By the way, that email could come from anyone. I can disguise myself any which way. Then, you open the attachment. The virus gets into the system via your own computer. I use it immediately to download all the audit files I need, plus all your email files as well."

Shi Tsu was incredulous:

"You can do that?"

"Yes, my friend, and it would not be the first time. . . . In many instances, I leave the virus active until the whole problem has been solved. But in others I can erase the virus right after the first inspection and no one would ever know it had been there."

"What do you recommend?"

Hai Chock asked Countess Renate for her opinion. She replied:

"As you know, this is not my specialty. Yet, something tells me that we have so many balls in the air now that we cannot know what we do not know. So, I would probably lean toward leaving the virus in there, regularly check whether there is any risk of discovery and be done with it. We can always erase it later."

Hai Chock nodded and offered the solution:

"Let me do this. First, I'll leave the virus in the server. However,

I will erase any way of finding out how it came into the system. So, even if someone should identify the virus, no one would be able to trace it to Shi Tsu's email."

Shi Tsu was smiling broadly:

"Brilliant. Then, let's do it."

■ ■ ■ ■ ■

"Simon? Jack here."

"Hey, how are you?"

"Well, pretty well. We have just planted the disinformation via the Pentagon. BACL must have received an email telling them that the Pentagon has found a way to detect the underwater transmitter and take it over."

"Is that possible?"

"Who knows? What I know is that it is not totally implausible. So, we expect two things. First the group should be working on a solution. Second, the leaker, if he is in the group, should warn Beijing."

"What if he decides to wait a while?"

"Obviously, that's a risk. It all depends upon what he knows. If he is senior enough to know of the sale of the drone to Iran, then he should warn them quickly. He already knows that Israel has located the transmitter though he thinks nobody knows where the drone is. Other than Hezbollah, obviously, but he probably does not know that either. So, he must be worried that they could take the drone over, . . ."

"That's a lot of assumptions, my friend."

"I know, but do you have a better idea?"

"In truth, no. Let's hope he takes the bait. By the way, I know from Countess Renate that they have started to highjack BACL's computer server. So our timing should be great if whoever it is sends the information by email."

"That does sound good, though, my guess is that any email would go from his private server."

"True, but our contact will be monitoring both emails and uploads from the server. My hope is that the leaker uploads something from the server, like the Pentagon email, and then forwards it to his controller, in China or elsewhere."

"Hey, I buy that. Keep me in the loop Simon. I'll do the same."

■ ■ ■ ■ ■

Simon placed one last call before calling it a day. He tried to reach Ariel, who, as usual, was still at his desk. He shared with him the various thoughts he had entertained the prior evening with Jennifer. He really needed to know whether he could both serve as Head of *Mossad* and keep his role as Head of Disruption. Ariel's answer was unequivocal:

"You would not have the bandwidth, my friend. Even you. There's too much to do in my job and in your current job for the two of them to be handled by a single person. May I ask what gave you the idea?"

"Sure. You know I'll always give it to you straight. I worry that I might not get along with the new boss if I do not get the job."

"I seem to recall we discussed that."

"We did and Jennifer made me see that I was kidding myself thinking I could."

"But you can't let go."

Simon hesitated for a second and then blurted out:

"Right. I love what I do, and I think I would really miss it."

"Let me park that one for a second, Simon. People who are good at what they do, often enjoy their jobs and feel they're happy just staying where they are. But let's not discuss that. Let me ask you. Hypothetically . . . You take my job. Who do you appoint to succeed you?"

"My first choice would have to be David Heller. But I was very impressed by Mark Levi as well."

"Good guy indeed. But he is young, David has much more experience. I think Mark can wait his turn. So, let's assume it's David Heller. Now, how would you feel if you were in his shoes. He's seen you get pretty much carte blanche from me. And now that he has your job, you're on his back? D'you think he'd like it?"

"No, of course not. You're right. So, back to square one, right?"

"Not quite. Not quite. You have a few more facts to consider. Keep thinking. I'm sure you'll come up with the right answer. . . . By the way, how are things going on the current big investigation?"

"Well, look. So far so good. But we are getting to a crucial point: uncovering the leaker in the U.S. I've been told that the fishing boat has left Tyre and as expected, she seems to be going straight for the Suez Canal. Bet you she's sailing for Iran. The sea route is just shy of thirty-three hundred nautical miles, but that's ten days at sea at an average speed of 15 knots per hour."

"You're on her, I'm sure."

"Absolutely. We have a plan, rather complex, but, frankly, I was able to "think complicated" because we have all the equipment we need to handle the complexity. Want to know any more?"

"Simon, my friend. I trust you. Keep me in the loop but focus on things that are very important. I know the project in is excellent hands. By the way, I heard you gave the assignment to Mark Levi."

"I did. I knew I would stay quite involved. David Heller might have objected to having me on his back. Plus, he's got a lot on his plate anyway."

"So, you see my earlier point on having the boss too much on your back. Anyway, glad to see you're still on the ball, Simon. Cheers."

CHAPTER.09

Hai Chock did not have too hard of a time penetrating the BACL server network once Shi Tsu had allowed the virus into his own computer. This made it possible for Hai Chock to retrieve virtually every file on the network, though his analysis was chiefly focused on communication files: emails coming in, emails going out and any form of upload or download of files. He whistled when he saw the number of files involved and thought to himself: *many days' work my friend . . .*

For his first pass, he focused his email inspection just on the names of senders and those of recipients. He was hoping to run screens based on Chinese names. His insight was that any link to the Chinese secret service would likely involve someone with a Chinese name. Obviously, a controller could have a western name, or a western pseudonym, but the odds were against that option in his view. With his current choice, he knew that he was surely going to miss a lot, but it seemed the easiest route. And, as he said to himself: *once in a while, you've got to get lucky.*

■ ■ ■ ■ ■

Jack Turnbull and Clay Mitchell were on a video conference call to review the initial findings of Clay's work on the BACL partners. He had essentially focused on the background checks which had been conducted on the partners when they were about to receive a contract from the Pentagon. Clay conceded that the information was a bit dated: The Pentagon approved the research contract with BACL at least a year ago. Yet, it contained interesting information. Clay started with Xi Shi Tsu, as he was supposed to be the one with the lowest likelihood to be the leaker they were after:

"Xi has had a relatively straightforward life. He came to the U.S. when his parents emigrated from China, not too long after the 1949 Communist takeover, in 1950. They originally settled in Seattle, but very quickly moved to the Boston area where the family has lived ever since. There are clear indications that they did not intend to stay in Seattle, no real estate purchase, no formal job though who knows if they did some work on the side, and a number of trips from Seattle to other major cities. His parents had some money, and it is believed that they managed to escape with bars of gold, but the notes clearly say that there is no hard evidence. The notes say nothing of the background of his parents before they left China. So, the gold bar story may be true, but it could also only amount to one or two, which is not unusual with immigrants. Now, clearly, if they were wealthy before leaving China, then there could be quite a few bars."

He paused to take his breath and continued:

"What is clear is that they were able to buy a home in the Cambridge area near Boston and to start a business. Though it's a bit trite, they first went for a laundry shop which they quickly expanded into a small chain; at the time of the background check, the chain had twenty stores and a processing factory."

Jack could not contain himself. He whistled and said:

"Not bad."

"Correct, but the story doesn't say how long it took him to go from here to there. Anyway, that's when the story takes an interesting twist. Xi's father went back to university to validate his Chinese medical degree. He then practiced medicine, internal medicine, while his wife was taking care of the chain of laundry stores."

"I see. You've got to give it to so many of these immigrants: they work themselves super hard, just so that they can give their children a normal life. They're prepared to sacrifice their generation for the benefit of children and grandchildren. Pretty impressive!"

"Absolutely. The rest is a bit more complex, but not out of the ordinary. They had two sons after they arrived in the U.S. of whom Shi Tsu is the oldest; his brother is Shi Wah."

"Both were born in the U.S.?"

"Yes. Shi Tsu was an excellent student. After high school in Boston, he went to the West Coast. He studied at both Stanford and the California Institute of Technology. At Stanford, he studied engineering. He obtained a PhD from Caltech in fluid mechanics. He stayed there as a researcher for some time, and then went to Singapore after which he was hired by MIT. His stint in Singapore involved a paid research and teaching assignment at the Nanyang Technological University."

Clay concluded:

"He has an excellent reputation. His wife, Xi Chun Hua, is of Chinese descent as well, although her parents emigrated later. She and her brother came to the U.S. in their very early teens. It seems her parents never worked directly for the Communist Party, though her father had some official role in local government."

"Could that be a problem?"

"It surely could. But you told me that he should not be on the list of suspects."

"Correct. I'll still mention it to Simon. I'd like him to ask Countess Renate what she makes of his wife's ancestry and potential government links. Though I bet she knows, it can't hurt anyone for us to have her angle. We'll see what Simon wants to do with the information, if anything. Now, how about Frank Lord?"

Clay continued his recitation:

"Classic American story; nothing special, I am afraid. Quiet family background from New England, New Hampshire, actually. His parents were both teachers, his mother at the college level and his father in high school. He has two siblings, both sisters. His schooling was all in New England, undergrad at Dartmouth where his mother taught, and graduate work at MIT. He was picked up as a superior research assistant by his thesis director and the rest is history. Eventually became co-Head of the fluid mechanics department with Xi."

"Nothing more?"

"Very little. He is divorced and re-married, with three children. His first wife was an MD at Massachusetts General, where she still is and is well-respected as a solid internist, with a specialty in diabetes. Their divorce was of the no-fault variety. Suspicions are that he may have cheated on her, as some claim that he had a bit of a reputation as a ladies' man. Remember, in those days, there was a lot less of a focus on professors dating students or research assistants. The notes say that he may well have been caught red-handed. So, he agreed to give his ex-wife whatever she asked. Yet, nobody knows."

Clay went on:

"Recently, he married a former Thai student of his; in fact, he was her thesis director. She goes now by the name of Mary Lord, but her maiden name was Chaem Choi Sae-Chin. The notes say that her first name means "gracefulness." Her undergraduate degree was acquired in Bangkok in mathematics. She is twenty years younger than he, and a note to the file says she is smashing. People were surprised when they married, as it seemed that Jack enjoyed his status as eligible and desirable bachelor."

"So, nothing too remarkable . . . other than the remarriage."

"Well. Yes. But I'm afraid that I've heard of many of those. If I was to look more deeply into someone, it would be Shi Tsu rather than Frank."

"How about Michael Lennon?"

"Well, his background is a bit more complex. He is Australian born, from Freemantle, just south of Perth, in Western Australia. He was a solid engineering student but did not go to work immediately after receiving the Australian equivalent of his BS. The notes say that his parents had some money, allowing him seemingly to have goofed around for a while; in Indonesia and Thailand in particular. He "got religion" in Singapore."

"Got religion? What does that mean, Clay?"

"Oh, simply, that he returned to school . . . He got his PhD from National University of Singapore. He is married to a Singaporean woman, whom it seems he met around the time he was enrolling at NUS. Is she the impetus behind his sudden interest in resuming his studies? We don't know. However, it seems that she came from a relatively wealthy family, whose principal interest was in property development."

"How did he eventually end up here?"

"Good question. The story does not tell what caused it. Yet, about fifteen years ago, he, his wife and their son came to the Boston area. We believe that he was recruited by MIT, but we don't really know more than one thing: doing research and further studies at MIT were listed as the reason for his visa request, and there was a letter of recommendation from MIT. Now did they happen on him or did he actively solicit the job, we don't know. He seems to be close to Frank, and I've read speculation that he may have met Frank's wife in Thailand, but we have absolutely no proof."

Jack could only note, sighing:

"Yeah right. Thailand is a big country. . . . So, he looks quite clean. Correct?"

"Certainly does. I wish I knew more about any links with Frank through his second wife or otherwise, but I have absolutely nothing. Their immigration interviews, the three of them still are resident aliens, green card holders, contain nothing of substance."

"Did he overlap with Shi Tsu in Singapore?"

"No, the dates don't work. By some real margin, like ten years or so."

"Well, I can't resist wondering whether there is more here than meets the eye. Whatever looks too good to be true usually is."

"I'll grant you that, Jack. We would need a much more thorough investigation to find out more and we can't do that without some judge's orders, as you know."

"I know. I know. Well, this has been very helpful, Clay. Let me process all that information and see where it leads me. So far, I would not zero in one any of them, other than Shi Tsu if I was not told he is above suspicion. Can you try to do a number of Ng Ho Lim too please? I know that we seem to have a lot of that information already. Yet, it'd be interesting to see if there are any discrepancies."

Jack paused and then asked:

"Anything on the Pentagon front?"

"Well, at this point, very little. It's awfully hard to do anything without drawing attention. I am working on a list of people who got access to the work product of BACL. Then, we'll see. I'll keep you in the loop."

■ ■ ■ ■ ■

"Hai Chock?"

"Yes, Countess . . . I was going to call you."

"Really, about BACL server?"

"Yes."

"Well, before you get into it, I have a question for you. Do you remember the fellow at the Security Intelligence Division in

Singapore?"

"Yeo Yap Min? You bet. We've gotten together a couple of times.

■ ■ ■ ■ ■

About a year earlier, the Military Security Department of Singapore had made contact with Countess Renate. They could see that their main server had been hacked but were unable to counter the criminal intrusion. Yeo Yap Min, a deputy director who reported directly to the Director of the agency who in turns reports to the Permanent Secretary of Defense had sought Countess Renate for help.

Singapore has three intelligence services which, like many things in the Republic, are known by their acronyms: ISD, SID and MSD. ISD, the Internal Security Department, looks after domestic and counter-intelligence issues. SID, the Security Intelligence Division, officially under the Ministry of Defense, is the agency responsible for gathering and analyzing intelligence related to the country's external security; its director holds a rank equivalent of Permanent Secretary and reports directly to the Prime Minister's office. The MSD, the Military Security Department, reports directly to the Permanent Secretary of Defense and is responsible for deterring, detecting, and neutralizing evolving security threats. Its mission is to protect the secrets of the Ministry of Defense and of the Singapore Armed Forces and to be an independent platform to help them advance their strategic interests.

The three agencies had been brought together when the initial breach was detected. In fairness, each had a reason to get involved. The ISD viewed it as a counter-intelligence operation, as everyone assumed, at least initially, that the threat came from overseas. The SDI saw it as within its purview because of the element concerning the country's external security. The MSD, which had initially detected the intrusion, received the mandate from the Prime Minister as it seemed that the challenge certainly involved protecting national secrets. Though this might make it sound as if bureaucratic infighting was ripe, it would be a serious misunderstanding of how Singapore functions to believe it was. In short, all three agencies have one goal and only one: serve the Republic.

Yeo Yap Min was as surprised as anyone when Countess Renate told him that her best expert on cyber issues was Singapore-based. She had hesitated a short while before revealing the detail, as the strength of her network was its secrecy. Therefore, she initially worried that effectively "outing" Hai Chock to his country's secret service was not a good idea. Hai Chock, in a quick conversation with her, made it clear that the government was bound to find out. It would therefore be better, in his view, to have a contract that stipulated that his identity was not to be revealed beyond those who absolutely needed to know. He felt that he could trust the officials to live by their words. Countess Renate took his recommendation, not without having warned him that he was the one running the risk. As she put it:

"Any pressure, if it comes, will be on you. I can sever all connections we have with you in a split second, however much I would hate to do it. Yet, as you know, Hai Chock, the network comes first."

Hai Chock nodded with a sad look in his eyes. They agreed that they were on the same wavelength however much he hated the potential outcome. Hai Chock and Yap Min agreed to meet at the Ministry of Defense. Yap Min started the conversation:

"Isn't it a bit awkward that the agency responsible in Singapore for counter-terrorism and cybersecurity has to call on an outside cyber-security expert?"

"You know, Yap Min, on the surface it might seem that way. But, in truth, the value proposition behind our network is that we bring the 'best' experts to those who need them. With all due humility, I am supposed to be it on the cybersecurity front. But, in truth, I never take myself seriously. It's just that I haven't seen a hack that I haven't been able to break."

CHAPTER.10

The mystery was still as deep as ever. The leaker or leakers had yet to be identified. Without that crucial piece of information, Simon and Jack Turnbull felt they were powerless. Anything which they might do was exposed to the risk first of being leaked and second of leading to some retaliatory action. The enemy, whoever it was, could choose to eliminate individuals that started to present some danger. Also, it could choose to lay low, interrupting whatever strategic move was associated with the placing of the armed underwater drone off the coast of Haifa. As Simon had said as the group got together:

"We don't even know if the drone we found was the first or the last one in a series, or anything in between."

The group comprised Countess Renate, Xi Shi Tsu, Jack Turnbull, Hai Chock and Simon. They had called a conference call to review the initial analysis of the BACL servers which Hai Chock had been able to perform. Hai Chock was careful to preface his presentation:

"Thankfully, the company did not have a policy of getting rid of emails on a periodical basis. That's the good news. The bad news is that there are literally thousands of files in the email folder."

Cross talk ensued which Simon brought to an end with a simple question, focused on two elements:

"Hai Chock, what have you been able to do and what have you found?"

Hai Chock replied that he had only worked on the email files so far. To save time given the number of entries, he focused on two criteria only:

"I checked for counterparties with oriental names and for correspondence with oneself. I applied these criteria, both to incoming and outgoing emails."

There was a bit of cross talk again, as Hai Chock's comment with respect to correspondence with oneself was not clear. He apologized and clarified what he had done and what he had meant:

"By correspondence with oneself, I mean emails sent or received by the same person. Say, for instance, emails which Shi Tsu would send to or have received from his personal address. Is that clearer?"

Everyone agreed that the process made a great deal of sense. Hai Chock went on:

"By the way, I eliminated all correspondence that involve the four partners in BACL corresponding internally. I kept emails where there might have been only two of the partners, just to see if there was a pattern. In short, the largest number of emails in that group was between Frank and Shi Tsu. No surprise here."

He paused and seeing that this raised no question, he continued:

"The bottom line is that there is not so much on which to hang our hats. Obviously, Shi Tsu has the most emails flagged, because he qualifies on all counts. Anything which he receives, or he sends by definition will make the screen."

"Did you learn anything?"

Hai Chock smiled, as he could see that Shi Tsu was the one asking the question:

"Well, Shi Tsu, you'll be happy to know that I did not see anything in there that looked suspicious."

Countess Renate chimed in:

"Not a big surprise. Tell us, Hai Chock, what did you do with the emails that you screened out? I mean, for instance here, Shi Tsu's email.

"Good question, Countess. I created a folder into which I copied all the emails that came out. That folder is on one of our servers."

"You mean Shadow Experts?"

"Absolutely, Countess. We can get back to them any time we want. Oh, while I'm at it, the same is true for absolutely all emails that were sent or received through the BACL server. So, we can go back to the data if we need more analysis."

Simon thanked him for his caution. He then asked:

"Who came in second in your search?"

"The second largest number of emails involve Michael Lennon, and a few of those merit some attention: it looks as if quite a few of them involve addressees that are abroad."

Shi Tsu commented:

"You know that Mike's wife is from Singapore . . . These emails could involve her family."

"Didn't know that. That could be an explanation, but for whatever it is worth I would have expected him to correspond with his in-laws from his home server."

Shi Tsu remarked that the conclusion was quite logical. However, he added:

"He spent a long time in Asia, and he may have made a number of contacts. Also, I believe he studied at National University of Singapore. He could also have contacts there."

Hai Chock conceded the point. Yet, he reinforced the conclusion he had drawn that if it was up to him, he would look into the email files with a bit more care. The group agreed. Hai Chock turned to the last partner:

"Frank Lord stands out as having very few emails sent to people with oriental names. There is quite a bit of traffic between his official and his private server though."

Jack Turnbull asked the first question:

"Have you been able to analyze these yet?"

"Not really, Jack. My initial focus was on seeking patterns, and secondarily on filing the emails into distinct folders to allow you all to do the analysis. Frankly, I am a bit uncomfortable peering into things that could be private. I saw a number of emails between Jack and his wife, Mary, for instance. I have no idea what they're talking about, but I do not feel it would be right for me to study them; their privacy, you know?"

Countess Renate interrupted to emphasize the importance of what Hai Chock had just said:

"This is very important gentlemen. We are not in the business of spying on anyone, unless there is a special permission officially granted to us by some authority. I believe that in the U.S. you call it something like "probable cause;" is that correct, Jack?"

"Absolutely. I understand. Now, this raises a very important issue for Simon and me at least, and possibly for Shi Tsu. The server is on U.S. soil and the individuals are, for a large part, either U.S. citizens or permanent U.S. residents. Clay had warned me."

Simon interrupted:

"Clay?"

"Sorry, Clay Mitchell, my opposite number at the FBI. He had warned me to be careful with anything that could be viewed as a federal crime, and this is over the line, I'm afraid. So, how do we get permission to review the material in some depth?"

Shi Tsu replied that he was neither ready, nor did he have the authority, to ask for some official wiretap. Jack said he understood and asked a simple question:

"Hai Chock, can you give us a count of the email traffic each of the four partners received or initiated once the recent news of the problem with the system came out?"

Shi Tsu asked:

"Why is that relevant?"

"Well, to be honest with you, Shi Tsu, it was disinformation which Simon and I decided to plant. If anyone from within the firm was leaking to the Chinese, you would expect this to be something he would have wanted China to know immediately."

"A trap?"

"Absolutely, Shi Tsu, a trap."

"Why was I not in the loop?"

Simon replied:

"Frankly, we felt that not having you in the loop was the best way to ensure that any discussion that might take place within your group was totally genuine. We did it to protect you."

"Nice. Thanks, I guess."

Simon added that they also had not put Countess Renate in the loop either. She asked why. Simon replied:

"Please, don't take this personally, Countess. It was never meant to have you out of a loop. But in this case, as you've told me in other instances, I guess I'd argue it was a need-to-know thing."

"Understood, Simon. Fair."

Hai Chock asked for the date when the news came out and how it did come out. Jack gave him the date and said that it was in an email sent to all four partners directly from the Pentagon. Being a bit more precise, he said:

"It was sent to Jack with copies to the other three partners."

Hai Chock paused for a few seconds as he was looking at his computer screen. He was apparently performing a number of manipulations, which the others on the call understood were most likely a variety of searches and counts. He blurted out:

"Well, taking out any email sent by one of the four partners to the others, the only person who sent emails to Chinese sounding names was Michael Lennon. The only other meaningful traffic was between Frank and his wife. Don't see any email to or from Shi Tsu."

Shi Tsu asked:

"Anything from Ho Lim?"

"No, None."

Simon asked the next question:

"Good, how about any upload?"

"Same two people: Frank and Michael. Ng Ho Lim had absolutely none and Shi Tsu only a couple."

Shi Tsu thought he needed to add:

"Don't know about the others, but, in my case, I can easily explain my traffic and uploads. When Frank first discussed the email, I had offered a possible interpretation of the problem. More than that, I said that I would look for a solution. You may not believe this, but I would rather work on issues on my system when I am home rather than working remotely on the office server."

Hai Chock added:

"Unless you have weak security on the office server, you are safer using it remotely than a presumably relatively unprotected domestic one."

"Good to know, my friend. Thanks. But I was worried about the connection that would be opened between my server and the office. Is that not a good idea?"

Hai Chock replied that he could argue it from both sides, but would always advise clients to work on the server that was the most carefully and fully protected, adding:

"I've seen exceptions, but transmission intercepts."

Turning to Shi Tsu on the video conference, he added:

"This is what I'd call someone trying to get stuff while you're communicating with the office server."

"Thanks, Hai Chock. You were saying . . ."

"Ah. Yes. Transmission intercepts usually occur when people know that something will be coming. Putting someone on such a watch would be expensive if you're simply trying to catch a particular transmission . . ."

Simon interrupted:

"Interestingly, Hai Chock, that's what we do in our business."

"I can see that: you have reasons to believe something might come out."

"Absolutely. But, here, assuming that someone is spying on Shi Tsu, I could imagine that he would be subject to ongoing surveillance. Anyway, we do not know. But, Shi Tsu, I would suggest you get a cybersecurity specialist, and you have one on the line, to look at your procedures and check them; plus, I thought you said it was against your own policies."

"Fair point. Thanks, you two. Hai Chock, can we find some time to chat?"

"Why not now? I'll call you right back."

Simon asked Jack what he would like to do next. Jack replied:

"We know the facts, two of the four partners seemed to communicate more with the outside just after the disinformation news release. In terms of next step, it seems that, first, we need to have a bit more of what Hai Chock rightly called a probable cause before we do anything. I suspect we need to wait and see what happens on the Chinese front. Shi Tsu, please, act as if you did not know it was disinformation and look for a hypothetical solution. I think that the second wave of disinformation might well focus on whatever idea you suggest. If we see the same two people communicate again in the same pattern, then we may have probable cause for looking at the relevant emails."

"Makes sense."

Simon moved to bring the conference to a close, adding:

"If we are through, thank you, everyone. Jack, could you stay on the line a few minutes more please?"

When Simon and Jack were on the phone by themselves, Simon asked point blank:

"Shouldn't be thinking that way but can't help it. Can we dig a bit more into the past of Frank and Shi Tsu. Countess Renate will be mad if she finds out, but I think we must at least have done the most elementary work. Maybe we can't do it officially, but a private investigator might. What do you think?"

"Frankly, I'm glad you mentioned the bit about Shi Tsu. You know Countess Renate better than I, but I would have hated to give him a complete pass. The conversation on his server preference when he works from home looked quite suspect to me."

"Unfortunately, I can't disagree."

"What do you think about giving a soft warning to Countess Renate, Simon?"

"It's tempting, but I'd rather wait until we know a bit more. Though, as they say, "note to self" we have told him about the disinformation."

"We have, and it means that, if he is the leaker, we won't catch him this time. We can certainly give the whole thing a second try, with a different idea. At the same time, we'll learn something about the other two. After all, based on my trust in Countess Renate, they are the ones that should be our suspects, particularly Michael."

"I can see that, but we've got to keep our eyes wide open."

"Agreed. Also, beyond Michael, I'd want to know when Frank got married to his current wife, how long he stayed divorced, how many of these romances lasted more than a couple of weeks and so forth? Maybe there's nothing to it, but we should at least look under that stone."

"Agreed, Simon. I'll investigate the idea of the PI."

"PI?"

"Yes, Private Investigator . . . Sorry. We may be able to have some work done without triggering all sorts of alarm bells about invasion of privacy and the rest. One thing your question triggered when I recalled the report which Clay gave: is there anything in his personnel file that talks of complaints by students or other professional females?"

Jack paused and, as if the proverbial light bulb had just come on, he said:

"You know what, Simon?"

"No, but you're going to tell me."

"Absolutely. Let me look into which PI could do the work. In the end, he or she should be hired by *Mossad*. I don't want to know who pays the bill, though I assume that it would have to come from the Israeli Embassy in Washington."

"I get it. If it's us spying on a private U.S. citizen, neither you nor Clay are involved. . . . And if we get caught?"

"You won't. But if you do, an apology and repatriating an agent that had gone rogue. The routine what?"

They both had a good laugh.

■ ■ ■ ■ ■

Countess Renate asked Hai Chock to call her right back, after he had dealt with the issue he wanted to discuss with Shi Tsu. She wanted to discuss the "new assignment" as she called it. Within a couple of minutes, he was back on the phone with Countess Renate. She asked:

"Returning to your friend Yeo Yap Min, I wonder whether we could look into a couple of things."

"It'll have to be off-the-record."

"Understood. I'm thinking of checking into the family of Michael Lennon's wife. Who are they really and is there anything interesting to learn about her?"

"I see. You said a couple of things."

"Yes. The other one is a bit more difficult. I wonder whether Yap

Min could find out about the family of Frank Lord's wife. On the surface, it looks quite clean, if I can call clean the fact that Frank was having successive love affairs with students. Yet, I'd love to know more. It could be a simple coincidence, but she ended up dating and then marrying a very important man, didn't she? Would be interesting to know how long the courtship lasted. Was their first meeting an accident? Or a part of a very careful plan?"

"Well, you tell me, Countess. Do you know how many conquests he made before getting to her?"

"Excellent question, my friend. Anything you can find out from Yap Min will be much appreciated. After all, they owe you big time."

"They owe us, Countess. But one caveat though: we do not know whether the lady ever visited Singapore. I assume that we're counting on his connections with his opposite number in Thailand, but that may be stretching it a bit. Anyway, it's certainly worth a try."

"Thanks."

■ ■ ■ ■ ■

Though the story was never revealed in the press, Hai Chock had indeed discovered that the hacking which the Ministry of Defense was experiencing originated in China but was facilitated by an insider. He was able indeed to follow the tracks left by the hacker all the way to a group in Beijing. That group appeared to be affiliated with the PLA, the People's Liberation Army, operating out of the Ministry of State Security and the Ministry of Public Security. That group, created within the Army itself, had been known to operate a number of classical tools to gain access to a wide variety of public and private information, with their targets ranging from the U.S. to Australia to the Vatican.

Yet, their traditional way of infiltrating systems, taking advantage of reported failings before they were fixed, could not possibly apply to the case in point. Singapore's Ministry of Defense was all over the issue and would fix any problem within hours of it being identified, failing which they would simply shut down that system until a fix was found. So Hai Chock dug further and using a secret tool he had developed found a way to trace what he called "echoes;" those would come into play when a computer on the target network actually contacted the hacker or when the hacker contacted it. This work pointed to an individual, relatively low on the totem pole, who had become dissatisfied with Singapore.

Singapore has a multi-party electoral system, although one party seems more often than not to win a wide majority of the seats in Parliament—the opposition retaining only a handful at most. While one might argue that this could be evidence of some measure of trickery, the answer seems to be considerably simpler. The Majority selects its candidates with utmost care and these candidates work very hard for their constituents. This is true most of the time, but it is particularly true at election time. Thus, certain adherents of minority parties have felt that the system was stacked against them. Chiang Wah Siu was one such individual. He had supported the opposition for a long time and eventually, though rising to the rank of lieutenant in the army, found himself attracted to China. Whether this was before he had chosen a recent immigrant as a bride, or because she was sent to seduce him, was never found. He was quickly caught, tried, condemned, sentenced to death and executed. His widow had left the Republic before the condemnation, suggesting to observers that she may have been bait.

Yeo Yap Min had been delighted and was all the more impressed that he did not have to say anything in terms of confidentiality. Countess Renate had been categorical:

"Secrecy and confidentiality are our foundation stones, alongside doing what is right. You will never hear a Shadow Expert leak. It would immediately mark him or her as an ex-Shadow Expert. And we would do whatever we could to repair any damage."

CHAPTER.11

WASHINGTON, DC, USA, AND TEL AVIV, ISRAEL

Simon was calling Jack Turnbull to finalize the details of the tail they were placing on the *Sea Crescent* as it had left Tyre. They both had a pretty strong conviction that she was going back to Iran but wanted to track her all the way. They agreed that she would need to refuel about every other day or so, assuming she was running at somewhere between ten and fifteen knots per hour. She would likely sail through the Suez Canal, all the way down the Red Sea and then through the Gulf of Aden, the Arabian Sea, the Gulf of Oman and eventually into the Persian Gulf via the Strait of Hormuz. Simon and Jack knew that they could call upon U.S. Navy resources. The Sixth Fleet operates in the Atlantic Ocean and the Mediterranean; more importantly, the Fifth Fleet is south of the Red Sea, and effectively covers the entire region the *Sea Crescent* would have to use after leaving the Red Sea.

While this would allow them the use of aerial drones which could take off and land on the aircraft carriers of either fleet, it was not enough in the eyes of either Simon or Jack. They also wanted to know what the ship would do along the way. Would they meet anyone? What would they do, if anything, while in port? They therefore organized to have a couple of supply ships which, with a length of 110 feet, were slightly larger than the Lebanese vessel and would take turns shadowing her while she was at sea. They also carried a lot more fuel than *Mossad* assumed the *Sea Crescent* carried: about 20,000 gallons. *Mossad* had one trick up its sleeve, in that a few of their ships could change their names on the bow of the vessel or could raise a crane (which otherwise was kept lying horizontally on the deck) in the middle of the ship to give her the appearance of a fishing boat. Though a very careful eye would most likely not fall for the subterfuge, that and the fact that they were flying Maltese flags would be enough, at least initially.

The plan was that the ship charged with the direct tail, one or two nautical miles behind the target but keeping the boat constantly on their radar, would contact headquarters as soon as the *Sea Crescent* gave any sign of going into port. In fact, they had already made assumptions as to where she would have to refuel, though they surely would not rely on them. There were indeed key unknowns such as the size of the fuel tank and the fuel consumption rate. They assumed that she carried about 2,500 gallons, simply because that's what comparable ships in the 75- to 80-foot range did, but there was always the risk that she could have been fitted with additional tanks or that she needed to make stops for other reasons. When the *Sea Crescent* gave an indication that she was veering toward a port, a surveillance drone would focus more sharply on it. The ship tailing the vessel would stop shadowing her, effectively seeming to go on her original course southbound on the Red Sea. Once out of sight of potential prying eyes, it would shift its appearance and refuel from a tanker which was the second boat in the three-ship surveillance group. The third ship, similar to the first, would position itself in such a way that she could start the shadowing as soon as needed. Simon and Jack had decided that, for the first port stop, the ship which would take over the surveillance on the following leg would not enter the harbor area.

They wanted to know what activity was going on within the harbor before taking the risk of placing a vessel in harm's way.

The surveillance aerial drones they were using were Eitans from the Israeli Air Force. The Fifth Fleet had allowed Israel to "park" a couple of Eitans on the deck of an aircraft carrier. Though Eitans had never landed on or taken off from an American aircraft carrier, Jack and Simon felt the remote pilots had experience with landing on runways that had to be shorter than those of a large U.S. carrier. Israel indeed has no aircraft carrier at present: too much of a sitting duck target. Thus, the disadvantage of that lack of experience was much more than offset by Simon's ability to issue virtually direct orders to their pilots. The Eitan's speed was modest—about two hundred and fifty nautical miles per hour—but that would be plenty to catch up with a ship that sailed at less than five percent of that speed. They flew higher than forty thousand feet, and with a length of about forty feet and a wingspan of less than eighty, they were very hard to pick up, unless someone was obviously looking for one knowing its general location. Its mission would be to create a movie of the activity of the Lebanese vessel while in the harbor. Simon hoped that the stop would last less than thirty hours or so, as the drone could not stay aloft a lot longer than forty hours. Armed with the movie, analysts in Israel would be able to get as good a feeling as possible of all that the ship and her crew did while in port.

Simon and Jack had asked to be kept informed of the progress of the *Sea Crescent*. They had said they would be glad to take any call if anything unusual was happening. Yet, quite frankly, they were not expecting anything until the Lebanese vessel got to Bandar Abbas, on the East Coast of the Persian Gulf, which they assumed was its destination.

Simon and Jack were therefore quite surprised when they received a call six days into the return trip of the Lebanese vessel. Marl Levi, who was in charge of the mission on the *Mossad*'s side, called Simon, who, upon getting the news, conferenced Jack on the call right away:

"Jack we've got news. . . . Go ahead Mark. Please summarize what you told me. We'll get to details when we have more time; it's nighttime for Jack."

Mark apologized, but Jack replied:

"No worries. Please go ahead. I'm wide awake now."

"Well, gentlemen, the ship followed the routine we more or less expected all the way to the Gulf of Aden. It stopped for fuel in Hurghada in Egypt as the Gulf of Suez becomes the Red Sea, in Port Berenice still in Egypt, in Massawa in Eritrea and in Aden in Yemen. However, it never went to Bandar Abbas . . ."

Jack interrupted:

"They store the stuff in Aden?"

Mark replied:

"Well, not really sir. As it sailed from Aden, instead of going east-northeast as it should have to minimize the distance to the Strait of Hormuz, it sailed east-southeast, in the direction of the island of Socotra. There, it was met by a Chinese cargo ship; by the way, there's no question that she is Chinese, we've checked. They sailed alongside each other for a short while, just enough, as the pictures from a high-flying drone revealed, to load what looks very much like a new underwater drone onto the *Sea Crescent*. The cargo was promptly moved below deck. They also transshipped an elongated box, which we assume is the transmitter. The vessel then sailed in a northerly direction for a couple of hours until it was met by an Iranian Navy ship which, similarly, seemed to be tied up with her and unloaded what the pictures revealed to be two missiles. At that point, it did not continue sailing toward Iran, but retraced its steps, stopping first in Aden and going then into the Gulf of Aden and through the Bab-Al-Mandab Strait back into the Red Sea. We assume it's on its way back, probably toward Tyre, with some pitstop somewhere to threaten Israel."

Jack could not hide his surprise:

"What do you make of that, Simon?"

"Well, my friend, it seems that both the Iranians and the Chinese are being very, very careful. But, at the same time, I think they're not terribly smart. They've clearly not taken into account the notion that the *Sea Crescent* might be tailed or the subject of aerial surveillance. Imagine the movie footage we now have."

"I can see that, but, at the same time, they're still running the risk of being found out. . . . And there could be trouble, with our Fifth Fleet not all that far away."

"True enough, Jack. But let's assume that the rendezvous points are selected at the last minute, by the Chinese first and then by the Iranians. You'd have to assume that these guys can check the immediate surroundings."

"I get that, Simon. But what about drone video footage?"

"As I said a few seconds ago, my guess is that they simply haven't thought of it."

They agreed that they needed more data points to come to a reasonable conclusion. Simon suggested that they needed to place "tails" on both the Iranian and the Chinese ships. Matter-of-factly, Jack asked:

"Do you have their names?"

"Yep. It's on the pictures I've sent to you."

"Great. Thanks. I'm sure that the Fifth Fleet can take care of that without being too obvious. We can even send one of our own drones up to do that. What do you want to know?"

"Well, everything. Thinking out loud, I want to know where each ship goes from there. I've got to assume that the Iranian military ship is probably going to return to Iranian territorial waters. They have no business being there, though, on the basis of the picture, she looks like a patrol boat and could claim to be on patrol. She's in international waters after all."

"Reasonable. What about the Chinese ship?"

Simon replied:

"Well, that's my real question. I can't believe she would make a trip from China just to carry one underwater drone. So, we need to figure out what she is doing, and we must do that without attracting her attention."

"Leave it with me, Simon."

Simon cautioned:

"They're making these transfers in international waters. It'd be real hard to try and stop them unless you were absolutely sure of what they're doing. And to make things even worse, what they're transshipping is not illegal."

He paused for a second or two and added:

"Embarrassing, if discovered, but certainly not illegal. No arms embargo violation for the Chinese. Same for Iran, I'm afraid."

"Absolutely. Come to think of it, back to Mark's earlier comment. I wonder where they plan to drop the drone?"

Simon replied:

"Don't know, my friend, but there are plenty of places. One thing we'll have to monitor is whether the ship goes back through the Suez Canal or sails up the East branch of the upper Red Sea toward Eilat. By the way, I also wonder why they're only carrying one underwater drone at a time. Could surely carry two or three, Any disagreement. Mark?"

"None, sir. Though the transhipment images we have do not suggest more than one. Maybe, they were contained in the same box."

■ ■ ■ ■ ■

The *Sea Crescent* retraced its steps pretty strictly on the way back. It made stops in exactly the same ports as it had done on the voyage to the Gulf of Aden. It sailed through the Suez Canal and dropped its drone in the same general area as before, though somewhat south of the earlier one. Then, she sailed on to Tyre. This proved to be important information for Simon and Jack. They had initially opined that the ship could veer to starboard when she got to the branching in the upper Red Sea. The main branch goes to Suez and is called the Gulf of Suez, while the right is called the Gulf of Aqaba and goes to the point where Israel and Jordan meet. On the Israeli side, one has Eilat, and one finds Aqaba on the Jordan side. To Simon, this meant that Hezbollah wanted to plant at least one more underwater drone aiming at Israel from the Mediterranean. That did not mean that there would not be anything planted later around Eilat, but that did not seem the current priority. Then, Simon caught himself thinking: *Unless they bring that one in differently. Yet can't imagine them smuggling it through Saudi Arabia. No, Simon, it would also have to be by sea.*

The interesting new element was that, this time, a closer examination by *Mossad* of the happenings in the Tyre harbor revealed that the crew was being changed. This made sense to Simon as the crew had to be based in or around Lebanon and comprised of Hezbollah troops. Another insight which he got from the information to-date was that there seemed to be only one ship carrying weapons like the drone. Simon indeed knew that many other weapons were carried by road, via Iraq and Syria. The setup made sense for as long as the drones were to be used against Israel.

After spending two days in Tyre, the ship started on a new voyage. She followed exactly the same route as two weeks earlier. It sailed from Tyre toward the Suez Canal. By now, *Mossad* and the CIA had their routine well sorted out and they followed the ship, from a bit further away, as they felt they knew its likely route. They also felt they knew where the ship would refuel and had therefore used local *Mossad* or CIA resources to track movements of the boat and her crew when they were docked in the harbor. Truth be told, the extra resources did not provide much new information, that they recognized as such at the time. Yet, in Massawa, in Eritrea, something surprising happened.

While in every other port, the crew had nonchalantly milled around the harbor as the ship was being fueled and a couple of sailors had gone to buy fresh food supplies, they seemed quite rushed in Massawa. No one could identify what caused them to behave differently, but their pit stop was shorter than usual and looked rushed. Simon and Jack were in for another surprise.

There were no rendezvous with the Chinese ship or with the Iranian Navy. The *Sea Crescent* went directly from Aden, where they also refueled quickly, to Bandar Abbas, in Iran. Simon called Jack as soon as he found out. Jack blurted out:

"What the hell is that?"

"Don't know any better than you, my friend. Let's see. We've shadowed the Chinese ship. Basically, she's anchored at sea in that same general area. She remains in international waters and there is nothing anyone can do about her. Ostensibly, she's going nowhere, but probably does not want to use extra fuel pretending to be moving. In short, she seems to be on some sort of holding pattern."

"Makes sense. Will she need to refuel?"

"Honestly, Simon, your guess is as good as mine. We don't know how much fuel she carries. My own guess is that it makes little sense to carry enough fuel to do a complete round trip from China. But there's no law against that. Anyway, she's not showing signs of any activity now. Plus, they could always bring in a tanker to refuel her at sea."

"OK. What about the Iranians?"

"Well, it was initially on some sort of holding pattern as well. Slow patrol along the coast of the Gulf of Aden. The big news is that it suddenly made a U-turn and sailed directly for Bandar Abbas, at some speed. Can't explain it. But now, with your news, I'm sure the whole thing is one big development . . . Don't know what it means though."

Simon thought for a minute. Then he asked:

"Do we know the date of the U-Turn?"

"I don't know as we speak, but I can find out in two seconds flat. What are you thinking about?"

"The impact of disinformation, my friend. Disinformation."

"What do you mean?"

"Remember, the Pentagon sent an email to BACL to tell them they had a problem with the system."

"Oh. Sure. I see it. It's not terribly hard to imagine that the same leaker or leakers let the Chinese know who would in turn have let the Iranians know that there had to be some delay. They would not want to deliver a faulty drone or a faulty transmitter."

Simon followed where Jack had stopped:

"Then, the Iranians could have told the *Sea Crescent* to stop and return to Tyre. But since she was on its way, why not simply re-route her to Bandar Abbas. There she'd be safe, and they could all wait the "all clear" from China together."

"Surely holds together, Simon. Naturally, there are other explanations. Correct?"

"Sure there are."

"Well, for instance, the *Sea Crescent* may be picking up other forms of armament and preparing to carry them into Lebanon."

"Agreed, Jack. But two things argue against that."

"Two things?"

"Yep. Two things. First, they typically carry their armament supplies via land, you know cutting across the north of Iraq and through Syria."

"That's one."

"The second has to do with the movements of the Iranian and Chinese ships. Why would they have initially at least for the Iranians stayed in the neighborhood if this was the last drone delivery?"

"Grant you that one as well. I'm not saying it is likely; I'm just saying it's possible. The only way we could know would be to board both ships and see what they carry. After we've done that. we could get ready for World War Three."

"No. You're right. Let's do this. Let's prod Shi Tsu and ask him to help us. He now knows the original information was fake. Let's have him say that he found out some indication that it was a false alarm. Then we'll see. In the meantime, can you press on with the investigations into the leaks in Boston please?"

"No problem."

"One last thing, Jack. We need to have surveillance of Bandar Abbas and the Chinese ship."

"Yeah. I see. We've got to know when the *Sea Crescent* leaves Bandar Abbas and see where she goes."

"Right. We also need some warning if there is any movement by the Chinese ship."

"Simon, where are your two spy ships?"

"You mean the tails?"

Jack nodded. Simon carried on:

"They're in the Gulf of Oman, just south of the Strait of Hormuz. We have a submarine in the area; so they have no issue of food or water, but there're gonna need fuel."

"Let me see with the Fifth Fleet. I'm sure we can get a tanker to refuel them. I'll let you know the details when I have them."

"Thanks."

CHAPTER.12

BOSTON, MA, USA, WASHINGTON, DC, USA, AND TEL AVIV, ISRAEL

Shi Tsu called a partners' meeting to inform them that he had the response to the question raised by the Pentagon. Frank Lord was ecstatic and asked him to explain. Shi Tsu obliged with all the more ease now that he knew that the original "complaint" had been a fake.

He went back to his earlier statement, arguing that what the Pentagon was complaining about was not a bug, but a feature. It was a part of the design of the system that communications could be read or initiated by anyone who knew what to do. He added:

"Imagine the mess it would be if you had to have a special transmitter or a special radar for each location."

Michael asked:

"Why didn't we think of that earlier?"

"Well, in a way we did, but I know that I said it at the time in a defensive mode. Now, I think it's all to our credit; we want perfection, and we were stunned that someone might have found a flaw. But, nevertheless, there is something that can be done to make communications more secure. That's what I propose to send in an email form to the Pentagon. It will not require any hardware modification; it's just a question of code."

Frank asked what Shi Tsu meant. Shi Tsu replied that they should provide for usernames and passwords, adding:

"Simple as that."

Frank seemed delighted, but still said that he did not fully understand the implications. Shi Tsu asked:

"Well, as far as we know, neither the Pentagon nor *Mossad* has deployed the system. Correct?"

"Absolutely."

"So, Frank, at this point the question is moot."

Shi Tsu could see that both Michael and Frank were still hesitating. He exclaimed:

"You can't be thinking of the drone which we have been told was placed by Hezbollah off the coast of Israel."

Frank immediately replied:

"Of course not. Well, in fact, I should say, not directly. My question deals with the future. If we are going to have to provide for usernames and passwords to grant access, that must mean that there will be maintenance needs."

He paused for a second, as if to see the reactions in his partners' eyes. Ho Lim was the first to react:

"That's true. So, does it mean that the usernames and passwords are in effect hard coded before the drones and transmitters are placed in the water, or can they be modified from time to time?"

Shi Tsu smiled and replied:

"Excellent question Ho Lim. To me, the issue is trivial with respect to the transmitter."

He could see the quizzical look on his partners' faces. He clarified his thought:

"Simple, gentlemen. The transmitter can receive and emit regular radio waves. We simply have to instruct it to rise to the surface. Remember, they hold a certain quantity of air in a special pocket inside the equipment. The depth at which they remain stationary is a function of the amount of air in the pocket, the more air, the higher they go. When the compressed air they hold in the four corner tanks is getting low, they automatically rise to the surface, replenish their air supply, compress it and return to the prescribed depth. So, any change in username or password can be orchestrated at any time."

Frank reacted the most quickly and asked the next question:

"What about the drone?"

"That's a bit harder, but I believe it can be done by the transmitter."

There was a really puzzled look on three faces. Shi Tsu did not show it externally, but he certainly had a good internal chuckle. He simply said:

"Think about it. It communicates with the drone through sonar signals. So, if it has the initial username and password for the drone, it can easily instruct it to go through a change, just like you or I would do with our own computers or laptops."

"Brilliant!"

"Thanks Mike."

Frank still looked like something was not right. He asked:

"So, the drone which Hezbollah dropped off the coast of Israel cannot be retrofitted."

"Well, that I don't know because we don't know how the Chinese, if they are indeed the guilty party, have configured it. But it's just a case of providing for there to be a username and a password in their own communication software and you're home free."

Frank smiled. He had understood.

▌▌■▌▌

Shi Tsu informed Countess Renate that an email response had been sent to the Pentagon in reply to their comment. He could not know it, but the original email did not come from the Pentagon, nor did this email reach the Pentagon. The CIA and the FBI had worked to create a fictitious address which looked like it was from the Pentagon. Jack and Clay received the email as soon as it was sent. They read it and were delighted.

Jack called Simon to bring him into the loop, before he, Shi Tsu or Clay could even talk to Countess Renate. Simon was equally happy but for a somewhat different reason. On a hunch, when Jack called him, he had asked:

"Jack, is there a way you can monitor the radio communications of the Chinese ship?"

"Well, up to a point. I'm sure they have pretty strong encryption."

Simon conceded the point, but offered a convincing counter argument:

"I'm sure of that. But I don't believe they could encrypt a change of software instruction to be incorporated into the drone's program. As well as the transmitter's, by the way. I can't imagine they would spare such a valuable resource as a top-flight programmer for a secret project by having him or her at sea for the whole time."

Clay interrupted. He conceded that Simon's point was excellent, but rhetorically asked why they would even need to do that. He immediately answered his own question:

"An easy way out would be to have a programmer fly from wherever he or she is in China to the ship. I know what you guys think. I know it's not an aircraft carrier. But it shouldn't be rocket science to fly the person to a nearby airport in a friendly country and helicopter him or her out to the ship."

Simon exclaimed:

"Brilliant. I'm sure that's what they'll do. Give me a second."

He paused as he was ostensibly working on his computer. He continued:

"Bingo. There's a commercial airport on Socotra Island. I can't find any airline that flies there, but I'm sure that China could land any sort of plane there. So, they could do a whole lot of things.

They could ship modified drones and transmitters to the ship, and presumably bring back whatever cargo she already holds. They could fly a programmer to the ship to modify the program on the drones and transmitters."

Simon paused again for a second and added:

"Or they could choose to do nothing. My own guess is that they will modify whatever other drone they will want to plant but will not take the risk of dealing with the one that's already off Haifa or any other if they have others."

"Makes sense, Simon. But what would the Iranians or Hezbollah ask for?"

"That, we don't know. We don't even know whether they have the leverage to ask for anything. We know that the Chinese, the Iranians, and the Russians conducted joint navy exercises off the Gulf of Oman. So we know that there is some form of alliance, though, here, I would bet that the Chinese will not have brought the Russians into this scheme, if they, the Chinese, are indeed officially in it."

He paused to see if anyone had anything to add. Hearing no comment, he continued:

"So, my strategy would be to keep a close watch on Bandar Abbas, Aden, Socotra, the Chinese Ship and the drone off the coast of Haifa. A bit more difficult, but I'm sure already in place is the need to monitor the Chinese Navy in the Gulf of Oman. Who knows whether they would go as far as being official in this affair? But it's a bet we cannot afford to lose. In short, no idea how they'll proceed, but we must be ready for just about any move. This is a game of go, my friend, not chess. Many more possibilities."

"A heck of a program, Simon. What do you need from the CIA?"

Simon went on to describe the surveillance which he would like to have the CIA provide, mostly from the Fifth Fleet, and via geosynchronous satellites. He felt that Israel would be ready to shadow the *Sea Crescent* virtually on command. Jack raised his eyebrows, which Simon could see on the videoconference. Simon said:

"There are a couple of things you probably don't know about those spy ships of ours."

Jack and, but to a lesser extent Clay because he was much more down to earth than Jack, seemed quite interested. Simon started his explanation with a simple affirmation:

"The vessels look like supply ships and can, within a minute, be made to look like shipping boats, when the crane that lies horizontally on the aft deck is raised. However, they are anything but either of these two."

He explained that, for a start, they were more than regular supply boats. Sure, they looked like regular boats with the bridge toward the front half of the boat and the middle and aft sections above deck suitable to carry many different loads. However, in reality, they were fast boats which could transform into hydrofoils with a couple of simple maneuvers. The foils, which at rest were folded into the hull at the bow of the boat, could be extended; at speed, the boat riding on these foils would rise higher on the water and have both less friction and thus more speed. To accommodate the fact that the boat could rise higher on the water, the angle and length of the two propeller shafts could also be altered so that they would still operate at full power at top speed. That alone made them quite different from any supply boat and would allow them to outrun virtually any boat, particularly as their twin engines were double the power which boats of that size would normally have. Unfortunately, with the need for more power came the requirement that fuel capacity be substantially raised as well.

Another series of modifications would never be visible except to those who knew where to look. First, the vessels were equipped with an air lock which allowed the boat to pick up or deliver loads underwater. Usually, this feature was used to transfer loads from one boat to another, but it also allowed the boats to be resupplied in food or water from a submarine without the operations being visible to anyone not underwater. Also, the lower level of the front deck, under the bridge tower, hid a full gamut of electronic surveillance equipment; it offered space for a couple of operators to work all the while allowing them to move from that space to the modest living quarters on the bridge without being required to step out in the open.

Finally, in Simon's words: "the vessels can easily change identity." He explained that they each had three names on rotating supports on each side of the bow of the ship. Simply rotating the support would allow the ship to change name. At the same time, each of the names corresponded to a country of registration. Currently, they were using Malta, Panama and Gibraltar. Thus, the flagpole at the very aft of the ship would display the correct flag through a clever mechanism inspired from the multi-color ball point pens of the past: each flag would roll around its own axis and the whole retract into a sheave. The captain could therefore "dial up" the flag he wanted." The cherry on top of the cake dealt with the color of the middle section of the hull. The top of the hull would always be white, while the bottom, the part most often immersed into the water would always be black. The middle section, however, comprised vertical rotating triangles which could display one of three colors: red, dark green and white.

Summarizing, Simon concluded:

"Nobody would guess what they can do, and we are very careful not to use their stealthy power in full view of any adversary, except if escaping is the point. Yet, each ship can in fact look like three different ships, with each name matched to a flag and a hull mid-section color. That greatly facilitates any escape, as the ship can decamp at fast speed and then seem to vanish when she is out of sight and executes her change of identity.

■ ■ ■ ■ ■

Three days later, Simon received an urgent call from Palmachim Base, where the surveillance drone control center was located. The message was short and sweet.

"The *Sea Crescent* has left port. She's sailing toward the Strait of Hormuz."

In the meantime, he had organized with the help of Jack Turnbull for both Israeli supply vessels to be refueled. They had also been resupplied with fresh food and water. This had taken place in international waters, with the food resupply provided via the airlock by a submarine drone—an Orca. The refueling had required the boats, one at a time, discretely coming alongside an American tanker from the Fifth Fleet.

Simon's instructions, relayed to the ships' captains by the Israeli Navy command, was to remain in the general vicinity of Socotra Island. They were both invited to train their surveillance systems to a specific frequency which allowed them direct communication with the command center which was in Haifa. The center's principal task was to plot the course of the *Sea Crescent* so that they could figure out when the Israeli boats should begin to sail toward her.

Jack, who had flown from the U.S. on a navy twin-seat jet to be with Simon for the operation, complete with one inflight refueling, was looking at the course of the Lebanese boat as broadcast by the Israeli internal radar system. Suddenly, he exclaimed:

"Hold it, Simon. This boat ain't going anywhere near Socotra. She's remaining way north of that route. I bet you she's going straight to Aden for her usual refuel."

Initially, Simon looked puzzled. He could see what Jack saw, but wanted to wait a while longer, just to be sure. A few minutes later, he conceded:

"Darn right my friend. Where is she going to get the cargo?"

"You mean the drone and the missiles?"

"Absolutely."

Jack was still straining his mind when Simon jumped up and exclaimed:

"Darn it. They've outmaneuvered us. Crafty bastards."

It was then Jack's turn to be surprised. He blurted out with a still incredulous look on his face:

"What in the world do you mean?"

"I'll tell you in a minute."

Simon was very excited and was forgetting pure teamwork. He was almost barking orders initially to his troops. He caught himself and asked a bit more calmly:

"Can AWACS detect and track helicopter flights?"

Simon was referring to the U.S.'s Airborne Warning And Control System, a mobile, long-range radar surveillance and control center principally for air defense, but which could also function in the current kind of mission. It involved equipment loaded onto a plane which stayed aloft patrolling a given surveillance area. Jack did not understand:

"Why are you asking?"

Even more calmly and politely, Simon said to his friend:

"Trust me. Again, I'll explain later. Can they?"

Jack, who knew Simon well, elected not to keep asking questions despite Simon not having answered them. He had been with him enough to realize that Simon was normally a mild-mannered individual who was quite sensitive to the ego and the feelings of all the people around him. For him to be almost barking orders or fail to justify why he was doing something had to mean that he had an important and urgent need. He knew that Simon rarely got excited or flustered as the case might be. So, he thought: *"must be serious. May have a great idea. We'll see."* Calmly and simply, he replied:

"Hold it. Let me find out."

Jack called a number in the U.S. which had an operator on duty 24/7. It was a liaison desk at the CIA which could establish contact between any senior U.S. government parties virtually anywhere in the world. Jack explained that he wanted to find out something about AWACS capabilities in the Fifth Fleet. Within less than a minute, Jack was connected to the officer in charge of the AWACs management within the Fifth Fleet, Lieutenant Colin Harris. He introduced himself and asked the question raised by Simon. To his surprise the answer was a simple:

"Of course, it does. Hmm, let me be a bit more precise. It does unless the helicopter uses radar evading techniques. For instance, if it flies very close to the ground."

"Thanks, Lieutenant, could you hold a second please?"

Jack relayed the information to Simon, who immediately asked:

"Can we find out whether there has been any helicopter flight from the Chinese cargo ship to Bandar Abbas in the last couple of days and if yes, when?"

Jack relayed the question again. The answer did not come as quickly. It took Lieutenant Harris a couple of minutes to identify the position of the Chinese ship, which thankfully had not moved, and to review the logs. He came back on the line, mildly surprised that Jack and his confrere had guessed right:

"Absolutely gentlemen. There was one flight to and from the cargo ship. I cannot tell you where the helicopter had come from or was flying back to, but, judging from his vector when we lost him, Bandar Abbas is totally possible. As to where it came from, with the number of ships in the area, I can see that the helicopter that landed on the ship followed quite a circuitous route in the last few miles."

Simon asked:

"When was that?"

"Early last night. It was under the cover of darkness here and he should have arrived in Bandar Abbas, if that's where it was going, under dark skies as well."

"Thank the lieutenant, Jack. I think we have the answer. They simply got the cargo to the *Sea Crescent* while she was docked in Bandar Abbas. They used a helicopter to bring it from the Chinese ship to the port. Smart. Quite smart."

Jack hung up the phone and, with Simon, started to plan their next move. Simon remarked that they needed to change their tactics as they did not anticipate the last move by the Chinese and Iranians:

"That's what I meant when I referred to the game of go as opposed to chess. These guys are masters at go, which requires considerably more forward thinking. By the way, there may be another surprise in this move by the Chinese. Let's keep all our options open! So, we need to catch the Chinese ship red-handed if we are going to do anything at sea about it."

"Agreed, Simon. The Fifth Fleet would not engage in what would otherwise appear as an act of war."

"Understood. With that in mind, we need to ensure that they make at least one other delivery to the Iranians."

"Absolutely and we cannot play again the disinformation game."

"Surely would look trite. I have an idea though."

CHAPTER.13

Hai Chock called Countess Renate to report on the analysis he had conducted of BACL's email traffic in the twenty-four hours since the starting time she had given him. She had not told him what the reason was that led her to pick that time window. It was not a question of lack of confidence in anyone, but Countess Renate operated as always on the principle that you should have the information you needed to do your job, but not more. Every associate in Shadow Experts understood the principle, as it was clear to all of them that the policy was, in large part, designed to protect each of them. You cannot be accused of anything if you did not know about it. In this particular instance, Countess Renate had not mentioned that the starting time she had given corresponded to the moment Shi Tsu had informed his partners that he had found a solution to the query raised by the Pentagon.

"Countess Renate?"

"Yes, Hai Chock. Anything interesting?"

"Well, in truth, not really. We have the same pattern as the last time we looked, but a lot less traffic. Maybe, it's because the window is shorter. A couple of changes though: Michael did not have nearly as much outgoing traffic. Shi Tsu had his usual traffic, but no significant up- or download. Ho Lim sent and received emails, but, again, not out of the range of expectations. Finally, Frank seemed only to be corresponding with his wife. The interesting thing about that, by the way, is that his first email to her was sent virtually at the very start of the period. There were a couple of emails later, but on the whole very little."

"Thanks. An odd question for you. Can you tap into their telephone system?"

"Why?"

"I'd love to know whether there was oral traffic."

"I can only do it if their telephone provider is the same as for their internet needs."

"Well try and see. In the meantime, thanks anyway, Hai Chock. I'll get back to you after I've talked with Simon. On another issue, any news from your friend, Yeo Yap Min?"

"Come to think of it, no. Let me give him a call and I'll report as soon as I have anything."

"Thanks."

■ ■ ■ ■ ■

"Simon?"

"Renate here. Everything OK?"

"Well. Up to a point. I think the Chinese outfoxed us."

"How?"

"I am willing to bet that they delivered the submarine drone to Bandar Abbas rather than have the *Sea Crescent* collect it in the Gulf of Oman."

"Well, I have a feeling we've been outfoxed in another way as well."

"What?"

"Well, Hai Chock just reported on the email traffic into and out of BACL after we broke the disinformation news."

"And?"

"Well, very little. Same patterns, but a lot less traffic. The only one that looks interesting is that Shi Tsu did not have much upload/download activity."

"What do you make of that last point?"

"You know I trust him, Simon. He has helped us in other assignments and assuming he is a Chinese spy is a really tough step for me. I still can't take it. My answer is simply that he took Hai Chock's security advice seriously."

"May be. May be. I have no reason to think differently, Countess. I must tell you, however, that when Jack and I were reviewing Hai Chock's initial findings, Shi Tsu looked like a primary suspect, as did the fact that he would prefer to work on a home server."

"You did not tell me about that, correct?"

"You're right. I didn't because I did not feel we had enough information. And, frankly, I would not have told you today if you had not shared your own hesitations. One thing though: can Hai Chock look at whether there were uploads or downloads, most likely the latter, onto thumb drives rather than via email?"

"I think I see where you're going Simon. Quite smooth. Should have thought of that myself. I'll let you know when I find out."

"Many thanks."

■ ■ ■ ■ ■

Jack called Clay Mitchell from an office close to Simon's. He wanted to get an update on the official snooping which Clay had been able to conduct. Clay had indeed promised to look for a reliable and discreet private investigator which could be unofficially recommended to Simon. Clay reported that there were two people that came close to each other in terms of references and could both be suggested.

William Martin was a very experienced private investigator, and in fact had helped the FBI in a couple of cases where there needed to be official as well as unofficial investigations. The problem was that he had a number of connections, which would cause difficulties if anything was ever revealed. As Clay summarized:

"How do we know that we are his highest loyalty?"

"I can see that. What's the other person?"

Clay explained that she was a totally unexpected individual, as, in a world dominated by men, she was a woman. He added:

"She is as tough as they come and has a license to carry a weapon. They call it an LTC in Massachusetts."

"How original."

"You said it. Anyway, I know she has helped us particularly in cases where some softness was required; you know, the woman's touch. Her downside is that she is younger and thus has less experience."

"We'll present the choice to Simon. Thanks Clay. By the way, I hope that we shall soon be able to do something official. Simon was telling me of a call he received from Countess Renate. We may need to have their phones bugged."

"Who's they?"

"Sorry. The four partners and anybody in their immediate entourage."

"You know the drill, Jack. Tell me when you have the information, we would need to get permission. . . . You know, the probable cause. By the way, so far, our digging into the potential for leaks at the Pentagon has produced nothing of value. Turns out that BACL is not providing them with day-to-day reports. They only report when something big has taken place. The last such report dates back to when they had completed their prototype."

"That could be interesting, though. What did the report contain?"

"Well, my friend, surprisingly little. It discussed the functionality of the communication system and had a few pictures of the prototypes.

Now, from what you've shown me, the submarine drone and the transmitters you photographed look a lot like the prototype. But I'll be darned if you can create a copy of a prototype just by looking at pictures. Now, one interesting thing I thought I'd mention . . ."

"Yes?"

"The prototype did not have any apparent missile launching capabilities. The only thing they showed at the front end of the submarine tube was an underwater camera, and obviously a couple of fixed headlights."

"Interesting. Thanks. Anything else?"

"Not really. I saw a few emails between one or the other of the partners and the Pentagon at the time they reported on the successful completion and testing of the prototype. But there were no attachments or other information. They did talk of discussing blueprints and the like, but almost made it a point to say that they would not use emails to share these kinds of documents."

"What do you make of that?"

"Not much I am afraid. It's still possible that they shared hard copies or even electronic copies on thumb drives. But we certainly were not able to detect any of those. We would have to get permission to investigate their own computer systems. And you know what it means?"

Jack nodded and said:

"I do. I do. An army of lawyers on their side to fight it, which means we have to have our own army. And in the end, it would be in the media before we knew anything useful."

"Jack, you're probably too cynical, but you know that I'm just behind you on that.

■■■■■

Countess Renate called Simon, who told her that he should get Jack Turnbull on the video as well. They went and sat at the coffee table in front of the sofa in his office. Renate explained:

"Gentlemen, our tracking of the email traffic, as you know, did not produce much. Jack, are you still prohibited from looking at all these emails?"

"Up to a point, yes. Obviously, there's a moment when I can call it a national security issue. But, at that time, I must bring the NSA, the National Security Agency, into the loop. I have nothing against them, they are good, and I have a good friend there too. However, as you know, the more people are in the loop, the greater the risk of a leak."

Simon added:

"That's what I thought. What do you think we can do? We need to find some way of penetrating behind the screen so to speak."

Simon took his own point even further. He explained that there would almost by definition be a moment where the whole issue would need to be escalated, noting:

"I'm sure Jack isn't in the position to order the Fifth Fleet to apprehend the Chinese cargo ship."

"Sure ain't. You're closer to the top of your pyramid than I, Simon."

"May be, but I'm sure our government wouldn't do anything without bringing the U.S. into the loop. So, we're all in the same boat. Tell you what Countess, let's keep digging and monitoring. Any news from Hai Chock's friend in Singapore?"

"Well, yes and no. On the positive side, he has been able to learn quite a bit about Michael Lennon's wife. Her family is indeed quite wealthy, though they have been through ups and downs. The early ups were when the local property market was doing very well. That was also the cause of their downs as they acquired too much land for future projects. I'm told they came quite close to folding. They were sort of saved by the Government which gave them a contract to build public housing. Very prevalent in Singapore, nearly everyone owns their own apartment there I'm told. Anyway, that got them through the crisis. It may not have provided much profit, but certainly enough cash flow to cover all their operating and financial expenses. They have come back from the abyss and are doing well now."

"If I may interrupt, the only thing of interest I pick up here is the government's connection."

"That's exactly right, Simon. So, there might be some possibility that she or her family feels in some debt to the government and thus may be sharing some information. But I can't imagine Singapore in bed with China to go help Iran."

"Sounds fishy indeed. Now, why did you say yes and no?"

"Well, the process is hellishly slow as far as Frank's wife. Our contact is having a terrible time finding anything on her family. On the surface, by which I mean officially, she looks quite clean. But below the surface, they don't find traces of her prior to the time when she met Frank. The one interesting bit is that there is no trace of her degree from University of Bangkok Metropolis."

Jack jumped into the conversation and exclaimed:

"Wait a minute, that's big. Very big."

Countess Renate interrupted:

"True, Jack. But she may have graduated from another university. I'm told there are over twenty public universities in and around the city of Bangkok, and many more that are private. So, it may be that she graduated from a university in Bangkok and not the University of Bangkok. It would be an easily explained error, particularly since whatever information we have must have originally been written in Thai; it had to be translated into English."

Simon interrupted:

"Quite a good point. Thanks, Countess, but are we continuing to dig?"

"You bet, Simon. In fact, we have offered some help to Hai Chock's friend, but he politely turned it down. I know someone there, though, and I'm going to ask them to look into this degree bit."

"Don't tell me you have an associate in Bangkok too."

Countess Renate replied with the nicest most charming voice, and a little giggle:

"Simon, you know I can't tell you that."

"I know. But let me summarize. We believe that Michael's wife is clean. There might be some connection to the Singapore Government, but we can't see it as a negative. For Frank's wife, the jury is still out, but the only thing we found out is that her degree is not from the University which we thought delivered it."

Countess Renate agreed that Simon's was a fair summary. Then, she added almost as an afterthought:

"Oh. By the way, still on Frank's wife, her full name is Chaem Choi Sae-Chin and there is an interesting bit in there. Her last name, Sae-Chin means that she is of Chinese origin and that her last name in China was Chin. Sae is one of very few prefixes that are placed in front of a Chinese name to make it into a Thai name."

"Quite interesting, Countess. You do have a solid contact in Bangkok, or at least someone who knows a lot about Thai. However, there must be thousands if not millions of people in China with Chin as a last name."

Countess Renate ignored Simon's joke and only replied to the second part of his point:

"Correct, Simon. But maybe not that many with an advanced degree in mathematics. We're checking on that too, starting in Beijing and Shanghai. But there are plenty of other places."

■ ■ ■ ■ ■

Simon and Jack were comparing notes after they had hung up with Countess Renate when Simon's assistant knocked at the door:

"General Landau on the phone for you."

Simon apologized to Jack and walked to his desk to take the call. The call was brief, and Simon walked back to the sofa to ask Jack if he could be excused for a while, adding:

"Ariel is calling and when he does, I've got to drop what I'm doing unless it's so important that he agrees to postpone his request. Not the case here, I'm afraid.

■ ■ ■ ■ ■

Simon walked to Ariel's office on the top floor of the building. Ariel ushered him in with a broad smile. He initially asked a few questions on the current project and looked pensive when Simon started to brush for him a few of the potential implications, effectively concluding:

"Unfortunately, there is no easy ending I'm afraid. If we were alone in this, I could easily imagine blowing up the drones and finding a way to destroy whatever installation Iran had to deal with them."

Ariel looked a bit puzzled. Simon replied that he could not believe that Iran could not build the submarine drones themselves. After all, as he said, they have built aerial drones and those are more complex. Yet, in the end, the only part which China might want to keep to themselves might be the communication hardware and software. Ariel nodded that he understood. Simon returned to the broader train of thought:

"The issue is what to do with whatever the Chinese are doing. They're not our problem, at least not directly and we cannot do anything without total concurrence from the U.S."

"Totally in agreement, my friend. And I know what that means in terms of delays and the like. Now, I don't want to take too much of your time but would like to ask you for an update of your thoughts on my proposal. As you know, I'm putting some pressure on myself to get this resolved as soon as reasonable."

Simon replied that he was seriously considering it and that he had in fact managed to get over a couple of the mental hurdles. Yet, he said that there was one question he wanted to ask:

"Have you ever considered what part of your job you could delegate if you felt you were too stretched?"

"Simon, this is a great question and I'm glad you asked it. The truth is that most everything can be delegated except the ultimate responsibility for any decision and the reporting to the PM. The way I've been operating is a result of both what I like to do and where I think my strengths are. You might choose something quite different. Remember, in my job, you're the boss. So, you've got to have only two key goals on your mind. First, you must always ask: "will that decision help discharge the responsibility of the agency efficiently?" Second, the next question must be "will it maintain all the relationships you need to nurture to do your job well?" Makes sense?"

"Totally, sir. May I chew on this a bit more?"

"You sure may, but I'm hoping to go public in the next couple of weeks."

Ariel paused and looked Simon straight in the eyes:

"I know I don't need to tell you that, but I still will."

Simon was unsure of what was coming and tried to hide his discomfort. Ariel continued:

"I will delay my announcement however long it takes if you are too busy with the current project. That is your first priority."

Simon broke into a wide smile. Ariel, as usual, was coming through. He was asking himself the question: *Could I be as smooth and sensitive as he in the same circumstances?*

CHAPTER.14

BOSTON, MA, USA, WASHINGTON, DC, USA, AND TEL AVIV, ISRAEL

Simon and Jack were in Simon's office discussing their latest success. Following the discovery that the Chinese and Iranian had outfoxed the surveillance that the CIA-*Mossad* team was conducting, they had decided to follow on Simon's latest idea. He had suggested that they should go back to the first submarine drone planted by Hezbollah and remove it. They were to bring it back to the Haifa Naval Base and keep it there. They initially debated about the transmitter and hesitated bringing it as well, but, in the end elected to leave it there, though untethered from the submarine drone. That latter activity required a simple "trap." They were going to connect the transmitter to a weighted waterproof unit they would leave where the submarine drone had been. Simon's logic was that leaving the transmitter gave them a "free option" in his words:

"Since it's so close to the surface, collecting it is not a difficult task. We can load it into one of our spy vessels through the airlock and with the help of one or two divers. Yet, for as long as it is on location, Hezbollah will not assume that anything has happened to the submarine drone. If we removed it, Hezbollah would know that something had gone wrong and might scrap the whole strategy, or at least postpone it."

The idea of removing the submarine drone was that, once it was somehow made official to the Hezbollah crowd, they would feel the need to replace it. They surely would question who might have done it. Yet, since the transmitter would still be in place, they would probably discount the possibility that *Mossad* might have done it. They might even simply assume that the submarine had drifted because of currents or some malfunction in its guidance system. There surely was a risk that they might decide to fire the missiles. For that to work, they would have to assume that the submarine had not drifted far enough from the transmitter to lose contact with it. Seeing that the missiles did not respond to their command, they could begin a more comprehensive search or simply choose to replace the submarine and its transmitter. They would need to replace the transmitter as well, because they could not instruct the remaining transmitter to communicate with the new submarine, without somewhat complex instructions and maneuvers. The simplest approach would be for the Lebanese vessel to make at least one more trip to collect the drone, its transmitter and the missiles. This might allow the team to catch the Chinese red-handed, or at the very least to learn more about how they operated. But the real key was that Simon felt that he controlled the timing of when Hezbollah would learn they had lost the drone and would start whatever process was needed to replace it.

The rescue of that submarine drone took place following almost exactly the same steps as when it was first discovered and brought onshore. The Israeli submarine and the underwater deep-sea rescue vessel left from Haifa, already submerged. They went straight for the location of the drone, captured it with the rescue vessel, dropped the waterproof unit to tether the transmitter at the surface and returned to port. Simon and Jack had been categorical. They had asked the crew to disconnect any communication device that they found on the submarine drone and to remove both missiles from the drone as soon as they had control over them. The last thing anyone wanted indeed was to have a missile explode in Haifa or to have missed a self-destruct mechanism on the drone.

At about the same time, an Israeli spy supply ship navigated to the same location, but on the surface. Two divers went down through the airlock and retrieved the transmitter. A communication engineer who had been brought along reprogrammed the tether for the transmitter. Once he had verified that the communication between the two units was as it should be, the divers went back through the airlock and replaced the transmitter at its desired spot. Any helicopter which would try to communicate with the transmitter, to give instructions to the underwater drone or simply to conduct a check would not know that the switch had been made, unless it was trying to activate the drone: the helicopter could communicate with the transmitter, but it could not send instructions to the submarine drone.

So, they would figure out that something was amiss if the instruction relayed by the helicopter was to fire one or both missiles or less dramatically to bring the submarine drone to the surface. In that case, nothing would happen. Yet, the terrorists would still not know whether the problem was due to a faulty communication or to a defect either with the transmitter or with the drone. At best, they would have to waste time to come on location and check the transmitter. They would be able to verify that it worked, though they might notice a change in the address of the unit to which the transmitter was tethered. Most likely, because Simon was pretty sure they did not have deep-sea rescue capability, they would abandon the submarine drone and replace it with a new one.

■ ■ ■ ■ ■

Meanwhile, the *Sea Crescent*, which was returning to Tyre, presumably loaded with the next submarine drone and transmitter, had left Aden and was sailing up the Red Sea. One of the two Israeli spy-ships was following it from afar, while the other was twenty miles ahead of it. Mark Levi was assuming that the Lebanese vessel would stop at the same location as on earlier voyages. The speed of the Israeli ships was such that the ship leading the parade could correct course quite quickly if the Lebanese captain made a change to his routing.

In fact, on this trip, the Lebanese vessel stretched its leg from Aden. She did not stop at Massawa and rather went all the way to Port Sudan. Mark was initially puzzled by the strategy. He would have immediately understood it, had he known that the Iranians had loaded soft-sided extra fuel tanks in the belly of the ship to increase her fuel capacity and range, The Iranians had made that decision to allow her to speed up the voyage. Had Mark had that information and passed it on to Simon, they would not have worried about creating the opportunity for at least one other voyage. It turned out that the shipment which the Israelis had intercepted was the first and that at least six more were planned, including one which would have missiles located near Eilat and thus capable of striking Southern Israel.

In some ways, this was a big miss for Simon. The very fact that he was told by Shi Tsu that the submarine looked very much like their prototype, except for the change in the bow to allow it to fire missiles was the obvious clue. Shi Tsu knew when BACL had finalized their designs. This should have been enough for Simon to realize that there would not have been enough time for several of these to have been built and deployed. Yet, fortunately, the miss only led to unnecessary maneuvers, not to a completely erroneous analysis. Or did it?

Mark figured that something had changed when the *Sea Crescent* skipped its next refueling stop after Port Sudan as well and went directly to Sharm-Al-Sheik. He called Simon:

"Simon, for whatever reason, they have skipped two refueling stops and are almost a day early on their schedule."

"Interesting. They may be trying to catch up on lost time. You know, the time they were stuck at Bandar Abbas . . . That would explain the risk which the Chinese took to deliver the submarine drone and its transmitter to Bandar Abbas. If that's the case, we may need to be a bit tighter in our surveillance. The next real test will be how long they spend in Tyre this time."

He paused and immediately added:

"And I'm sure you all are ready to disrupt their drop off wherever that'll be."

"Oh. We are Simon. In spades."

■ ■ ■ ■ ■

A couple of days later, Mark called Simon again. Jack had gone back to the U.S. but was willing and able to get onto any conference call if he was needed. Simon waited to call Jack until he knew more. So, the call was only between him and Mark.

"Simon?"

"Yes, Mark. What's up?"

"We are never sure, but it does not look as if the *Sea Crescent* is returning to the same general location."

Simon had to ask:

"What do you mean?"

"Well, if you follow her on the radar map . . ."

Simon did not have the map on his computer screen at the time. He told Mark:

"Just a second, I'm calling it up. . . . I've got it, go ahead."

"She just left Port Said to enter the Mediterranean. But she is not sailing in a northeasterly direction. She's going due east."

"Interesting. Very interesting. Can you ask your people how long it would take her to reach our coastline, starting just north of the Gaza strip and then further north?"

Mark looked like he was missing something:

"Sure. May I ask why?"

"No secret between us my friend. If she's going to drop her cargo near our southern borders, we will need to send the submarine and the deep-sea rescue vessel early. There's at least a half-days' worth of travel for them."

Simon paused and then said:

"You know, and I have no idea what it means quite yet, but this may indicate some alliance between Hezbollah and Hamas. The Iranians may be trying to get them together against us, the common enemy."

"I see. Totally possible. Mischievous, but possible. Anything you want me to do?"

"Not now. Please keep tracking the ship and warn me when she is at most a day's sailing from Gaza."

He hung up with Mark and called Ariel.

"Ariel, may I see you? Got to do with the project."

"Sure, come on over."

Simon walked to Ariel's office to discuss the latest news. The notion that this could be more than Hezbollah but extend to other Palestinian groups had made him quite nervous. Ariel listened intently to Simon's description. Then, calmly he said:

"One thing does not compute here, Simon."

"What?"

"Didn't you tell me that the first two missiles off Haifa were aimed at Tel Aviv and Jerusalem?"

"Sure did."

"Then why do they need to go south?"

Simon thought for a minute and replied:

"What if they are not dropping the drone this time, but just delivering it to Hamas?"

They went back and forth for a short while and decided that it was too early to come to any conclusion. Yet, Ariel told Simon that he would warn Aaron Spielberg, the Defense Minister, adding:

"That's a ship I'm pretty sure they will want to intercept if she comes within our territorial waters. And it would if she's going to dock in Gaza."

Ariel paused and then simply said:

"Thanks for this, Simon. Please keep me in the loop. We will need to widen the circle if our assumption with respect to Gaza turns out to be correct. And it'll go beyond Aaron."

■ ■ ■ ■ ■

Simon then called Jack, time zones be darned, to let him know of the new development. He did not share about his visit with Ariel, as this was in his view internal Israeli politics. Yet, he had to mention the risk that the enemy list might be widening. Ariel had told him they would need to widen the circle in Israel. But Jack immediately replied that this would require bringing in U.S. political leaders as well, starting with the Head of the National Security Agency, and then onto the National Security Council all the way to the President.

Neither Jack nor Simon was particularly excited at the prospect of having such a broader group with which to deal. There would simply be too many loose ends, and both felt that the last thing they needed at this point was political interference. Yet . . .

Jack surprised himself:

"Hey, Simon. What if it's not an effort to work with Hamas, but a desire by Hezbollah to threaten Hamas?"

Simon saw right away where Jack was going with his idea. The three groups representing the Palestinians were not particularly friendly to one another. Hezbollah was by far the one that was best politically organized, as it had focused its activities on Lebanon, where it had gained actual political representation and thus power. Thus, rather than working to lead refugees, it was an influential political force in a country member of the U.N. Now one could begin to wonder whether Hezbollah were trying to become the unquestioned leader of all Palestinians. This would make all the more sense, as the relationship between Fatah and Hamas was frayed, at best. One could even take this further and imagine a political motive on the part of Iran. Their strategy might be to make Hezbollah the de-facto leader of all Palestinians, the one over which many people thought Iran currently exercised the most control. One could begin to imagine a whole number of tactics.

Simon offered one possibility:

"What if they are not delivering the equipment to Hamas, but planting it off the Gaza strip? Then, what if the missiles do not have Iranian markings, but something that makes it believable that they belong to Hamas? Next step? Hezbollah fires one or both of these missiles into Israel, say Ashkelon or Ashdod, two semi-coastal towns, for instance. Israel would retaliate against Hamas."

Jack could only admire Simon's imagination, but his down-to-earth nature took over:

"Tell you what, Simon. We're now talking of something that could lead to World War III. And we're doing it on speculation. Why don't we wait until we have a few more hard facts. Israel retaliating against Palestinian missiles is no longer front-page news. It's great for us to anticipate, but at some point, there are simply too many balls in the air."

"Totally agree, Jack. I'll keep you in the loop. By the way, sorry it's so early your time."

"Don't worry. I'll just have a bit more time to exercise this morning."

■ ■ ■ ■ ■

The Lebanese boat had indeed approached the southern coast of Israel. It had not dropped its cargo opposite Gaza or even Palestinian territory. Rather, it had settled opposite Ashkelon, about ten nautical miles up from the border between Israel and the Gaza strip. Mark had appropriately requested careful surveillance by an Eitan drone which was therefore able to see and film the maneuver: first the drone with its two missiles was lowered into the water and second the transmitter was placed on the surface of the water in about the same area. The Lebanese vessel had then resumed its course, following the Israeli coastline in a northerly direction. Mark and everyone else assumed it was going to Tyre, to change the crew, refuel and reprovision before going back to the Gulf of Oman. Now Mark was back on the phone with Simon:

"Simon, there is serious news."

"What is it Mark?"

"Well, the Lebanese boat is stopping and looks like something is very wrong."

"Can you patch me on the video feed from the Eitan?"

"Sure can. Wait a second."

The line went silent for a short while, then Mark came back.

"Simon, you should be receiving an email on your secure server. It has the URL for you to use."

Simon followed the required steps and very soon was looking at the same images as Mark. He joked:

"Can't see much at all, my friend."

"In the lower left of your screen, you'll see an electronic switch for light enhancement. It'll transform the infra-red image into something we are more used to. Won't be like daylight, but close enough."

"OK. OK. Now I see. So, the *Sea Crescent* looks like it is stopped. But wait a minute. You know what? It's preparing to make another drop."

"Sure looks like it. So, on this trip, he had two drones and two transmitters . . ."

"And four missiles. . . . Holy mackerel. New tactics. Speed on the water was not enough. They now must be trying to speed up deliveries. What in the world could this mean?"

Simon paused to give himself time to think. His mind was racing. His major concern was that somehow the news that there might be a spy within BACL might have gotten back to someone, the Chinese most likely, but potentially to the Iranians and Hezbollah as well. This might mean that the actual missile strike was planned in the near future. The fear that the scheme might be discovered too early might be leading all participants to speed up deliveries and that the strike was imminent. Simon added for Mark's benefit:

"OK. Keep watching. For all I know he may have another one or two on this trip. We don't know how many "packages" they onboarded in Bandar Abbas."

"Unfortunately not. We've already called for the deep-sea rescue effort, though we'll have to wait until the helicopter comes to instruct the drone. By the way, Simon, do you know if they can load a drone in a submarine?"

"No problem. It fits into the airlock and that's the binding constraint. I see where you're going. The answer from my point of view is that we can probably retrieve the two drones in one trip and thus, eventually reposition them in one trip as well. Might be tougher to retrieve more than two and that could be a serious problem. Leave it with me. Focus on whatever they do on this trip."

"Thanks, Simon. By the way if you look at your screen now, you'll see it clearly. The ship is lowering the drone into the water."

The next thing he saw was the lowering of a transmitter. The Palestinians had decided to recover the lost time by having the same ship carry out two missions instead of one. Simon took his earlier analysis a bit further and thought:

I must understand why they would need to hurry up. Is an attack really imminent? Depends on how many submarine drones they felt they needed. Anyway, I think Ariel needs to know, but I don't want to scare anyone quite yet. I need to choose my words carefully.

■ ■ ■ ■ ■

Simon called Jack to give him the update. He also needed to ask him a question:

"Jack, how do we get ahold of the usernames and passwords which we have to assume they're using if the leaker has done his or her job?"

"Funny you should ask. I had a call from Countess Renate, and I asked her that very question. She came back within five minutes after having talked to Shi Tsu. He's given her a set of procedures to follow. I'm sure she'll send them to you. Question, by the way: do you want your guys to do that yourselves or do you need a specialist?"

"I assume that by specialist you mean either Shi Tsu or Hai Chock."

"Actually I was thinking of Shi Tsu. He's the one who designed the process, so he's got to be the best one to deal with it."

"Agreed. Let's ask him whether a gifted computer engineer can follow his instructions. If not, we'd need to have him here."

CHAPTER.15

As in all instances where it was not necessary for him to divulge his identity, Simon had decided to stay in the background with respect to the Boston investigations. In fact, so had Mark Levi, his right-hand man on this project. Joel Miller, officially a diplomat in the Israeli Embassy, a financial attaché, in Washington, took care of hiring the private investigator in his un-disclosed capacity as senior *Mossad* representative in the U.S. Joel had interviewed the two candidates who had been introduced to him via Jack Turnbull, as on this occasion, Clay Mitchell also preferred to stay in the background. Though quite impressed by both, something made him lean toward Rachel Acker. Although she was relatively young, as he had been warned by Jack, she was bouncing with energy. She also had that "kind of charm" which tends to lead people to confide in her: people, subconsciously, did not move their guard up; rather they dropped it a bit. More importantly, she had no pressing assignment at the time and could start, as she had put it: "like, yesterday."

Her mission was to dig into the past of both Frank Lord and Xi Shi Tsu. The team had indeed decided that work on Michael

Lennon would be best carried out abroad, as the intriguing elements of his life seemed to have taken place between his graduation from University in Perth and his hiring by MIT. What they already knew made for interesting reading, though everyone has the right to goof off for some time before finding his or her ways. So far, the sheet on his wife seemed totally clear as well, though there were possible links to the Singapore Government. Ho Lim was also not a part of Rachel's mandate. He had "come clean" to Shi Tsu and, unless the findings on Shi Tsu came back surprisingly incriminating, the only doubts that remained were as to whether Ho Lim was truly trying to defect or was just pretending so that he could play the role of a double agent. The "disinformation test" the team had just ran seemed to point to the conclusion that Ho Lim was not a double agent: he did not seem to be the one who alerted the Chinese to the hypothetical transmission problem. Thus, though doubts had to remain, he was gradually moving closer to being in the clear. At any rate, Rachel would probably not be able to identify anything more incriminating on him by herself; there were more chances to uncover something in China.

The mandate regarding Shi Tsu was quite broad, as Mark and Simon were totally unsure of what they might be looking for. There were, of course, the stints as research assistant in Asia. Yet, there is nothing inherently suspect in a student broadening his horizons, particularly in the case of a student of overseas Chinese ethnic background wanting some experience with people with the same cultural traditions rather than those of his adoptive country, the U.S. As a part of the Shi Tsu mandate, Joel still had asked Rachel to take a look at Shi Wah, Shi Tsu's brother, just in case.

The mandate concerning Frank was quite broad as well, though there were at least three obvious directions in which to go. The divorce and his life prior to it were one such direction. Though there were official versions which Clay had been able to uncover, Joel wanted to find out whether there was something more specific that unconventional digging might reveal. The other direction related to Frank's somewhat cavalier dating prior to meeting his wife. Though most of it surely happened before the Me-Too movement came to the fore in the U.S., dating students and colleagues had long been viewed as sailing quite close to the wind. Finally, anything which could be found regarding the circumstances prior to and since his second marriage deserved close attention.

Rachel Acker was a stunning woman in her late thirties. She was quite tall, and her body demonstrated her interest in athletics. She had been a varsity volleyball player in high school and had continued when she went to the University of North Carolina at Chapel Hill. Chapel Hill is also the place where she became acquainted with firearms and had become an excellent marksperson. Though born and bred in New England, her stint in the south had mellowed her manners and taught her the use of female charm as a tool, although this never extended to granting sexual favors to anyone "for business." Her first marriage had unfortunately only lasted a very short time, when she had realized that her husband was cheating on her on every occasion available to him. Thankfully, they had not had any children; that made the split easier. At the same time, it reinforced in her the sense of the need to evaluate everyone very carefully: indeed, she tended to blame herself for not having picked up earlier that her then husband-to-be was not as dedicated to her as he might proclaim, particularly as it seemed that the cheating had started before they were even married.

She was not at present in any long-term relationship, though she was well-aware that her body clock was ticking if she wanted to start a family. She had a strong desire to be a mother and was often asking herself whether she should take a break from her current activities to dedicate her time to find "Mr. Right." So far, she had preferred to assume that she would find him like everybody else: without looking too hard. She wore her dark hair relatively short, which combined with a very discreet use of make-up gave her a highly professional look. This preference was matched with a tendency to avoid all forms of extravagant clothing; she preferred discreet dresses in solid colors or discreet patterns or suits.

■ ■ ■ ■ ■

For some reason, Rachel started her digging with Shi Tsu. She justified it to herself on the basis of the many dimensions of his family. His father's change of career, his mother's business success, their having come from China allegedly with some money, in gold, and others. She found someone who knew Shi Tsu when he was in Singapore: another Chinese student. The way she stumbled on him deserves telling, as the coincidences were just too crazy. Tony Lee Wah Kwong, as this was the fellow's name, was a good friend of Shi Tsu while they were both in Singapore; Shi Tsu went to Singapore from the West Coast of the U.S. while Wah Kwong actually had received a comparable degree to Shi Tsu's but from MIT rather than Caltech. Coincidentally, their paths diverged from Singapore, as Wah Kwong stayed for a while and then went to Caltech, while Shi Tsu went to MIT, effectively switching their alma maters. As Rachel was calling Caltech to get some more information on Shi Tsu, she was directed to Wah Kwong. She told him that she was a freelance reporter working on a background piece on Shi Tsu, following the forming of BACL. Wah Kwong told her that he had lost touch, but that he would be happy to talk to her, adding:

"Don't expect any dirt, he was a wonderful guy. Our wives did not get along as well as we would have liked. So, we stopped seeing each other. But I've followed his work. . . . Quite impressive. Your phone call reminds me that I should send him an email. We could rekindle that old relationship."

She met him in Pasadena for lunch and returned to Boston on

the red eye flight that very night. She was able to fill in a few of the blanks which Joel Miller had identified but could not come up with any indication that Shi Tsu was any different from the picture he was projecting. Interestingly, she learned a lot about Shi Wah, Shi Tsu's brother. She found out that the academic tradition ran deep in the family. He had become an orthopedic surgeon practicing and teaching at Massachusetts General Hospital on Fruit Street. Yet, he did reserve at least half of his time to teaching duties. He was apparently quite appreciated by both his students and the residents with whom he worked. One comment seemed to come again and again: "a simple, very approachable fellow who does not take himself too seriously."

Joel briefly hoped that something might be unusual when Rachel gave him the report, in particular when she said that Shi Tsu was known to have some association with foreign research programs in fluid mechanics, though he did not seem to work more closely with one than another. He asked:

"Do you know whether they are principally in Europe or in Asia?"

"Not really. The people I talked to tell me he travels abroad quite a bit, usually to participate in some research symposium. But that's about it. For instance, I found out that he visited Singapore in the last twelve months but has not seemingly been to Europe or the Middle East, except one trip to Zurich in Switzerland."

Joel thanked Rachel and asked where she was on the Frank Lord front. She replied:

"He did have a reputation all right . . . I have not seen anything that could be serious yet but managed to contact someone in the human resources department of MIT. There may be something in his file, though I may or may not get access to it. They're pretty strict usually. But that source owes me something, so . . ."

■ ■ ■ ■ ■

Hai Chock was quietly working in his office when he received a call from Yeo Yap Min, his friend, the Deputy Director of the Military Security Department:

"Hai Chock, I may have really interesting information."

"Really?"

"Yes. The story of Mrs. Lord, or should I say Chaem Choi Sae-Chin, is definitely turning out to be full of surprises."

Without giving Hai Chock a chance to interrupt he continued:

"It turns out that she did receive the Thai equivalent of an undergraduate degree in mathematics."

"So far so good."

"Absolutely. However, she did not get it from the prestigious Bangkok University. She graduated from Siam University, which was once a technical college."

"OK, but we don't have anything under her direct control that mentioned Bangkok University. The document we have says "the University **in** Bangkok." We're leaning toward a translation mistake."

"Understood, but there is a big caveat."

"Ah. What was it?"

"Well, turns out she did not study there for the whole time."

"Really? What does that mean?"

"Simple. She transferred into Siam University from Tsinghua University, in Beijing."

"Hold it. That's big. What do you mean?"

"Well, simple. The large part of her degree was "earned" in China. To me, this suggests she is probably not really Thai. She is most likely a Chinese citizen who was sent to finish a degree in Thailand."

"A spy?"

"Interesting you'd get to that conclusion. My thought is that, if I had to guess and that's what I am working on right now, I'd bet that she was sent to Thailand to be able to portray herself as a Thai student."

"A spy?"

"Could well be."

"That's huge!"

"Well, it could be huge. But, so far, we're really only hardly beyond speculation. I'd suggest that you ask someone to find her application to MIT. It would be very interesting to see whether she is described as Thai or Chinese. Oh, by the way, her real name is not Chaem Choi Sae-Chin, but Chin Chang Ying. At least, that's what it was before it was changed to the Thai name, as she needed to become a Thai subject. I have a friend who knows someone in the Thai Ministry of Home Affairs. He's digging up her naturalization file. Very unusual to get naturalized that quickly."

"Any chance she never was?"

"What do you mean Hai Chock?"

"Well, the quickest way to get a new nationality is to get a fake passport."

"You're devious my friend. I work in the secret service and hadn't thought of that one. But that may well be true. However, how come no one discovered that in the U.S.?"

"With respect to your last point, don't know. On the first, just call it beginner's luck. Many thanks, Yap Min. I owe you a big one."

"Let me finish the assignment. I'll let you know when I have more to share."

After a short minute of banter, Hai Chock hung up and immediately called Countess Renate.

"Countess, we have interesting news on Mrs. Lord."

He proceeded to tell her everything which Yap Min had reported. She thanked him and called Shi Tsu after they had hung up:

"Shi Tsu?"

"Yes, Ah. Countess Renate. Anything interesting?"

"Well, we found something unusual with respect to Frank Lord's wife. Did you know that she was both Thai and Chinese?"

"Well, I certainly knew she was of Chinese descent. Her name gave that away."

"That's not what I mean, Shi Tsu. She was still a Chinese citizen a year before she received her bachelor's degree in Bangkok."

"How can that be? It's a four-year course."

"Well, she transferred to Bangkok from Tsinghua University in Beijing. She transferred as a senior."

"Oh. How unusual. You usually transfer earlier, way earlier. In fact, I'm surprised that she was allowed to do it. Anyway, when you don't transfer earlier, you transfer to complete the first degree in the university where you intend to get the second. So, I would have assumed that she was going to go for her PhD there as well. Something does not compute here, Countess."

He paused and suddenly it was as he had been hit by a ton of bricks. He exclaimed:

"Oh. No! Tsinghua University . . . That's where Ho Lim and Adrian Lee Yeo Min got their degrees as well. . . . Too much of a coincidence. Way too much of a coincidence. We know that both Ho Lim and Adrian worked for the Chinese government. Could she? That couldn't be. Do you think Frank knows that?"

Countess Renate understood what her associate was going through. She could clearly hear that he was deeply troubled. She understood that he had just conjured up an image in his head that would lead him to suspect a good friend, a partner. They may have had differences of opinion on the need for personal visibility and on leadership by mandate rather than by example. Yet, they were still friends. And now that . . . Countess Renate could only reply:

"I can't tell you, my friend. But my guess is that she's just become our prime suspect. The question would be how she got the information from Frank. Whatever you do, Shi Tsu, do not mention any of this to Ho Lim."

"Why?"

"Who knows whether he is really trying to defect or just working to become a double agent? Remember, three of our characters have spent time or studied at Tsinghua University."

Shi Tsu let go of a deep sigh. He was fully aware that this was a possibility. Yet, he had just started to trust Ho Lim. Now, he had to think again. He was now pretty much alone. He was sorry that he never really developed a personal relationship with Michael. Maybe, it was because Michael's Singaporean wife did not fit with his own wife. Shi Tsu's wife may have been Chinese, but never really adopted the relative flashiness which certain overseas Chinese can have, more often in Hong Kong, but also to a degree in Singapore. Aside from her obvious physical features, she could have been a midwestern girl who did not like excessive consumption or display of financial means. Thus, while she would never "fight" with or simply be anything but hospitable to Michael's wife, Chun Hua did not enjoy spending time with her: she was busy managing the laundry business of which Shi Tsu had inherited one half from his parents—the other half going to his brother—and which had grown quite significantly, now covering most of the Boston metropolitan area.

Countess Renate added:

"I know I don't need to say it, but not a word of this to anyone in BACL quite yet. We don't want to point to anyone or lead anyone to feel they have become suspect."

■ ■ ■ ■ ■

Renate completed the call and dialed Simon right away. After she had told him the headline of what she wanted to discuss, he asked that Jack Turnbull be conferenced in, saying:

"Jack needs to hear that."

When the three of them were on the phone together, Renate repeated the main point of what she just heard. Jack was the first to react:

"Son of a bitch. She is playing him like a violin."

Simon agreed, but also added:

"Unless he is a willing party."

Countess Renate interrupted adding:

"Gents, there's no point speculating when we don't have the facts. Yet, one thing is clear, we need to find out a lot more about Frank and his wife."

Jack conceded that speculation was not necessarily useful, but he still added:

"Remember, when Hai Chock was tracking the emails from BACL."

Simon cut him off:

"Hey! You're right. He would send emails to his wife. That's what you were going to say, right Jack?"

"Bingo. Well, at any rate, it's giving me plausible cause. I can ask Clay to set up a telephone tap."

"Totally agree. Makes a lot of sense Jack, but I'll leave all these U.S. legal issues entirely up to you. Should someone tell Rachel Acker?"

"It in your hands, Simon. Remember, she was hired by Joel Miller."

"I'll talk to Mark Levi who'll talk to Joel."

CHAPTER.16

The *Sea Crescent* did not seem to hurry its visit to Tyre. *Mossad*, via physical assets as well as Eitan pictures, was able to confirm that she and her crew seemed to follow the same routine as the last time she was in port. A new crew came aboard; the fuel tanks were filled up, thought it took about twice as long as the prior time; and provisions were loaded. The boat waited until the early morning hours and set a course that appeared to take her directly to Port Said, from where she would go through the Suez Canal into the Red Sea and beyond. Pictures from the Eitan confirmed that she seemed to be floating lower than usual: that had to be due to the extra fuel she was carrying. It also meant that the front sensor placed by *Shayetet* 13 might be partially submerged until some of the fuel was burned.

Mark Levi had retained the two same spy boats as earlier, though he had ensured that they carried different names and different flags and had a different color hull than the prior time. Ships must indeed register as they enter the Canal, and it was important for *Mossad* that its vessels did not appear to make the trip too frequently. *Mossad* was in fact surprised that the *Sea Crescent* had been used for all voyages so far. Someone in the Port Authority would be able to report the trips. Was there some sort of local complicity? Though that would not change much in the current situation, it could become a serious issue if any form of local complicity was to prevent Israel's ships from using the canal on one of their next voyages. Clearly, this would assume that the secret of these foreign-flagged boats would have been pierced, but the possibility now had to be incorporated into *Mossad*'s calculations.

The white *Mossad* boat, the *Charm of the Sea*, was pavilioned in Malta, while the other white boat, the *Sailing Princess*, was pavilioned in Gibraltar. The *Charm of the Sea* was given the regular appearance of a supply boat, while the *Sailing Princess* was "disguised" as a fishing boat, with a large crane standing right behind the bridge. The initial close surveillance duty was given to the *Charm of the Sea*, while the *Sailing Princess* had sailed directly to Port Tawfik, the harbor in Suez, at the southern end of the Suez Canal. Mark had indeed deduced that it was quite unlikely that anything unusual was going to happen while the *Sea Crescent* was in the canal.

■ ■ ■ ■ ■

The Suez Canal is almost 120 miles long, with a depth of about 75 feet and a width of about 220 yards. The canal itself is a single-lane waterway, with passing places in the Ballah Bypass and the Great Bitter Lake. In fact, ships travel in two convoys, one southbound and the other northbound under relatively regimented conditions, which would make it quite difficult for any vessel to deviate from its normal, forward progress. In fact, as was recently observed, any incident with a ship which has to stop or, worse yet, obstructs the passage of other ships, as was the case when the Panama-registered Ever Green blocked traffic for six days in March 2021. Additionally, principally for larger ships, captains employed by the Canal Authority usually board the ships during their trip in the Canal to ensure smooth operations, though they never, technically, take control of the ship.

■ ■ ■ ■ ■

After exiting Suez, for some reason, the *Sea Crescent* used the same ports as on her earlier southbound voyage, without seeming to use the higher speed she had shown on her last northbound leg. Mark and his team could not understand why she was still making the stops she was making if she did not need them given her larger fuel capacity. He thought:

Why would she take twice as long to fuel if she does not have additional tanks? And why would she not use that extra fuel if she indeed bought it?

He instructed the *Sailing Princess* to sail directly to Massawa and dock there. A couple of her sailors were supposed to go ashore so that they might tail whoever from the *Sea Crescent* would be going ashore to purchase the fuel and re-provision the ship. This is where Mark had a really big surprise which might even lead him and Simon to revise their tactics.

The one thing which they did not expect at all was that the stop was used by the sailors on the *Sea Crescent* to sell some merchandize they carried with them ashore. It turns out that the sailors were conducting two separate businesses. The first was what everyone had been able to observe: they were ferrying submarine drones, missiles and transmitters north from the Gulf of Oman. The other involved, at least on the southbound trip, raising funds by selling drugs along the way. Mark assumed that the drugs made it from Afghanistan to Lebanon by road and were then distributed by boats like the *Sea Crescent*, principally in Africa. In fact, that also helped him understand why Hezbollah did not use different boats on successive missions: theirs was a well-established commercial route. There might be differences in terms of the northbound cargo, but the southbound goods were all the same. He made a mental note to report that to Simon: curbing that drug trafficking activity might be a way of cutting back on the financial resources of the terrorists. He further noted in his own mind:

"They must keep their speed and the extra fuel for cases when they need to take flight in a hurry."

■ ■ ■ ■ ■

Rachel Acker called Joel Miller:

"Any chance we can meet. I've got news, on Frank. I can meet you on the Mall in about thirty minutes. Let's say at the corner of 15th Street and Madison Drive. We'll be near the Washington Monument and should be lost in any crowd that's there. We can walk and thus avoid any prying eye."

Joel was surprised by the request. Rachel seemed implicitly to feel that they needed to be more careful than usual. Joel immediately agreed.

Joel saw Rachel from the corner of 15th Street and Constitution Avenue and had to accept that she definitely was quite a nice-looking woman. She was wearing a dark, conservative dress, a light-colored jacket and a scarf wrapped around her neck and her right shoulder. Joel checked himself:

Joel, you're married.

His mind put back on the right track after pushing away the thought that had crossed it, he reminded himself that he was most impressed by her work ethics and her ability to get results. After they greeted each other with a chaste kiss on the cheek, he asked:

"So, what's new?"

"Well, it is very, very interesting. Here's what I found. Frank had a few problems at the university, as a few of his conquests did complain that they had been placed in a situation where they had to do things—they might have preferred not to do."

"Sexual harassment?"

"That's right, though what I was told is that the harassment part came from the fact that situations lacked clarity. There was apparently no outright quid-pro-quo or threat. Only some flirting which ended up going too far before the ladies had a chance to revisit their stance, as they say in bureaucratese."

"I see. Was there any disciplinary action?"

"Not per se, but there was a difficult one-on-one conversation between him and the Dean. The file says that he was informed that there would be no further discussion if the problem was to recur."

"And . . ."

"Well, at this point, nothing, other than the fact that the files do not disclose any further infraction on his part."

"Do we know when that warning was issued?"

"I see where you're going. I do, but I do not know how close it is or is not to when he met the one who was to become his wife."

Joel could not help concluding that this was good news: at the very least, they may have found some lever that could be used to put pressure on Frank. He thanked Rachel and told her to keep going, adding that he would call her if he needed more.

■ ■ ■ ■ ■

Joel called Mark to brief him on the current conclusions of Rachel's work. Mark in turn called Simon, who had Countess Renate patched into the conversation. Mark simply repeated the message which Joel had conveyed and was quite surprised when Countess Renate started laughing out loud.

'Is it something I said, Countess?"

"No Mark. Absolutely not. Let me bring you up to date on our own findings, relating to Mrs. Lord."

Countess Renate went through the conversation Hai Chock had had with Yeo Yap Min, his friend, the Deputy Director of the Military Security Department:

"In short, the story of Mrs. Lord, or should I say Chaem Choi Sae-

Chin, is definitely turning out to be full of surprises. She is probably not really Thai, although, who knows, maybe she did get the Thai nationality through some local Thai connection. She is most likely a Chinese citizen who was sent to finish a degree in Thailand, so that she would be able to portray herself as a Thai student as she subsequently tried to get into MIT. We're pretty sure she is a Chinese spy named Chin Chang Ying."

Simon interrupted:

"Really! Really. Very interesting. What do you make of that, Countess?"

"Well, we have no proof yet, but it seems that one could create an interesting scenario based on what I know and Mark found out. Let me give it a try: Frank Lord, a known philanderer, appears to be close to an important invention. He has been told by his Dean that he would not be allowed any further misstep with a student. China organizes to have Miss Chin apply to be in his program, with the goal of seducing him. She succeeds based on credentials which may or may not be totally correct. He falls for her, despite having made valid efforts to control his instincts. Note that here I'm kind to him; at any rate, that assumption really doesn't matter. But there, the roles were inverted; he was no longer the one trying to charm a student to get the "pleasure of the conquest;" now, she's the one who charms him. Somehow, Miss Chin succeeds but then starts blackmailing him: you marry me, or I say you forced me to have sex with you. He marries her and then is forced to spy for China."

"Wow! Not bad. Not bad. You write spy novels? The worst about it is that it looks totally plausible."

"Thanks, Simon."

"On that basis, Countess, do you believe we have our guy?"

"It would seem that way. But what we do not have is any proof to link him to any of the leaks. Until we have that, frankly, we have nothing."

"Let me talk with Jack on that front. I'm sure he can help."

∎∎■∎∎

Frank Lord was resting comfortably on his bed, when his girlfriend, Chaem, who was sleeping naked by his side woke up:

"Frank, Darling, I am tired of this secrecy."

"What do you mean, honey?"

"You know, us meeting here or at your place and not being able to be in public together."

"But we have been in public together; restaurants, plays and concerts. Don't you remember?"

"I do. I do. But I would like to be known as Mrs. Lord. You know? We've discussed it, haven't we?"

Frank swallowed hard and sat down on the bed, revealing an athletic upper body, at least for a man his age. He had fallen in love with Chaem, but he was not sure "it" could work given the age difference. Chaem insisted:

"We've now been together for quite a while and we seemed to have stopped in our tracks."

"What do you mean?"

"Well, initially there was progress toward something; I thought we were moving to some more permanency. But then looks like we've ground to a halt."

"I know it's a bit my fault, Chaem darling. Don't you worry about the age difference?

Chaem's face became harder. She knew she had been sent to the U.S. by the Chinese government with the clear instruction to find a way to enlist Frank Lord as a spy for China. At the outset, her bosses had allowed her to take her time. It may be trite, but it is a fact of life that most Chinese individuals live in a longer time frame than westerners who always seem to be in a hurry. Yet, she was now somewhat caught in the middle. On the one hand, she had fallen in love with Frank and truly enjoyed their relationship. On the other, Beijing was pressing. She felt trapped and blurted out:

"Frank, I want to become your wife. . . . Soon."

"What's the hurry, darling?"

"It's got to happen. My past is catching up with me."

Right after saying this, she got up, almost in a huff, and added:

"Let's get dressed. Let's go get some lunch. Too late for breakfast!"

Frank was quite puzzled but decided at the time that there was no point arguing any further. He replied:

"Fine, get dressed and brunch it is."

■ ■ ■ ■ ■

Simon and Jennifer had agreed to resume their conversations on Simon's possible career move. Simon was still confused, which was quite a novel feeling for someone who was perceived as having such clarity of thought when it came to his "business." Jennifer noted it jokingly. Simon replied:

"I know exactly what you mean, dear. I'm confused in part because I'm noticing the obvious contradiction."

"You'll have to explain that, my friend."

"I am used to seeing an issue in somewhat of a dispassionate frame of mind, although I cannot eliminate feelings when it comes to the safety of the members of my team. Here, I can't seem to be dispassionate."

"I've been thinking about that. Let me try and help with a thought."

"Go right ahead."

"I think the reality is in fact simple. You love what you do, and you love doing it under Ariel."

"Couldn't agree more. Where are you going with that?"

"I've been reading a psychology book which talked of the process of selecting top executives. I stumbled on something which could help you, because I saw a direct parallel."

"You'll always surprise me, Jenny, but I can't wait."

"It's all about motivation when there may be some fear of the unknown. It's also about what they call negative emotions."

"Well, that's certainly not any clearer to me."

"I know. Let me explain."

Jennifer went on to explain that individuals who are to be considered for a promotion to the most senior ranks in a company tend to have at least two traits in common. The first is that they love their current job and its circumstances. The second is that they have been quite successful at it and enjoy the positive feedback they receive or are even giving themselves in the face of these successes. When presented with an opportunity to move on, there may be some initial excitement; yet it does not matter whether they're risk seeking or more conservative, they always have to deal with the fear of the unknown versus the knowledge of what they are leaving behind. Successful headhunters find ways of selling the new job and its excitement to generate a positive pull toward it rather than simply work on taking advantage of any push from the current duties. She added:

"It's obviously more complicated than such a trivially simple summary. Yet, the issue I see is that you have a major fear of some of the duties of the new job. And also, you would miss some of what you're doing, but that's not unusual. I bet you would quickly learn to enjoy your team's success vicariously. But your blockage is with the political dimension of the new job."

"I can't disagree, but I thought we had already covered this."

"I know. I know. What we had not covered is what comes next. In your case, you may need to flip the situation around."

"Flip the situation around?"

"Yes. I think you may need to convince yourself that there is more to fear from the possibility of a new boss if you do not take the job, than the fear of the uncertainty of another new boss if you take it.

Am I making sense?"

"Well, I think you do, but I'm not sure. Let me try to paraphrase. The issue, as you're seeing it, is that whatever I decide I'm gonna be faced with a new boss, Ariel's successor if I don't take the job or the Prime Minister if I take it. I get it. Interesting twist darling."

"That's only a part of it, Simon; the other is that anything that is new, like the boss here, causes some discomfort if not fear. So, you have to stop in some ways demonizing politicians one of whom would become your direct boss and others who would be influencing him. If you don't take the job, you'll have the same uncertainty plus the risk of your troops being somehow surprised or even disappointed that you did not get the job."

"OK. Assume I understand that, which I think I do. Very useful, by the way. What about some of the duties that I know are part of the new job and I know I don't particularly care for?"

"Remember, honey, what Ariel told you: You're the boss. You can choose to structure your job the way you want. You could appoint an administrator to take care of the bits you don't care for. You might be more of an action-focused head of *Mossad*, rather than Mr. Inside."

CHAPTER.17

MASSAWA, ERITREA, ADEN, SOUTH YEMEN AND TEL AVIV, ISRAEL

On her next southbound trip, the *Sailing Princess* arrived in Massawa and her captain, Moshe Aaron, decided to dock near where the *Sea Crescent* had docked the prior time. Massawa's harbor is a complex comprising three islands and three promontories jutting out from the African Continent. Only two of the islands are used, with the third, appropriately named Green Island or Sheikh Saeed Island, designated as an ecological reserve with its large mangrove park. On her prior voyage, the *Sea Crescent* had docked on Massawa island, a roughly rectangular island on which the old city of Massawa was originally located. While the center of the island continues to be inhabited and features the fifteenth century Sheikh Hanafi Mosque, the whole of its northwest side serves as a massive harbor, with, in particular, a container port accessible to large ships. It also offers additional docking facilities right near the eight-hundred-foot-long causeway that links it to T'Walet Island, which houses the Port Authority and the ruins of the old imperial palace, built in the second half of the nineteenth century for Werner Munzinger. T'Walet is linked to the mainland part of Mitsiwa by another, much longer, causeway measuring at least three-thousand feet. Additional docking facilities are offered on Ras Gherar and Abdel Kadir YeMidir Lank'a, the only two of the three promontories to have any significant activity.

The *Sailing Princess* chose to dock on the northeast side of T'Walet Island. Though, on his previous trip, the *Sea Crescent* had moored on the opposite side of the channel, on Massawa Island, Moshe had chosen the spot because it would allow him to observe any activity around the *Sea Crescent* from the seaside. At the same time, he had sent two sailors across the Causeway on foot so that they could monitor what was happening on the land side. He had made sure that both sailors had a pocket monocular with night vision capabilities, as the night had already fallen. They were also equipped with handguns with silencers and enough rounds that they could defend themselves if attacked. At least, the guns would give them the time to resist and await the arrival of reinforcements from the *Sailing Princess*. Thankfully, there were refueling facilities on both sides of the channel. The *Charm of the Sea* which was tailing the *Sea Crescent* from a couple of nautical miles back would inform the *Sailing Princess* if there was any need to make change to their setup. For instance, if it appeared that the *Sea Crescent* was not going to dock in the same location as on the prior voyage.

Fortunately, everyone's guesses proved correct. The *Sea Crescent* docked pretty much opposite the *Sailing Princess* across the river. The first thing which she did was to start her refueling; that was exactly as expected. The *Sailing Princess* sailors were able to observe the various interactions between the sailors on the Lebanese ship and the employees of the port services. While Moshe Aaron was beginning to wonder whether anything interesting would in fact happen, he caught the sight of a strong projector moving over the sea in the general direction of Massawa Island. His binoculars helped him identify it better: it was a headlight projector carried on top of a black semi-inflatable boat, a Zodiac, making its way toward the *Sea*

Crescent. The boat's body was totally black, and its sailors all seemed dressed in black as well; the color of their skin suggested they were Eritreans. Moshe asked the other two remaining sailors on the *Sailing Princess* to train their strongest binoculars onto the semi-inflatable boat and to listen to any radio contact that it made with the harbor or the *Sea Crescent.* Eventually the Zodiac came to a stop along the water side of the *Sea Crescent.* One of the three sailors on the black Zodiac called on the radio. Moshe assumed that he was asking the *Sea Crescent* for permission to moor, as the sailor was speaking in a dialect which Moshe did not understand.

Soon after the Zodiac had moored alongside the *Sea Crescent,* the sailor who had spoken on the radio, whom Moshe assumed had to be the captain, was offered a flexible ladder to climb onboard the *Sea Crescent.* He carried a suitcase with him. After a couple of minutes, during which Moshe had switched to other binoculars, a 20x digital zoom with night vision, twice as powerful as the most powerful civilian product available, he signaled his crew to be ready. Moshe could clearly see that four cases, each about half a cubic meter, were being discreetly lowered from the Sea Crescent into the Zodiac. Though he could not make out the exact markings on the cases, not because he could not see them, but because he did not read the language, Moshe immediately imagined the cases had to contain drugs. More specifically, given what he knew of the drug trade in and around Africa, he assumed they contained more or less refined heroin. They would have looked much heavier if they had contained small arms, and, at any rate, why would a Palestinian ship be supplying arms to the Eritrean rebels. There had to be more convenient sources. Fortunately, his binoculars contained a recording feature which would allow *Mossad* eventually to work on a more detailed analysis of the film of the incident. The captain climbed back down into the Zodiac; Moshe noted that he no longer had the suitcase with him.

Moshe called, Barak Decker, his opposite number on the *Charm of the Seas* and asked him to go around Massawa Island and toward the tip of T'Walet to see if he could intercept the Zodiac. He told Barak the whole story in as few words as possible and suggested calling Mark and get more specific instructions. He assumed that Mark would not want them to stop a foreign boat in foreign waters but wondered whether something could be done anyway. With the delivery of the cases apparently completed and its captain back onboard the Zodiac, she sped away, toward the south side of T'Walet Island, most likely going back to the newer part of Mitsiwa.

Mark Levi agreed that his team could not play the role of international police. Ostensibly, they had neither the equipment nor the manpower. Yet, while the *Charm of the Sea* could not behave like a police-boat, Mark noted that another boat could play a different role, still leading to the same outcome. Thus, he instructed Barak to switch the name, hull color and pavilion of his boat and to see if he could steal one of the cases from the Zodiac. The boat was not going to police the area, she was going to be pirating. Mark knew that, once the boat had captured a case, she could escape at high speed. Then, still while traveling at high speed, the crew could return the boat to its original appearance.

Everyone was surprised at the speed with which the *Sea Dragon*, a dark-green-hulled boat with a Panama pavilion, which minutes ago was seen as the white-hulled *Charm of the Seas*, with a Malta pavilion, arrived on the scene without its navigation lights on. It made it easy for her to ambush the Zodiac, which ostensibly was not prepared for a fight. A couple of automatic rifle shots across the bow brought it to a standstill and two powerful projectors were trained right onto the Zodiac. The small crew of three appeared completely lost: they clearly never anticipated pirates in that area. The *Sea Dragon* came alongside the Zodiac and used Arabic to ask for one of the cases with a bullhorn. The crew of the Zodiac had no way of knowing how many sailors were on the pirate ship. They assumed they were vastly outpowered and did not put up much of a fight, particularly when they saw four semi-automatic arms pointed in their direction—How could they know that this was all the firepower that was available?

The Zodiac crew motioned to the *Sea Dragon* that it was ready to comply with the instructions. The *Sea Dragon* positioned herself alongside the Zodiac and lowered a line with its crane. The rebels placed the hook at the end of the line on the spot which was designed to have the case moved up or down. The *Sea Dragon* raised the case and simultaneously started its engine so that it would be some distance away from the Zodiac by the time the case was up on deck. Barack, the captain of the *Sea Dragon* was conducting a classic maneuver: he had the motors operate in opposite gears, which allowed the boat to spin on its own vertical axis. Back on the bullhorn, Barack instructed the Zodiac to go on its way.

The three Zodiac sailors were initially quite surprised and did not react immediately. They had not understood the original instructions and were fully expecting the next request to call for another case, and that until the four cases had moved from one boat to the other. This explained why they did not understand why the *Sea Dragon* was moving away from their boat as quickly as it did. Yet, when it became painfully obvious that the *Sea Dragon* was speeding away, the sailors started to smile at one another. They were celebrating the fact that they had kept three quarters of their precious cargo. Their leader meanwhile was starting to think of how they could manage reinforcements for the next transshipment, which he fully expected would occur on the next voyage of the *Sea Crescent*.

Meanwhile, on the *Sea Dragon*, Barak ordered the ship back to the hydrofoil configuration she had abandoned, before being visible from the Zodiac and sped in the direction of the mouth of the harbor. While on the water, he changed the *Sea Dragon* back to the *Charm of the Sea*. She eventually went off the hydrofoil mode back to the normal configuration. Several boats indeed could say that they saw a white-hulled boat emerging at normal speed, from the harbor channel near the southern tip of Massawa Island. Nobody could remember ever seeing a dark-green-hulled boat named *Sea Dragon*. While enroute, Barack went on the aft deck of the boat to check on the case: he made a small cut in the wrapping around the case and immediately saw some white powder seep out. Back in the command tower, he called Moshe using their satellite phones, as they could not use the radio for that kind of message:

"Excellent guess, Moshe. White powder. I'm no expert, but I'll bet it's neither flour nor sugar, even if it doesn't seem super refined yet."

"Many thanks, Barak. Can you please brief Mark? *The Sea Crescent* looks as if she about to leave and I don't want to miss it. Feel free to go straight to Aden. By the way, you will need help to get rid of the samples."

"You bet. I'll tell Mark to inform the Fifth Fleet. Hopefully, they can have a boat meet me in the Gulf of Oman. Have him let me know as soon as he has it lined up, please."

■ ■ ■ ■ ■

The *Sea Crescent* continued her "normal route," traveling at around twelve to fourteen knots and probably planning for her next stop to be in Aden, through the Bab Al Mandab Strait. Ostensibly, any stop between then and Aden would be a huge surprise as the total distance between Massawa and Aden was hardly more than four hundred nautical miles. On the other hand, sailing directly to the area around Socotra Island where the ship had been supplied on the first trip that *Mossad* monitored would be very close to nine hundred and fifty nautical miles, enough to stretch the *Sea Crescent's* fuel capacity. Yet, no one really knew how much fuel they were carrying in their incremental soft reservoirs.

■ ■ ■ ■ ■

The *Charm of the Sea* which was not on current "tail" duty had sailed at high speed through the Strait and in the general direction of Socotra Island. She had organized to rendezvous with a tanker from the Fifth Fleet which could remove the case of opiates she likely carried. Mark had made it clear that it was dangerous enough to conduct the kind of operations they were conducting; they did not need to be trafficking drugs to boot. *The Charm of the Sea* took advantage of being near a tanker to fill up her own fuel tanks, as her high-speed traveling while practical from the point of view of the mission more than tripled her fuel consumption. With a full load of fuel, she travelled still at high speed into the port of Aden and moored where *Mossad* had noted that the *Sea Crescent* had docked on her prior visit: in the small gulf past the Alfanar Lighthouse, in the At-Tawahi section of Aden. The docking area was a single T-shaped jetty. *The Charm of the Sea* moored on the East side of the jetty.

The *Charm of the Sea's* mooring permit noted that they would likely buy provisions, though there would not be much more to buy in that location in Aden; they had indicated on the permit that they would not need fuel. Repeating the scenario which Moshe had followed in Massawa with his boat, two crewmen went ashore to be able to observe any activity around the *Sea Crescent* when she would arrive, while Barrack Decker and his other two crewmen remained with the boat. Given the geography of the port of Aden, they had to be ready, if needed, to move to a different location. Looking at satellite pictures, Mark had warned the team that there were at least four other docking areas along the waterfront, not counting Aden Container Port, or Port Yemen, on its own island on the north side of the channel. He had thus recommended to both boat captains to be flexible, effectively saying:

"They'll go back to the old position if the only thing they do is fuel up. But you can almost guarantee that they won't go back there if they're picking up something else."

They had agreed in fact that since Barak's ship, the *Charm of the Seas*, was to sail ahead of the *Sea Crescent* while the *Sailing Princess* was following it, she should stick to the earliest location. Moshe and the *Sailing Princess* would in effect follow the *Sea Crescent* wherever she eventually docked. If Barak had to move, he was going to do it and fix a rendezvous point to the two sailors that were already ashore.

The area around the T-shaped jetty suddenly became quite busy. Indeed, the *Sea Crescent* offered no surprise this time. She went straight to her usual fueling terminal, on the west side of the jetty. This initially caused a bit of a problem for Moshe who would thus have to dock his own boat, the *Sailing Princess*, quite near the *Charm of the Seas*, currently docked across the jetty from the *Sea Crescent*. Barack immediately understood the challenge: the *Charm of the Seas* had to move. He told the two sailors he had dropped ashore that he was going to move from his current location, adding:

"I'll give you detailed instructions as soon as I can."

As he was sailing toward the back end of the harbor, he briefly went abeam the bow of the *Sea Crescent*. From there, he could clearly see that what he called the "Massawa scenario" was being repeated. A boat was coming alongside the water side of the *Sea Crescent* and Barack did not need much imagination to become convinced that some additional drug transshipment was taking place. A quick call to Mark made it clear to Barack that Aden was not a place where *Mossad* could repeat the approach followed in Massawa. Barack deadpanned:

"There are too many possible observers around. I could not change the appearance of the vessel without someone seeing it."

Mark immediately understood. He was sorry that they could not steal another case, if only to satisfy themselves that the *Sea Crescent's* cargo was solely comprising opiates. He asked:

"Can you find a way to loiter so that you can follow the boat carrying the contraband in the harbor?"

"Frankly, it depends upon how quickly they carry out the

transaction. At this point, I am ahead of the contraband boat if she turns my way. So, I could track her a bit. I don't know how quickly I could do a U-turn if she goes in the opposite direction."

"Understood."

Barack kept going in the direction of the large Aden Container Terminal, which was straight ahead of him, in the distance. He was going at as slow a pace as he possibly could, to keep his options open. Once he was far enough away from the *Sea Crescent*, he maneuvered the *Charm of the Seas* as close to the quay as possible and cut off his engines. Telling them where he was, he called the two sailors that were onshore:

"Can you get back here in five minutes or less?

"Less than that. We're quite close."

Barack then called Mark to tell him that the contraband boat had sailed in the opposite direction, adding:

"Got to get my men onboard and cannot go after her."

Mark appeared non-plussed:

"Not a problem. It's not as if we didn't know that this kind of trade took place in Aden. Plus, it's not our job to police the drug trade in these waters."

As Mark was still speaking, Barack interrupted:

"*The Sea Crescent* is coming this way."

"Follow it and report."

Thankfully, the two sailors just had the time to climb aboard before Barack started his engines and positioned himself to tail the *Sea Crescent*. Barack radioed Moshe:

"Can you tail the *Sea Crescent*? I'm still ahead of her."

"Should not be a problem, but you're in a better position. Let her pass you and follow her. I'll follow further back. Whenever she stops, if she does, keep going and I'll take over."

Within minutes, Barack was back on the radio with Moshe:

"I think you need to transform your boat and replace me."

"What are you talking about, my friend?"

"Well, Moshe, there's this guy I can see on their bridge which keeps looking back at us through binoculars. I've no way of knowing whether he is looking at us because he is suspicious, or simply because that's his job. But if you do take over from me you must have a different identity: he's got to have already seen the *Sailing Princess*."

"I see. I see. You need to veer off and let me get behind her. I'll be the *"Sea Riches"* with a beautiful red hull, and a Panama flag. I'll sail faster than you to catch up so stay in position. When you see me, slow down and pretend to dock near a fueling pump. You might even get a few hundred gallons of fuel, just for credibility's sake. Remember, the harbor dead-ends near the container terminal. You do not want to go anywhere near there."

"Agreed, Moshe. We wouldn't want both of our boats to be stuck in the harbor. We'd be sitting ducks."

"Precisely. If you have the chance without being too obvious, the *Charm of the Sea* may need to give way to another identity too . . ."

"Makes lot of sense. I'll select the red hull, with a Gibraltar pavilion and be the *"Sailing Joy."* I'll sail toward the mouth of the harbor at slow speed. You can call on me if needed, but otherwise I'll anchor just after I reach the sea."

Barack called Mark to make sure he was fully in the loop:

"Hey, slight change in Aden. I'm giving up tailing the *Sea Crescent* and Moshe is taking over, using the red-hulled *Sea Riches*. I'm also switching boats: I'll be on the red-hulled *Sailing Joy*."

"Why all that Barack?"

"*Sea Crescent* may have picked me up . . ."

"Say no more. I'll ask the Eitan to remain as close as it can. Also, I'll ask them to broadcast to both yours and Moshe's boat his pictures in real time."

"Do you suspect anything, Mark?"

"Frankly no. But I see this as a useful precaution."

CHAPTER.18

ADEN HARBOR, YEMEN, WASHINGTON, DC, USA, AND TEL AVIV, ISRAEL

Simon called Jack on the phone:

"Anything new on the Frank Lord front?"

"Very little, Simon. We got permission to place his phones under surveillance. We also received permission to go through BACL's email traffic. Shi Tsu was able to sign off on the subpoena and we downloaded the files which had been retrieved by Hai Chock. Nobody needs to know that we had done some digging before receiving these permissions. One person who does not know all these hot details is my buddy, Clay Mitchell."

"No need to know, right?"

"Absolutely. By the way, Countess Renate was immensely helpful in cutting all red tape. We owe her one."

"I think that we'll owe her more than that when all is said and done. And, frankly, not all of it will be covered by her fee."

"You're a cynic, Simon."

"No, just a realist. So, when do you expect news from the Lord investigation?"

"Hard to tell. It all depends on what we find on these emails.

From my point of view, the real nasty would be if we do not find anything. Then it would point the finger back to Shi Tsu or Michael, or even may be Ho Lim. . . . What a mess!"

Simon nodded. He fully appreciated the predicament described by his friend, Jack. For the time being, the only internal suspect was Frank, counting him as one with his wife. They would have to go back to square one if they could not back their suspicions up.

■ ■ ■ ■ ■

Meanwhile, in Aden's harbor, things were heating up. Moshe picked up his phone to call Mark:

"Mark, *Sea Crescent* is not making much sense. I don't see where they're going."

"What do you mean?"

"They're pretty close to the container terminal and there's nothing after that. You know? Absolute dead-end."

"What do you want to do?"

"With the Eitan surveillance as it is, I think I should abandon the tail as well and disappear from the scene. I'll look for a hiding place along the shore and move this boat back to being the *Sailing Princess*."

"Why?"

"Just a hunch. Can you instruct the Eitan to move even closer if it can. Either they were driving me into a trap and my making a U-turn will kill that plan, or, at some point, they'll turn around as well. Barack can pick them up as they exit the harbor. On the other hand, they may still be picking up something and we need to know what it is. Don't you agree?"

"You make a lot of sense, my friend. When you're back sailing as the *Sailing Princess*, why don't you dock near the earlier T-shaped jetty. With any luck, the *Sea Crescent* will believe you were there all along."

"Unless they have spies on the ground."

"True.

■ ■ ■ ■ ■

Mark called Simon to bring him into the loop. Simon immediately called the Eitan images onto his own screen to follow the situation:

"Mark. Look carefully. The *Sea Crescent* is approaching another boat."

""Delivery on the sea?"

"No! In fact, it looks as if it's picking up something. from that other boat!"

"I see. Strange. Very strange. What do you think it is?"

"I don't know, but I'll bet it is not any sort of white powder, not in Aden's Harbor."

"Simon, look, it seems it's two cases, large cases. They're placing them on the aft deck. They are not bringing them below deck."

"Correct. We can probably assume it is neither secret nor terribly unusual. Really wonder what it could be."

Mark stayed silent for a while longer and then exclaimed:

"Bastards!"

"Why do you say that, Mark?"

"I think I've figured their game out."

"Pray, tell."

"What if these were mines?"

Simon thought for a split second and came right back:

"Great idea, Mark. If you're right, I wonder whether they plan on using them against us."

"That's exactly my intuition, Simon. I bet you that they picked up the fact that someone has been tailing them. So, they went about their business because they could not do otherwise, but, meanwhile, on the radio, they ordered a few mines. Then, when they're back in the open sea and they see one of our boats following them again, they'll drop a chaplet of these mines behind them. They'll try to attract the boat following them into their trap."

"Excellent, Mark. Excellent. I 'll let you talk to the captains to warn them. While you do that, I'm gonna see if we can have a couple of anti-mine munitions brought to the boats by submarine. I don't know if it'll be via one of ours or one of the American's. At any rate, make sure that everyone is monitoring the Eitan images on a permanent basis. We want to see them when they drop the mines, if that's what they're going to do.

■ ■ ■ ■ ■

"Jack? Simon here."

"What's new?"

"Well, I need your help and I want to plan an additional operation."

"What's going on, Simon."

"Well, two things. First, we suspect that the Palestinians may have picked up the fact that we're tailing them."

"Really? Shit!"

"We're not absolutely sure. But we think we're going to need anti-mine munitions. If we're right, they're gonna try to blow up one of our boats following the *Sea Crescent*. In that case, we absolutely need the anti-mine munition. If not, the munitions will be surplus to requirements. We'll then need to figure out what they did pick up and what they're planning on doing with it."

"I see that. How can we help you?"

"Do you have any of these anti-mine munitions in the area?"

"I'm sure there's gotta be the right stuff somewhere within the Fifth Fleet."

"Could some be brought to one of our spy boats by a submarine so that the loading is done underwater?"

"I'll let them decide how to do it. Can be a submarine. Can be an Orca drone."

"Excellent."

Jack switched gears, going back to Simon's earlier point that he was going to start a new operation. Simon replied that this would entirely be carried out by *Mossad* and the Israeli Army. He explained:

"I want to disrupt their operations a bit more."

"Who's they?"

"Hezbollah. I have to assume that they believe that something is amiss. I'm sure they do not know for a fact that *Mossad* is on their tail. But they most likely suspect us. At any rate, we need to put pressure on them."

"What do you want to do?"

"We're going to remove a couple of their underwater drones. I want them to wonder what is happening. I'm hoping that they would simply try to replace them. We can then disrupt their procurement and get more insight on the Chinese and the Iranians."

■ ■ ■ ■ ■

Mark's next call was to Joel Miller. He knew that there would be no news on the Frank Lord front, but he did not want to lose sight of the other three partners:

"Joel, I need you to have your private investigator continue to look into Michel, Shi Tsu and even Ho Lim."

"You're not satisfied that you've got your man in Frank Lord?"

"Joel, you never know. . . . The Frank Lord track looks safe on the surface, but, below the surface, I can think of two things. First, what if there is more than one? They all seem to have a Singapore connection."

"True, other than Ho Lim."

"Correct."

"But they've had totally different paths since then."

"I know. I'm probably overthinking this. But my second point? I'd rather pay a bit more in fees to the private investigator than find out at some point that there was a really gaping hole we all missed. Looking at the others could create that opening that clarifies everything."

"So, Mark, what's the mission?"

"I would like Rachel to retrace as much of these people's life story as she can without opening a complete can of worms. My boss talked to Countess Renate earlier and she agreed that you could open up a connection between Rachel and Hai Chock in Singapore, provided she is not made aware of Hai Chock's relationship with the Shadow Experts. This should allow her, if Hai Chock agrees it can be done, to talk to Hai Chock's friend in the Singapore secret services."

■ ■ ■ ■ ■

Back in Aden Harbor, the *Sea Cres*cent was retracing her steps and sailing for the mouth of the harbor. Whether her captain saw or did not see the *Sailing Princess* moored to her port side may never be known, but Moshe could certainly attest that there was no one on her bridge scanning the horizon for other boats. He still decided not to move for as long as his boat could be seen by the *Sea Crescent*. He had two of his sailors scan the surroundings of the jetty with infra-red binoculars, in the hope of seeing someone hidden ashore that would be monitoring them and, potentially, inform Hezbollah at some later point. They were both categorical: they could not see anyone. Moshe knew very well that people could be inside buildings or even inside other boats moored here or there. He was thus painfully aware that he still did not know what he did not know. He called Mark:

"Everything looks clean at this point. I will wait for the *Sea Crescent* to exit the harbor before setting off. I can always catch up with her if needed in hydrofoil mode. I'll know when she is outside the mouth of the harbor from the Eitan images."

"Sounds excellent, Moshe. I'll let Barack know that he must tail the *Sea Crescent*."

"Agreed. However, Mark, two thoughts. First tell Barack to have one guy permanently watching the back of the *Sea Crescent* and the images from the Eitan. If they're going to try and do something funny, he needs to find out quickly enough. Second, when are we getting the anti-mine protection?"

"Good question, Moshe. I have not talked to Simon on this yet. All I know is that the Americans will have some underwater vessel, submarine or drone, deliver them to both of you guys."

"Where?"

"They will know your heading and general location. Someone will contact you and Barack when they're ready to deliver. At that point, you'll slow to a crawl and have a couple of divers ready by your airlocks to retrieve whatever they will be giving you."

"I hope this will happen soon. I am not sure I like the idea of someone following the Sea Crescent without any defense."

"Don't worry. It's in Simon's hands and very little if anything ever slips through the cracks."

Moshe hung up and called Barrack to brief him. As he was looking at the Eitan images, he could clearly see that the ship had cleared the mouth of the harbor. He turned his engines on and moved slowly away from the jetty. As he was maneuvering, he saw, in the corner of his field of vision, a small boat approaching. He yelled the command:

"Raise the stern and aft guns. Gunners at your stations."

The two sailors took their positions, well-protected by the sides of the deck. They had their earpieces on and were waiting for an order from Moshe. They first heard Moshe on the ship's loudspeaker, speaking in Arabic:

"Do not approach any closer."

A few seconds later, Moshe repeated, with a stronger emphasis:

"Do not approach any closer or I open fire."

The sailors took their firing positions, sitting next to the guns and protected by the shield in front of them. That shield was made of steel for the whole lower half and thick bulletproof glass in its upper section. Both sailors could see that the suspicious boat was still moving toward them. They heard Moshe:

"Fire. First just in front of them and then at them if they do not stop."

Two volleys of fire exploded into the quiet of the harbor. The smaller craft kept coming. The next two volleys struck just in front the boat and made it stop. Moshe ordered:

"Stay at your positions. I'm going hydrofoil. Be well-tethered."

While she was still in the Inner Harbor, the *Sailing Princess*'s engines roared into life and the crew could see the bow rising above the water, after which they could feel its aft section rise as well. Moshe was steering the *Sailing Princess* alongside Al-Ma'ala on the port side and quickly around the Prince of Wales pier and Tawahi, both still on the port side. Moshe could see the mouth of the harbor straight ahead, with so-called Little Aden on his starboard side. Moshe knew that he was not supposed to go as fast as he did in the harbor and regretted that he had shown whoever was watching a secret of Israeli spy-ships. However, he thought:

I regret that less than others might regret my not being alive and safe now.

He continued at a higher rate of speed than normal for another five miles at which point he was in the high seas and felt he could slow down. He instructed his crew to lower the guns into the belly of the ship, after he had shifted back away from his hydrofoil mode. He changed the name and the appearance of the ship another time, going back to the *Sea Riches*. The ship's hull went from the white of the *Sailing Princess* to the red of *Sea Riches*, while the Gibraltar flag was lowered and replaced by a Panama flag.

Moshe then calmly called Barack to brief him, conferencing Mark in so that the higher ups knew of the incident.

■ ■ ■ ■ ■

Mark called Simon on the videophone. He looked disappointed. He was obviously delighted to know that his troops had valiantly resisted and then won, but he was fuming:

"If they did not know we were behind these boats, they must now."

Seeing the quizzical look on Mark's face, he added:

"Who else in the region has that capability?"

"Honestly, I could only think of the Americans, but somehow someone would have picked up these small crafts before. They don't sail along with the Fifth Fleet."

"Well, it's all water under the bridge anyway. Our enemies now know or at least strongly assume we have an unusual capability, but the only things they've seen are first that our unarmed boats are in fact armed and that they are capable of much higher-than-expected speed."

For Mark's benefit, he added:

"We must quickly make sure that the two boats have their anti-mine defenses. And we've got to assume that the *Sea Crescent* will have been made aware of the danger. They now must know they cannot outrun at least one of our boats, so they're going to have to try to destroy it."

"You say one, but don't you mean two, Simon?"

"It could well be two, but they only know for sure of one. They haven't seen Barack's boat sail at that speed. Anyway, with respect to Moshe's, I would add that they think it's a white-hulled boat flying a Gibraltar flag."

Mark interrupted Simon:

"I'm getting a signal from the Americans that they're ready for us."

"Excellent. Let me get off the line and let you manage the exchange."

Mark called Lieutenant Charley Maxwell who had pinged him.

"You're ready for us?"

"Yes, sir"

Mark could not fail to notice the relative youth in the voice and the strongly stressed "sir" at the end of Lieutenant Maxwell's reply. He thought: *pure product of the Naval Academy.* Mark asked:

"What are your instructions?"

"We're delivering the defenses using an Orca. It's as fast as a regular submarine and much smaller and more discreet. Give me your ships' positions please."

Mark looked at his GPS screen and could see both spy ships. He gave the coordinates and said:

"Can you please contact their captains directly when ready?"

"Sure, Sir. Just have them place two sailors, in diving gear in the airlock, which they should open. The plan is for the Orca to sail alongside and below each ship and let go of a package which should float slowly up. Your divers should catch it, place it into the lock and close it."

"How is it floating up? Anti mine munitions are heavy."

"The packing is mostly air – it is bigger, but the air wants to rise to the surface."

"I see. Does not sound too terribly difficult, Lieutenant."

"It isn't, though everything is in the details as usual."

"What are these defenses?"

"They're small torpedoes which can be manually launched, dropped from the ship may be a better way of saying it. Once launched, they go forward and look for any magnetic field that mines should trigger. They explode on contact, clearing the way for the boat which follows."

"Quite ingenious. Any precaution?"

"Only one. Make sure when they are dropped in the water that they are pointed in the right general direction. You wouldn't want them to turn around and explode next to your ship."

"That's for sure. Thanks."

"You're welcome, sir!"

CHAPTER.19

WASHINGTON, DC, USA, TEL AVIV, ISRAEL, AND IN THE GULF OF ADEN AND THE RED SEA

Jack called Simon:

"Simon, my friend, there is some news on the Frank Lord front."

"Excellent, let's hear it."

"Well, I'm not sure I would call it excellent."

"Ah. What's the scoop?"

"Well, in a word, we have not found anything in all the material which we've looked at?"

"Nothing?"

"Yes. Absolutely nothing."

"Sharks. What's your next step, Jack?"

"Well, that's what I wanted to discuss with you. My friend, Clay Mitchell, remember, from the FBI, says that he can't take it any further, because what appeared like a probable cause has simply collapsed."

"So?"

"So, I am kind of stuck."

Simon thought for a minute and then asked:

"Tell me, Jack, Mrs. Lord, Chin Chang Ying if I recall correctly . . ."

"Yes, what about her?"

"Is she an American citizen?"

"God! You're smart, Simon. Hadn't thought of that. That does give us a potential avenue. At any rate, whether she is a U.S. citizen or just a permanent resident, there's gotta be a file on her in the Immigration Department."

"Probably worth looking at. . . . And if that fails, should someone have a chat with Dr. and Mrs. Lord?"

"On what pretense?"

"I don't know. How about something close to the truth, but with a small omission?"

"A small omission?"

"Yes; forgetting to mention what we know and that they're our primary suspects."

"Good thought, my friend. Good thought."

"Thanks. On our side, by the way, nothing new. The private investigator hired by Joel Miller has not come back to us with anything, though I hear from Countess Renate that she has had a conversation with Hai Chock in Singapore."

"So, Simon, I guess we are at some kind of standstill."

"On that front, yes, Jack, but the operations continue. Not that I'm not concerned, you know. We still have a number of missiles potentially pointed at us and BACL still has a problem with leakage of military secrets to China. However, we have removed two of Hezbollah's underwater drones and made sure that they know about it. They're bound to react in some way."

"Anything happened to your boats on their trip back from Aden?"

"Well, that's another story."

Simon explained that the *Sailing Joy*, under Captain Barack Decker's command, had eventually started to follow the *Sea Crescent* from further back than usual. In fact, Captain Decker was relying more on the images from the Eitan drone than on direct vision to trail the *Sea Crescent*. Thus, nothing happened initially. Then things heated up.

■ ■ ■ ■ ■

First, the *Sea Crescent* sailed in a southeasterly direction. Everyone assumed that she was going back in the general vicinity of the Socotra Island. They remembered that the ship had yet to pick up underwater drones, missiles and transmitters and were thus not surprised. Captain Barack Decker on the red-hulled *Sailing Joy* did not feel there was any need to get any closer to his target. He was well aware that he could close on the *Sea Crescent* in mere minutes if he switched his boat to the hydrofoil mode. Captain Moshe Aaron, on the *Sailing Princess*, was giving his colleague a wide berth and still going in the same general direction, sailing initially more easterly than south-easterly. The two captains were counting on the fact that neither of their boats had previously been seen in their current configuration to ensure them some measure of anonymity.

Mark, separately, had given a heads up to his contact on the Fifth Fleet, Lieutenant Charley Maxwell and had asked for them to provide a discreet escort to the two boats. Mark had nothing firm on which he could hang his concerns, yet he was worried that the two boats were vulnerable in the open sea of the Gulf of Aden. That proved not to be a useful precaution early on, as nothing happened until the *Sea Crescent* reached the small island due west of Socotra. There she was met by an Iranian ship which, surprise, was this time accompanied by another patrol boat. The Eitan dutifully filmed and transmitted the images of four missiles being lowered onto the *Sea Crescent's* deck and promptly moved from prying eyes and placed below deck.

The *Sailing Princess* was the first to arrive in the general vicinity of the *Sea Crescent*, shortly after the transshipment had taken place. However, Moshe was still several miles from the *Sea Crescent* when he picked up on his radar a craft approaching at a fast rate of speed.

He immediately radioed Lieutenant Maxwell who told him not to worry. One of their frigates had both his ship and the other on their radar. It was going to take care of it.

It certainly did, firing a single rocket that landed no more than one hundred yards from the bow of the Iranian craft. That did not make it stop, however. The Iranian craft kept going in the direction of the *Sailing Princess*. Moshe quickly decided that he was not in a fighting position. He thus shifted to the hydrofoil mode and simply disappeared from the radar of the Iranian craft in less than five minutes. Further, when he thought he was out of radar range, he turned sharply to port to be sure he remained in the correct general vicinity, though still well within the protection of the Fifth Fleet. Moshe also called Barack to warn him of the danger.

Yet Barack had in the meantime come close enough that the Iranian patrol boat started racing after him, though still a few miles away. Like Moshe, Barack followed Mark's instructions and called from help from the Fifth Fleet. Another rocket was fired, but, this time, it was calibrated to hit the water quite a bit closer to the Iranian boat. As it again failed to slow down, the next rocket hit right in front of its bow, which brought it to a total stop, with sailors plunging into the warm waters of the Gulf of Aden. They were rescued by an American boat. Barack returned on the distant tail of the *Sea Crescent*, which was sailing in the direction of a Chinese cargo boat.

Taking advantage of the cover of darkness, the Chinese boat unloaded two submarine drones and their transmitters onto the deck of the *Sea Crescent*, without realizing that she was starring in a movie taken by the Eitan drone to be eventually released to a broader audience at the appropriate time. Simon smiled as he saw the clip, thinking that it would be a great hit on certain social networks. That the clip would be censured in China was not a problem. At the very least, the world would know what China was up to, and Israel could lodge a formal protest at the United Nations. Again, that it would certainly be vetoed within the Security Council by China, and probably Russia, was not going to diminish one of their few Israel public relations successes: catching China red-handed providing advanced equipment to Hezbollah, equipment which could not be used for any purpose other than attacking Israel.

Once the submarine drones were camouflaged on the deck of the *Sea Crescent*, she turned north and west and proceeded back on her route via the Red Sea.

■ ■ ■ ■ ■

Captain Barack Decker was somewhat in front of the *Sea Crescent*, leaving the rear guard to Captain Moshe Aaron. Both Israeli captains were still totally aware that there remained significant risks that they would be attacked during the trip, most likely by the *Sea Crescent* if they came a bit too close, but quite possibly by someone else. It was agreed that the Fifth Fleet could not go beyond the strait of Bab al-Mandab between Yemen on the Arabian Peninsula and Djibouti and Eritrea on the Horn of Africa. Israel sent a submarine which was already in the Gulf of Aden to patrol the waters around the two boats. An American submarine also came along as further support.

The relative narrowness of the strait made the passage somewhat dangerous though not dramatically so. The Strait of Bab al-Mandab is eighteen miles wide at its narrowest point, which leaves only two two-mile wide channels for inbound and outbound traffic involving very large boats. These restrictions surely did not apply to any of the three vessels, though they did restrict somewhat the margin of maneuver of the submarines. A couple of rockets fired from Yemen did fall in the general proximity but still short of the *Sailing Princess*, but Moshe saw this more as some form of intimidation than anything else. He suspected, rightly as it turned out, that the insurgent did not have the right equipment with the required range to fire with sufficient precision to expose his boat to any serious risk.

After the *Sea Crescent* had made a refueling stop in Massawa, the roles of the two Israeli captains were inverted. Moshe was sent ahead in the direction of the two most likely refueling ports, while Barack was left behind to ensure that Mossad knew exactly what the *Sea Crescent* was doing along the way.

This is when things really heated up, as they were sailing abeam Port Sudan. The *Sea Crescent* had inexplicably slowed down, thus allowing Barack to catch up to within a couple of miles, if not a bit less. Someone on the bridge of the *Sea Crescent* noted that the ship which they now assumed to be Israeli despite its misleading flag was closer than she had been. He informed his captain. Coincidentally, there was no boat travelling in either direction between the *Sea Crescent* and Barack's *Sailing Joy* at that time. The Eitan sent clear pictures of the crew of the *Sea Crescent* allowing Barack and others to follow the developments:

"Captain Decker, look?"

"What?"

"The guys at the stern of the *Sea Crescent*. I can't see them distinctly from here, but the images from the Eitan are clear. What in the name of God are they doing?"

"By God, you're right Hershel. Let's see. It appears they've got a few of what looks like small bombs together. What are they doing with that?"

"Bombs, Captain? Looks to me like they could be mines. . . . The mines they picked up in Aden."

Captain Decker thought for a few short seconds and exclaimed:

"You must be right, Hershel, mines make a lot more sense. What are they doing with them? Why would they plant mines in the middle of the Red Sea? A terrorist act?"

"Could well be, sir, but my guess is that it's too deep here to make any difference, unless they're supposed to stay at the surface or near it."

"I see. Are they dropping them now?"

"No, first, it looks like they are attaching them to some cord . . ."

"Wait, it's more like a net-like thing."

"You're right, Captain. It is a net. What are they doing?"

Barack smiled:

"Now I get it. It's so obvious. That's what Mark was worried about. These mines are for us. We wouldn't see them if we did not have the images from the Eitan. Look on the screen, they are preparing to drop them behind their boat."

"I can see that, but the net looks small. The trap they're setting seems incredibly narrow. Shouldn't be hard to avoid them."

"Correct, but remember, they hope we don't see them and sail directly into them."

"I see. You mean they'd be just below the surface. Still, are we following them just where their wake would have been?"

"Agree with you Hershel. Ah. Wait a minute, Look at the Eitan images. The ends of the net seem to be moving. Yes, they are moving. They're straightening the net. They're widening the trap."

"A motorized net?"

"Why not, Hershel?"

Barack slowed down his boat further. A last look at the Eitan images convinced him. He started barking instructions to the crew:

"Get two of the anti-mine torpedoes from the hold. The two of you with the torpedoes, stand on either side of the bow. On my count, release them. Make sure you've got them pointing straight ahead. . . . One, two, three, Drop!"

The two torpedoes hit the water at just about the same time. The two sailors that dropped them kept watching to check that they were functioning as planned. They were expecting them to ignite their motors and start going forward not more than a foot below the surface. Yet, none of this was happening. One of them called out:

"What's going on, Captain? Can't see the torpedoes anymore. At all. I don't see any sign they're going after their target. They've just plain disappeared."

Barack was initially surprised:

"Get me two more torpedoes. Let's repeat our last operation. Are you sure you had them switched on?"

The sailors were puzzled. They were convinced that they had done exactly what they were supposed to do, but now started doubting themselves. They quickly got the additional two torpedoes from the hold. One of them went with his to the bridge to show it to Barack, who asked:

"What did you do the last time?"

The sailor showed him without actually going through the full process."

"You're doing it right. Darn it, those must have been duds. Yet what are the odds that two out of two are defective?"

He added:

"Go to the bow and await my signal to turn them on."

Barack was about to bark the next set of instructions when he and his crew heard a first explosion. It was followed by several more, within seconds. He barked:

"Stand down. Put the next two torpedoes back in the hold. The other two did their job.

What Lieutenant Charley Maxwell had not told Mark was that the torpedoes would initially plunge about three feet, race forward and stay down at that depth until they somehow picked up the magnetic waves. At that point, they would move to the appropriate depth, up or down, and hit their targets. By the time the *Sailing Joy* arrived on the spot where the mines had been, there was nothing to be feared. He could still see the *Sea Crescent* in the distance. He was well-aware that Moshe could also see the *Sea Crescent* on his long-range radar. They had indeed received instructions from Simon via Mark not to tempt fate:

"Stay at a safe distance. We have you two. We have the Eitan filming above. We can afford to give them a bit more leeway. The only risk is that the *Sea Crescent* would slow down enough to transfer her cargo to another Palestinian ship. We are watching for that and will let you know if you need to get closer. With your speed advantage, either of you should be able to catch up with them in five minutes of hydrofoil mode or less."

Neither captain had any reason to disagree.

They kept tracking the *Sea Crescent*, one from the front, the other from the rear. They continued to watch for anything suspicious as nothing said that the *Sea Crescent* had only picked up a single load of the mines. Mark had warned Barack:

"I can't believe that they haven't figured out that there are at least two boats following them. They may first have targeted you, but I'd be stunned if they don't have at least one if not several other sets of mines."

Barack did not debate Mark's view. That nothing had happened immediately after the first ambush did not preclude another, possibly several other attacks. At this point, though, they were still plotting their course following the *Sea Crescent*, assuming that the next decision point would be when she would have to choose between the right or the left arm of the upper Red Sea. She initially veered to starboard. Moshe, who was in front, observed:

"We're on our way to Eilat and Aqaba."

He steered the *Sailing Princess* through the Strait of Tiran, at the mouth of the Gulf of Aqaba with Sharm El Sheikh overlooking it on the west site, at the southern tip of the Sinai Peninsula. He was still watching the moves of the *Sea Crescent* when he saw her seemingly slowdown. Eventually, she moved into the harbor. He wondered:

"What the heck is she doing?"

He called Barack on the radio to brief him. Barack decided to remain outside the harbor when he got there, relying instead on the

Eitan for intelligence. Both captains were in fact quite lucky as a new Eitan had replaced the one which had filmed so far. It was getting close to its full range and needed to return to base and refuel. The new images were just as good as the previous ones. Both Captains could see that the *Sea Crescent* appeared simply to be getting herself refueled. They were thankful that they had enough fuel to get through the Suez Canal and then some. Yet, Moshe placed a call to Mark asking for a floating fueling rig to be brought in their direction, as he would definitely not have enough fuel to go all the way to Eilat and back. Mark observed:

"You can always get fuel in Eilat if needed. Let's wait until we know better whether the *Sea Crescent* goes up to Aqaba or backs up to go through the Suez Canal."

"Turn around?"

"Yes. There was no refueling option for the *Sea Crescent* after Sharm al Sheik before Port Said. So, they sailed toward the East branch of the Red Sea simply because they needed fuel. Remember the multiple maneuvers around Socotra. By the way, if she does go back through the Suez Canal, don't worry. We'll have refueling facilities for you in the Mediterranean."

Moshe agreed and passed the message onto Barack. In the meantime, they both decided to stay in position, with only one engine turned on and at idle speed to boot. The *Sailing Princess* was north of the Straits of Tiran in the event the *Sea Crescent* would continue on the East branch of the Red Sea. The *Sailing Joy* went through the Straits and awaited the *Sea Crescent* if she was going to retrace some of her steps and aim for the Suez Canal. The *Sea Crescent* did not seem to do anything more while at harbor than get her fill of fuel. When she was through, but still without appearing to rush, she came out of the harbor at slow speed and initially moved south. Barack, who was watching on his Eitan screen, exclaimed:

"She's going for Suez."

He called Moshe:

"Let's reverse our order. I'm ahead of the *Sea Crescent*, so let me go through Suez first. I'll wait for the Sea Crescent at the mouth of the Canal."

"Fine. I will let her gain on me and will aim to be a few ships behind her while in the convoy in the Canal."

The Israeli and American submarines which had followed them since Bar Al-Bandar bid both captains farewell and returned to their respective positions around the Gulf of Aden. Meanwhile, Israel had sent another submarine in the vicinity of the mouth of the Suez Canal as well, together with a couple of frigates, just in case the Palestinians or the Iranians would be planning some sort of unpleasant reception for Barack as he reached the Mediterranean Sea. While the submarine was able to discreetly sail into Egypt territorial waters, the frigates had to remain outside to avoid any form of international incident.

CHAPTER.20

Jack called Simon on Zoom:

"You won't believe this, Simon, but I just got a call from my friend, Clay Mitchell."

Jack could clearly see his friend Simon smile as he said:

"Let's not exaggerate, Jack. I am sure you get several calls from him, if not each day, at least each week. However, I am indeed curious to hear what he had to say."

"Very funny. Well, in a word, Frank Lord and his wife want to talk to him."

Simon looked pensive for a short while and then blurted out:

"Wonder why. Do they want to confess?"

Jack conceded that he had immediately thought of that, with a U.S. legal twist: he considered whether Frank was seeking some form of deal. Something like limited immunity in exchange for talking. However, he added:

"No, at this point, nothing. He just wants to talk."

"So, what did Clay do?"

"The only thing that came to his mind. He said he would be

happy to and asked if he could bring me in with him."

"And?"

"Frank said he had no problem with that as well."

■ ■ ■ ■ ■

"Frank, I've got a problem."

"What is it, Mary?"

Frank and Mary were at home, having a quiet breakfast, when Mary surprised Frank with her statement. Frank, as many husbands would, immediately asked:

"Is it your health?"

"No, Dear. Could even be more serious than that."

Frank's face shifted in a second to displaying fear. Mary explained to him that she was being pressured by her "controller" at the Chinese Consulate in New York, adding:

"He left a message on my cell phone yesterday evening, I guess. I just listened to it after taking my shower and getting ready this morning. I don't like it. I won't offer to have you listen to it, since it's in Mandarin."

"What did he say?"

■ ■ ■ ■ ■

The morning when Frank and Chaem Choi Sae-Chin, as she was still known then, had decided to go get some brunch was pivotal in their relationship in many ways. Chaem had decided to open up to Frank. Love was getting the better of her. They settled at a table at the Brookline Lunch, in Central Square. Then she said:

"I want to come clean, honey."

"What in the world do you mean?"

She explained that she had indeed been specially trained to seduce him, adding:

"It's a long story, Please do you best not to interrupt me. The story is not fun, but, for me at least, it has to have a good ending. It started when they sent me to "finish" my degree in Thailand, remember at Siam University?"

Frank seemed totally lost. He blurted out:

"I'm sorry, honey, but you are not making any sense."

Mary paused and looked deep into his eyes. She was about to start her confession when the waiter came to their table to get their order. They both ordered waffles with fresh strawberries. The waiter asked:

"Anything to drink beside water?"

Frank replied:

"We'll have two coffees, both with skimmed milk, warm for the lady and cold for me."

Mary resumed her story as the waiter walked away. She started by admitting she was a Chinese spy. Frank could not believe his ears but decided that the smartest thing to do at that point was to listen and avoid interrupting. Mary continued her explanation:

"They wanted me to seduce a U.S. professor posing as a doctoral student. They made me say that I graduated from the University in Bangkok, but in fact I graduated from Siam University."

"What does that have to do with me, the Siam University thing?"

"Well, they assumed that it would be less obvious if I was Thai rather than Chinese. So, since in fact there is a bit of Thai blood in me, my maternal grandmother, and since I spoke some Thai that I had learned from her, they cooked up that scheme. They made me write the University in Bangkok because Bangkok University is better known and has a better reputation than Siam University."

"So, when we met, it was all a ploy? You seemed interested in the topic though."

"I was, but honestly at the very beginning, I was there to seduce you. But that's how it became a problem."

Mary told Frank that eventually she fell in love. She was not faking love. She was deeply in love with him and needed his help. She did not want to cause any problem for him, adding amid genuine tears:

"I am caught in a trap."

"Wait, rewind this a bit. What was the point of the whole thing?"

"Well, somehow, Beijing found out that you had a history of affairs with students and that you had received some warning from MIT."

Frank looked somewhat embarrassed but conceded that the facts were unfortunately undeniable. He still asked, again:

"What was the point of the whole thing?"

"Well, my love, they knew you were conducting very special research and they wanted you to spy for them."

"How did they expect to get me to do that?"

"Classic entrapment. They have a movie of our first night together and they were going to use it to threaten you."

Frank seemed crestfallen. Mary shifted closer to him on the semi-circular bench in their booth and said:

"I agreed initially, but very soon I really regretted it. But now, the pressure is getting too big. That's why I want to be your wife. I love you. Think about it: their video means nothing if we get married."

Frank was still having a very hard time making sense of the whole thing. He understood the general drift, but too many emotions seemed crazy and in contradiction with one another. The only thing he could reply was:

"You don't get married out of fear."

Mary had shifted further to his side and was now literally right next to him. He could feel the warmth of her leg against his. She simply said:

"I don't want to cause trouble. I want to fix any problem I might be causing. And I want to spend the rest of my life with you. Do you believe me?"

Frank could see that she was either a fabulous actor or was really telling the truth. He had himself fallen in love with her. The affair that they had been conducting for the prior three months had become quite different from the flings he had had before his divorce and since. He really enjoyed being with Mary and had in fact toyed with the idea of marriage a couple of times. Yet, he was a mature man who knew that one does not get married in these kinds of circumstances. He asked:

"Help me understand why being married makes things different."

"As I said Frank, the video becomes worthless. Whether you were seducing a student or not, the fact that we would be married would remove any leverage, wouldn't it?"

"I'll grant you that it would reduce the risk of MIT terminating my contract. But, . . . still."

They went around in circles a bit longer and stopped when the waiter brought their plates. They picked at their brunch and kept talking, until Frank asked the obvious question:

"They won't leave us in peace even if we're married. They've got too much invested in you. So why would a wedding make a difference? They'll find something else."

"Frank, my love. I cannot dispute your view. But trust me. I have been mulling over this for at least a month and I have a plan."

■ ■ ■ ■ ■

Jack called Clay back. He wanted to find out whether he had been able to schedule a meeting with Frank. Parenthetically, he was keen to hear whether he could attend or not. Clay literally floored him:

"I know it sounds crazy, Jack. But, as I told you earlier, he wants to meet and does not mind you being there. I told him who you were And what your current focus was."

"And?"

"Just as I told you earlier. I could not see his face, we were on the telephone, but his voice became almost cheerful. He said that it would be great to meet you. He imposed one condition though."

"Hmm. Let's hear it."

"He wants his wife to be with him and he wants to make sure that neither of them will be in any way prosecuted."

"That's what I feared. They're seeking immunity. They're our leakers. Now we know."

Clay appeared a bit more circumspect. He replied:

"Could well be, but I wonder why they would come out now. Something tells me that we should withhold judgment for a while longer."

"I'll believe it when I see it. Anyway, Clay, the deal must be off, right?"

"Why?"

"Can you give them immunity without anything in return?"

"Well, hold on to your chair, Jack."

"What is it now?"

"Something I was not supposed to disclose. I'll tell you any way, but you can't talk about it."

"Fire away/"

"They're formally seeking our protection."

"Witness protection?"

"Absolutely, and this may involve secret service stuff initially."

■ ■ ■ ■ ■

Jack had pursued the conversation with Clay a few minutes longer. His chief goal was to get Clay to allow him to be open to Simon. He felt that knowing that Frank and Mary were seeking federal protection was a potential game changer. He argued that he could not possibly keep working on the project with Simon if he had to withhold such a crucial piece of information. Clay argued that he did not see what had changed until they had talked to the Lords, but Jack would not budge. In the end. Clay grudgingly allowed him to share that piece of information.

Jack was with Simon on the Zoom in a flash.

"Simon, a big piece of news . . .

"Jack and Mary Lord are seeking Federal protection."

"What?"

"You heard me. They called Clay and said they wanted to talk to him. In the negotiation, before telling anyone anything, they asked for both immunity and protection."

Simon exhaled noisily and seemed pensive for what looked longer than the few seconds that it lasted. He asked:

"What do you make of that?"

"Frankly, I don't know. I could make sense of their asking for immunity: they spied and are now prepared to tell us about their activities."

Simon jumped up in the air. He exclaimed:

"That's it. They leaked. They want to come clean, and they want protection against any form of threat from the Chinese. I'd have no difficulty assuming that the Chinese will be fuming when they see the Lords have turned their coat."

Jack looked dejected:

"You're way ahead of me. As usual!"

Simon smiled but conceded that there were other interpretations that were possible. He said to Jack that he would talk to Mark and find out what Joel Miller's private investigator had found so far. Jack came straight back:

"You can't tell him about the federal protection."

Simon looked amazingly calm:

"I know that, my friend, I know that. Trust me. In my position, I can ask for an update from one of my guys without it becoming a case of my blurting out all I know.

Jack smiled and they hung up.

Simon suddenly looked troubled, then pensive, then visibly elated.

■ ■ ■ ■ ■

"Jenny?"

"Simon? From the office? It must be quite serious . . ."

"I think I've made a decision."

"A decision?"

"Yes. Let's talk about it tonight."

■ ■ ■ ■ ■

Mark picked up the phone at the first ring. The screen told him it was Simon:

"Simon? What can I do for you?"

"Mark, I need an update on the work of Joel's private investigator."

"You must be psychic. I was about to call you. Joel just gave me a rundown and I think there is interesting news. Are you in your office?"

"Sure, see you here in a minute."

Mark walked into Simon's office and as was customary went directly for the couch while Simon sat on the upholstered chair next to it. Simon asked:

"So, what's up?"

Mark started by making the point that he had news on two fronts. First, he knew a bit more, though not enough yet on Michael Lennon. Second, he had found out an interesting detail on Frank Lord.

"Why don't you start with Michael?"

Mark went on to explain that Rachel needed to go to Singapore in person. Joel wanted to go along, but she refused. She had to be able to move on her own. Hai Chock's friend, Yeo Yap Min, was willing to share some more information with her, but he would not do it on the phone or even on Zoom. Yap Min was able to fill in a couple more blanks. He confirmed that Michael's wife, Sew Lin, had somewhat of a relationship with the government, because her family felt indebted: the government had come to their help in the depth of a real estate market downturn, and she was paying it pack. She had an undercover job for the Singapore government who suspected China of having spies within the foreign student community. Mark added that it seems that Michael and his wife were introduced by one such foreign student. He added:

"The story doesn't tell whether he was a spy or not, but we've got to assume he was clean, if he had developed some relationship with Sew Lin."

Simon smiled:

"Anything else on Michael and his wife?"

"No, but she is digging into the student that introduced Michael and Sew Lin."

"So, how about the Lords?"

Mark sat back in the sofa after having taken a sip of water from the glass on the end table. He started by saying that there were many things which Rachel had unearthed that looked odd, adding:

"Not always odd per se, but odd in conjunction with other things."

"You'll have to explain, my friend."

"Take their wedding, for instance. It seems that they married quite quickly. We do not know exactly how quickly, because we don't know when they first met. One thing's for sure, they got married during the spring semester, and she could not have arrived earlier than for the beginning of fall semester. By the way, MIT operates on a 4–1–4 academic calendar with the fall semester beginning after Labor Day and ending in mid-December, a 4-week "Independent Activities Period" in the month of January, and the spring semester commencing in early February and ceasing in late May."

"Love at first sight?"

"Would seem like it. Not unusual for younger people, but not in a couple with a twenty-year age difference, with the husband divorced a few years earlier and known to have sequential affairs with his students. . . . Not so common!"

"I'll grant you that. Anything else?"

"Well, they immediately started an immigration process for her to get first her Green Card and then her U.S. citizenship."

"Anything of note?"

"Well, I talked to Clay Mitchell who allowed us to look into the immigration file. She had solid documentation for virtually everything she did in the prior decade."

"So?"

"You, know, Simon. If it looks too good . . ."

"It probably is. So, you think something is wrong there."

"Yes. I suspect she is a spy."

Simon smiled.

CHAPTER.21

TEL AVIV, ISRAEL AND MEDITERRANEAN SEA

Before the *Sailing Joy* came out to Port Said, effectively the mouth of the Suez Canal on the Mediterranean Sea, the two missile boats, *INS Javelin* and *INS Storm*, which Israel had sent could clearly see that something was not right. Though the harbor and the mouths of the multiple branches of the river in the Nile delta are always a hub of activity, the small flotilla of fishing boats concentrated at the mouth of the Suez Canal looked suspicious at best. After conferring with the higher authorities in Tel Aviv, the two captains of the *INS Javelin* and *INS Storm* agreed that they had to start maneuvers. They moved slowly in the direction of the mouth of the canal positioning themselves so that all ships would have to sail between them after they had reached the high sea. Radio communication with the Dolphin Class submarine *INS Dragon* ensured that she remained submerged but in the immediate vicinity as well, but more toward the middle of the channel.

When Captain Barack Decker saw all the activity in the harbor as he exited the canal area, he gave his crew instructions to raise the two guns in as unobtrusive a fashion as possible. The guns, one at the bow and the other at the stern, rotated around a horizontal axis which allowed them to be, upside down, below deck when non-operational and fully exposed above the deck when some firing capability would be needed. The gun turret, however, was small enough that it did not obviously protrude above the ship's railing. Barack still had his men ensure that they would have enough ammunition if they needed to fire.

Somehow, nobody seemed to be expecting *Sailing Joy*, a red-hulled boat flying a Gibraltar pavilion. When he saw that the way seemed clear, Barrack instructed his men to lower the barrel of the gun so that its tip was hidden by the railing. He also had them throw a dark green tarp over both gun assemblies so that his boat looked as innocuous as she could. He breathed a further sigh of relief when he saw the two missile boats on the horizon. He would be protected, though he would have to be careful: long-distance missile shots can miss their targets. He sailed through the flotilla and took a north easterly heading, at slow speed, thinking:

Don't want to be too far if Moshe were to need us.

About ten minutes later, the *Sea Crescent* emerged from the canal as well. A good number of boats in the flotilla sounded their horns, leaving no one in doubt as to where their allegiances were. The captains of the two Israeli missile ships maneuvered their boats to be as close as they could be to the place where the *Sailing Princess* and Captain Moshe Aaron might need their help while still in international waters. Captain Ayel, from the *INS Storm*, send a cryptic message to the Egyptian port authorities:

"Please ensure order in the harbor."

He was only mildly surprised when the answer he received seemed to have been written by a public relation firm: "we always do."

Less than five minutes later, the *Sailing Princess* with her white hull and Gibraltar flag started to make its way out of the Canal and into the harbor. Ominously, the flotilla formed a tighter cloud and moved directly in the direction of where the *Sailing Princess* would expect to sail. Moshe sounded his horn, but to no avail. He decided not to slow down. He had instructed his crew, just as Barack had done, to get the two guns into position so that they could fire if needed. With the flotilla becoming tighter and tighter, Moshe decided to fire a blank round into the air. The blanks were going to go above all the small boats, but the noise and the smoke should deter a number of them. Moshe smiled when he saw that the way offered to him was definitely a bit wider, but the respite was short-lived. Two boats were approaching and appeared quite threatening. He called for help from the Port Authority, which broadcast on its priority wavelength a message asking for free passage for the *Sailing Princess*. It also said that it was sending a couple of patrol boats to the area. Moshe thought:

Why did they not think of that earlier? Come to think of it, they probably did, but were hoping they would not have to take sides.

The *INS Dragon* fired an unarmed torpedo to the port side of the *Sailing Princess*, ostensibly to help create some space where Moshe could navigate. Moshe saw the *Sea Crescent* in the distance not too far away from his ship. He revved up his engines. He was accelerating both to intimidate the small boats around him and to get closer to the *Sea Crescent*. That move initially backfired. A few of the small boats thought the *Sea Crescent* was threatened and started firing small arms at the *Sailing Princess*. Moshe instructed his crew:

"Do not retaliate. Protect yourself as you were taught. The glass on the bridge is bullet proof and the gun assemblies should also protect you. Benjamin, aim the aft gun straight at our wake."

The sailor manning the gun at the stern did as instructed. He heard Moshe say:

"Fire a blank above their heads."

The noise and the smoke again got the flotilla to disperse somewhat. Moshe was now approaching the limit of Egypt's territorial waters when he saw a small boat that was coming his way at quite a rate of speed. He barked:

"Fire at that boat. Stop it. Could well be a suicide boat."

The captain of the submarine who had heard Moshe's command on the radio via sonar transmission decided to go into action. He fired a torpedo at the small fishing boat. It exploded with a much louder bang and much more power than one would expect from a simple boat. Moshe laconically concluded:

"She was full of explosives."

This opened an avenue for him to raise his speed even further without triggering his hydrofoil mode. He came within less than a mile of the *Sea Crescent* and slowed down to match her speed. Passing as he did in between the bows of the two Israeli missile boats, Moshe knew that he was now safe. He called Barack on the radio:

"Where are you, my friend?"

"A mile to the east of the *Sea Crescent*. Thanks for the fireworks."

■ ■ ■ ■ ■

The *Sea Crescent* continued to sail in a northeasterly direction. Moshe called Simon:

"Any idea what she's doing? Didn't you say that the submarine drones which you captured where closer to the Sinai than to the heart of Israel?"

"I did, Moshe. I did. How far out of Tyre are you?"

"About 150 nautical miles, Simon."

"Keep following her from a distance. Watch the Eitan screen to make sure she does not drop her cargo into another boat. Tell Barack to move east and let the *Sea Crescent* overtake his boat. I need both of you following it and seeing what happens on both sides."

"No problem."

"Give me a shout when you get within 50 nautical miles of Tyre. We do not want this equipment to go ashore."

Simon's main concern was clearly about the weapons which the

Sea Crescent carried. He felt he could control their fate for as long as they remained in the Sea Crescent or were deposited in the sea. Yet, once they were brought onshore, it would become next to impossible to track them, with potentially very serious consequences for Israel.

■ ■ ■ ■ ■

"Ariel? Simon here."

"Yes, sir, what's up?"

"Well, I don't know for sure, but we may have a situation developing."

"Tell me."

Simon summarized what he knew. He added that his worry was that the *Sea Crescent* which was carrying two submarine drones, two transmitters and four Iranian missiles, might not drop them into the sea as was the normal procedure.

"I worry that they know they have been identified and in some way unmasked. What if they took the equipment ashore and there transshipped it to smaller boats which could then place them where they are intended to be?"

"That would be very serious. They could also decide to reserve one assembly and drop it in a body of water onshore, somewhere in the region. . . ."

Ariel added:

"Let me call an emergency meeting of the War Cabinet. How much time do we have?"

"I'd say around 10 hours or less. We will need to make a decision when they are 50 nautical miles from Tire. 8-10 hours if they sail between 10 and 15 nots."

"Thanks my friend. Oh. By the way. Closer to any decision?'

"I will need to talk to you soon. I assume you agree this project takes precedent."

"Sure do. Told you so."

"You did."

■ ■ ■ ■ ■

Ariel was back to Simon well within the prescribed time frame. The message was serious, but implacable:

"The Palestinian boat must not reach Tyre."

"Understood."

"What about the cargo?"

"Have our team carefully note where it sinks. We'll send a deep-sea rescue mission to retrieve what can be retrieved."

"I assume that means that we should aim for some deep-sea area. We don't want the enemy to be able to retrieve anything using divers."

"Agreed, but isn't it where they are now?"

"Indeed."

■ ■ ■ ■ ■

Simon and Mark were quickly in touch with the Defense Ministry to coordinate their actions. They agreed that the Dolphin-Class *INS Dragon* should carry out the first part of the mission. Simon indeed argued:

"The fire power of either of our boats is insufficient to sink the *Sea Crescent*."

Simon and Aaron Spielberg, the Defense Minister, called Yael Orbach, the Head of the Navy, and put in place the plan. Yael noted:

"*INS Dragon* is close enough to carry out the hit. She's shadowing you all. Can you have one of your ships send her the message via sonar. It's easier that way for as long as she is submerged."

"Mark will relay the message to Captain Decker."

"Thanks, my friend."

Simon told Yael that he was going to ask both Barack and Moshe to keep a close eye on the *Sea Crescent*. He added:

"We have the Eitan images."

They had not finished that part of the conversation before a message came from the *Sailing Joy*. It was echoed a few seconds later by the officer in charge of monitoring the Eitan picture:

"Two small crafts approaching the *Sea Crescent*."

Simon ordered:

"Monitor very carefully. Moshe and Barack get closer to the *Sea Crescent* if you need to. Any sign that they're downloading anything from the *Sea Crescent*, advise *INS Dragon* by Sonar.

Within less than fifteen minutes, the Israeli forces were organized. The two spy ships were on either side of the *Sea Crescent*, less than a mile away and closing in at slow speed. The Eitan was positioned so that its "big eight" holding pattern would give it about as good and comprehensive a shot at the *Sea Crescent* as possible. Finally, the *INS Dragon* had taken a submerged position about a mile ahead of the *Sea Crescent*. That would give it as clear a shot at either her or the two small crafts that were approaching. At that point, they were still northeast of the *INS Dragon*, but they would have to pass over it in order to come anywhere close to the *Sea Crescent*.

Barak called on the radio, using a channel that Moshe, Mark and Simon were using as well:

"One of the two small crafts is within less than a hundred yards of the *Sea Crescent*!"

Simon replied:

"They have to be planning to get alongside it. Either they're delivering something, possibly heavier arms, or they are taking delivery of something else. My guess is the latter. They don't need to deliver arms; they can directly attack our spy ships if that's what concerns them."

Moshe could only agree. The Eitan sped up to be in as good a filming position when the small craft was expected to dock, temporarily, with the *Sea Crescent*. As expected, the small craft moored to the larger ship and the Eitan camera could see an individual climb a ladder to the aft deck of the *Sea Crescent*. He met up with some counterparty on the *Sea Crescent* and they disappeared inside the main bridge area. Minutes later, the individual came back and was followed by a few members of the crew of the *Sea Crescent*. The camera showed clearly that some large piece of equipment was being raised from below deck; the crane rotated in a counterclockwise manner and the piece of equipment was lowered into the small craft. Simon called out:

"This is what we worried about guys. They're taking delivery of the stuff which the *Sea Crescent* picked up near Socotra Island. Everyone keep a tally of their various operations."

The crane, in all, made four overall transshipments. The group assumed that it meant that the Palestinians had moved half of their cargo onto the smaller craft. One for each missile, one for the submarine drone and the last for the transmitter. They also expected that the other half would in turn be moved to the other smaller Palestinian gun boat. Simon ordered:

"Let's not shoot them down immediately. Let's wait for the other transshipment to have taken place. Barack, please relay to *INS Dragon* by Sonar."

"Yes, sir."

The first smaller craft was heading toward Tyre as the second sister boat came to moor alongside the Sea Crescent.

Simon exclaimed:

"Wait a minute. They are not following the same routine. They are in fact bringing in some heavier armament. The stuff they're lifting onboard the *Sea Crescent* looks like a bigger marine gun."

He paused for a few seconds. He added:

"Hey. This is a small rocket launcher. Barack, call *INS Dragon* and have them torpedo the first small craft. Bet you they have both submarine drones, with their four missiles and the two transmitters. Should have picked that up when what we assumed to be the transmitter was too big to contain only one of them."

The *INS Dragon*, which was almost right behind the first, small Palestinian craft, received the message. It launched a torpedo which hit the target right between the two propellers. The boat exploded. A few sailors were seen jumping into the water. Simon sadly said:

"I hope they'll be picked up by the other Palestinian boats."

He added:

"*Sailing Princess* and *Sailing Joy*, move away from the scene. Return to Haifa."

Mark asked:

"Do you think we have done all we had to do?"

"Why do you ask?"

"Well, I just had a very cynical thought . . ."

"What is it?"

"Well, what if the *Sea Crescent* only unloaded one of the two pieces of cargo?"

"What do you mean?"

"What if they still have the other submarine drone, two more missiles and a transmitter onboard?"

"Why would they do that?"

Simon paused and did not give Mark a chance to continue his thoughts. Simon added:

"I get it. Great idea. Quite cunning. They assumed that we would anticipate their game, and that we would let the *Sea Crescent* go to Tyre unharmed. Calling Barack Decker. . . ."

"Sir?"

"Have *INS Dragon* sink the *Sea Crescent* as well.

CHAPTER.22

"Simon? Jack here . . ."

"Hey, what's new, man?"

"Just talked to Clay. He reported on his first conversation with Frank Lord and his wife. Bottom line: they did some leaking but are seeking to come clean. Oh and, by the way, how are things going offshore Israel?"

"Probably over in terms of the risk of the current situation. We've sunk both the Sea Crescent and a small boat onto which they had downloaded some equipment. Now the question is what step will they take going forward."

"They?"

"Yep. Could be driven by Hezbollah, Iran or even China. Only time will tell."

■ ■ ■ ■ ■

Frank had indeed confessed that, after he had the famous brunch with Mary when she told him the truth, her plan had originally been to stop everything then. Frank had told her that it would require her to be placed in a witness protection program which might break their relationship. She had asked why, and he had replied that he could not abandon the work he was doing, and it was unlikely she could be protected in Boston. They had agreed that they would keep their current roles, passing information but making sure it was generally innocuous.

■ ■ ■ ■ ■

Simon replied:

"Well done. Is there a way that the next meeting with them might include Countess Renate, without camera and with a voice transformer, and me, in addition to Clay and you?"

"I'll ask, but . . . tell me, why Countess Renate?"

"Well, she may know a lot more from Shi Tsu. I would not mind having her there, and would tell her that it would be OK for her to have a parallel line including Shi Tsu, though he would have to remain totally silent."

"Silent? Parallel line?"

"Yes, I mean he could be talking to Countess Renate, but his voice could not be heard on our line. This way, he might come up with a question that Countess Renate could relay without ever disclosing where it came from."

"Simon, you always have a way of surprising me. You're even more devious than I."

"I'll take that as a compliment."

"By the way, Simon, you're making a crucial assumption."

"What?"

"In fact, it's two assumptions. First, the Lords are the sole leakers and therefore second Shi Tsu is in the clear."

"See that."

"What if there is someone else? What if that someone else is Shi Tsu?"

"Damn it. Let me mention this to Countess Renate. I think I know how she will react, but this has to be her call."

■ ■ ■ ■ ■

Somewhat to Clay's surprise, Frank had no problem with the proposed setup, except with respect to Countess Renate who had been introduced as an agent in Europe. Clay placed Frank on hold and called Jack. Jack immediately offered a simple solution:

"Tell him that we can remove the need for that other agent. We'll have Countess Renate and Shi Tsu on a parallel line with Mark, who will be seating right next to Simon. Countess Renate will be able to hear what is said on our line but will not be able to talk. Her questions will be relayed by Simon or Mark.

■ ■ ■ ■ ■

Mary started explaining her plan to Frank. She conceded that the risk of the Chinese government coming after her or after them was undeniable. She asked Frank:

"Promise me you will not get mad. That you'll let me explain."

"I can always try. But you know me."

She started with the idea that they could produce insignificant intelligence, adding:

"You know your stuff well-enough that you must be able to find things to say which are impressive but not immediately useful."

"I sure can. But don't you think that they'll have people reading whatever we give them. They'll soon figure out whether it is useful or not, won't they?"

Mary conceded that there was a risk, but she added:

"Yet, honey, I'm sure that the stuff on which you all are working now is so advanced that there must be the little detail here or there without which the information would not be readily usable."

"And you think they would not find out? They have battalions of

PhDs there, a few of whom were trained here at MIT. They would find out the error in a matter of weeks if not days."

This was happening before the three professors had founded BACL. They were still working on concepts and the theoretical side. The Chinese had gotten wind of their invention through a research paper which they had probably a bit carelessly published before they figured out the implications of their work. Mary was therefore correct to assume that details of the theory could be carefully edited and leaked without either endangering their progress or disclosing enough to the Chinese. Yet, Frank was also correct figuring out that a scheme of misinformation would not be a lasting solution. Mary came out with the clincher:

"Remember: as soon as we are married, they have no leverage on you. We will still need to be careful and tell them some of what's happening. But you will be out of the woods."

"You seem to be forgetting what we discussed earlier: they could decide to punish you or me or both of us for not giving them enough."

Mary looked pensive for a short while. She retorted that the whole point was to play for time, adding:

"If things get too bad, we can always go to the U.S. government and ask for federal protection."

"That won't be enough."

"Why?"

"You seem to be forgetting that we would have given intelligence to an enemy; it's called spying and it is a federal crime."

"Can't we ask for immunity? In fact, I have a better idea."

"What next?"

"Well, we could work with the U.S. authorities to pass on disinformation to the Chinese."

"OK, now you have us becoming double agents? You know, Mary, double agents usually end up dead, with both sides chasing after them."

"Do we have a choice? OK, Do I have a choice? I love you. I don't want to lose you. But if you don't play along to some extent, they'll either kill me or ship me back to China."

She started to cry. Frank was convinced that her tears were not fake. He cuddled her until she had calmed down. He then made the fateful decision to help her, in effect to spy on his own team and his own discovery.

■ ■ ■ ■ ■

Clay and Jack were sitting in a room at the FBI headquarters on Pennsylvania avenue in Washington, D.C. The massive, modern J. Edgar Hoover building covers a full city block, between 9th and 10th streets. The conference room was adequately furnished but offered no unnecessary luxury. Clay had taken great care to make sure that neither Frank nor Mary would be intimidated. He wanted the meeting to be friendly, and even had offered to pay for their roundtrip air-shuttle fare from Boston.

After some initial banter, Clay introduced Simon and Mark on the video-conference phone, explaining to the Lords that they were the people in charge of the investigation into a problematic discovery:

"As I may have mentioned earlier, your company's invention found its way to the Mediterranean sea floor off the coast of Israel. It had Chinese markings and carried two Iranian missiles."

Frank immediately replied:

"This is news to me, but I can categorically tell you that nothing that works could have been constructed with the intelligence we passed on to the Chinese."

Simon interrupted:

"Are you sure? If true, this is a very interesting piece of information. I suspect Frank, may I call you Frank?"

"Please do."

Simon continued:

"I'm Simon. I suspect that there is a lot more to this story. Could you, Clay, summarize what Frank and his wife told you and then invite Frank to build things up from there?"

"Good idea, Simon."

Clay provided a few initial insights and then asked Mary and Frank to take things over from there. Frank and Mary were quite forthcoming in their recitation, having earlier made the decision that the immunity and federal protection which had been granted to them warranted them telling all the truth and nothing but the truth. Mary started to recapitulate her past in a somewhat contrite voice, adding that she would need some help for her immigration dossier to be corrected, adding:

"I'm sure you'll appreciate that I did not have much to say on what was written there, other than accepting to sign where asked."

Jack immediately said:

"No worries. Your immunity extends to false declaration. And we promised to get you safely protected in the U.S. and that includes having a U.S. citizenship."

She went on with the early stages of the mission. She looked downright embarrassed when she described the way in which Frank had been presented as her target. Frank simply smiled at her and encouraged her to keep going. A number of questions were relayed by Mark to the Lords as to the exact nature of what they disclosed. Frank looked a bit surprised that Mark would know as much as he seemed to know on the physics of the transmitter. Mark noticed and apologized:

"I prepared for this with a great deal of care and quite a bit of help from physics specialists in Israel. I must confess that I am not sure I understand more than a fraction of what you are telling."

"Now, it makes more sense. In short, let me assure you that what we disclosed was enough to whet their appetite, but surely not enough to construct a working transmitter."

"How do you explain that they were able to construct one such object, even though it is admittedly a prior generation from the most current development."

"Frankly, Mark. I am stumped. I cannot."

Mary interrupted:

"If you will allow me, I would like to share with you a hypothesis. I'm sure there are others, and you would be perfectly right to believe I'm praying to my own saint. What if there was another leak?"

"Another leak?"

"Yes, Simon. The thing that got the two of us to come forward and seek your help is the last in a series of troubling phone calls I received."

"Ah! Why?"

Mary replied:

"Well, these phone calls were relaying increasingly precise threats against Frank and me. They were telling us that they knew . . ."

Mark interrupted:

"Who is "they," Mary?"

"Oh. Sorry. "They" refers to our Chinese controller. He had information which I did not have and when I shared with Frank what he was telling me, Frank could not figure out where he could have found out about it."

Simon interjected:

"I am not telling you that I buy this story in full, but I'll concede that it is totally plausible. Now, there are not that many people who could have provided the information. Are there?"

Frank chose to reply:

"Frankly, my first reaction was to believe it came from our company. Before pointing to my current partners, however unpleasant I find it, I could think of Adrian Lee, our prior research assistant. Yet, I don't see how he could know some of what he knows. Again, the only explanation there might be is that he had managed to trick Ho

Lim, our current research partner, to tell him things that he should not have. Yet, I can't believe that Ho Lim would do that."

Mark relayed a hypothetical question:

"What if the questions were asked in a way such that Ho Lim could have replied without appreciating the full impact of his insights?"

"I thought about that. I still don't believe it. Ho Lim knows much more than Adrian ever knew. He's at least as smart, at least in my appreciation. I can't believe he could be tricked, unless it was done after heavy drinks, or even the ingestion of some drug."

Simon joked:

"This is turning into a heck of a spy story."

Frank could not help himself:

"Is it not the way it started?"

Frank could see Simon's smile on the video phone. Simon added:

"Touché. But if not Ho Lim, who?"

The conversation went on for quite a while longer, delving into further details, which Mark relayed. Virtually no one else but Frank, and Shi Tsu who was listening in and asking the questions, could understand the full meaning of either questions or answers. At one point, Mark surprised everyone with his next question:

"Would Frank be prepared to hold another meeting, with the same people, plus his partners?"

Frank looked straight at the camera and replied:

"Absolutely. Do not get me wrong, gentlemen, I know that what Mary and I did was simply wrong. Believe me when I say that love for my wife made me agree to follow along. Yet, I never intended to help the Chinese or anyone else. My loyalty is to our country. Mary got trapped before I did, and I am sure that she would be prepared to share with you how and why it came to that. I believe that our leaks were stupid, but innocuous. I am stunned that the Chinese took them as far as they did."

He paused and then said, with his voice cracking from emotion:

"How can you all protect us and still have me involved in our work? At BACL? I do not want to abandon it and honestly believe I can still contribute."

Simon interrupted:

"Frank, this is a serious issue. I can assure you that what you are asking is possible. Your partners will have to know how to get to you, but they may not even know precisely where you are. Simply, please, trust us: you will not have to give up your job and the two of you will be safe."

"When does that protection start?"

"Now. We're going to make it as easy and unobtrusive as can be."

Mark interrupted:

"Frank and Mary, I can vouch for this. I just emerged from a year of protection which my wife and I spent away from our official duties. Yet, we kept contributing as we could and I am the living proof that, so far, nobody has gotten to us, or our child."

Frank seemed to be breathing a sigh of relief, but Mary remained quite tense. She asked:

"How can you be sure that no one knows where we are or how to get to us? What if the other leak is one of Frank's partners? You seem to have had help from our friend Shi Tsu. In normal circumstances, it would never occur to me to suspect him. Much too nice a man. But, with my life and Frank's on the line, what if?"

Mark could see her on the verge of tears and shaking with fear. He replied:

"Mary, nobody outside of *Mossad* will ever know where you are. Nobody. Trust me."

■ ■ ■ ■ ■

Once the meeting ended, Simon, Mark, Jack and Clay got back together on the video conference phone, with Countess Renate and Shi Tsu officially on the call as well. Simon asked:

"What do you all think of that?"

Shi Tsu was the first to offer his views:

"Well, Simon. Somehow, I am relieved. There is no doubt in my mind that what Frank says he provided, if that's all he indeed provided, is not enough to replicate our work. That leaves me with two main worries. The first, which may surprise you all, is whether Mary is as innocent as she appears to be. After all, she now has her PhD, and she could easily get her hands on some more information and pass it on. I cannot discount that at this point. The other is who else could it be. I know it's not me, but I obviously cannot prove it: it's nearly impossible to prove a negative."

He smiled and had a short laugh and went on:

"I believe Ho Lim, because I do not see why he would do what he actually did, if he was the leaker. At the same time, a cynic could construct logic that would point to him. As far as Michael is concerned, I cannot believe he is involved. We know that his wife was at some point involved in tracking Chinese spymasters; she would have to have the skills to find out if her own husband was a spy. Plus, why would they do it? She is wealthy, we know it as she shows a lot of it. So, they don't need the money. I've never heard Michael express political opinions which would appear to favor China. So, I am totally stuck."

Simon asked:

"Anybody else has something to add?"

Countess Renate added that she understood Shi Tsu's logic and felt dumbfounded. She arrived at a different conclusion, however, when she argued:

"The one thing we still do not know is whether Ho Lim or Michael have any skeletons in their closets. Mary's story, as abridged as it was when she discussed it, shows that people get recruited because they have a problem they're trying to hide or run away from. I think we need to do more work on the partners and on Mary, as I share Shi

Tsu's lack of conviction that she is totally in the clear."

Simon was very carefully listening and elected not to share his thoughts. Yet, one thing kept coming back in his head: *Mary fears Shi Tsu and Shi Tsu fears Mary. I agree that Mary is not totally in the clear, but I must have a chat with Countess Renate. To me, Shi Tsu is not in the clear either.*

CHAPTER.23

"Ariel? May I come to see you?"

"Sure, Simon. You mean . . . Now?"

"Yes, if you have the time."

"Come right ahead."

With the *Sea Crescent* crisis over, unless one considers the medium to long-term implications which were obviously far from over, Simon had agreed with his wife, Jennifer, that it was time to have a final chat with Ariel.

Simon walked into Ariel's office. Ariel, as always, was all smiles and offered a cup of coffee which Simon was happy to accept. Ariel only asked for a glass of water. Simon went straight to the point:

"Ariel, I have one final question and then I think I can give you my reply to your immensely generous offer"

"Between us, we can dispense with superlatives, Simon. It is an honor for you indeed, but you must be absolutely convinced—and I am sure you know that—that I would not have decided to put your name forward if I was not totally sure that you are the guy for the job. Anyway, that said, fire away"

"Well, I want to go back to an earlier question. I asked whether

I could choose what to delegate and you seemed to tell me that I could."

Ariel interrupted:

"I did not seem to tell you, my friend. I did tell you. As the boss, you have the freedom to structure your world the way you see fit. By the way, do not see this as imperial powers. Every head of anything must know both what the job requires and in which way he or she is able to discharge these duties. I seem to recall that you felt that you would not be the strongest candidate for certain aspects of my job. Believe me, I had the same feeling when I took that job."

"Really?"

"Sure. Only idiots think they can do everything."

Simon smiled. There was the Ariel he had known and appreciated for so many years: straightforward and direct, but also humble and sensitive. Ariel continued:

"Smart people, really smart people, know both their strengths and their weaknesses. They play to their strengths and, to the extent they can, they learn to alleviate their weaknesses."

"That's exactly what I had understood, Ariel. Thanks. Well, I am very honored by your offer, and I would like to accept it."

Ariel's face lit up like a Christmas tree. His protégé and friend would have the opportunity to lead the Agency which he had carefully directed himself for so many years.

"Simon, I cannot tell you how happy I am. First of all, you absolutely deserve the promotion. But second, I have learned to trust your instincts and your self-awareness. I remain sure that you will know how to surround yourself with people who will help you. And, and, and you will help them achieve their own potential."

Simon was visibly moved. He hesitated, but still had to ask:

"Would you be available from time to time?"

"Simon, I have no intention of disappearing from the face of the earth. I'll always be available to you but be careful."

Ariel instinctively moved a bit forward in his chair:

"I should not be your security blanket."

Simon smiled. Ariel went on:

"Organization behavior professors would likely describe your promotion as a stretch assignment. I do not disagree. At some level, I would like to be able to stay on for another two or three years, to groom you more fully. But Golda's health makes me speed up my plans. Wouldn't it be nice if everything always happened at the right time and on the right schedule?"

Simon looked quite serious again:

"But you do think I CAN do the job now."

"I do. I do, my friend. Sure, I do. But you're gonna have a steep learning curve. Oh, by the way, what organizational change were you considering when you came into my office?"

"Well, I think I would need a solid administrator next to me."

"So, you do not worry about the political dimension? I thought you would, in truth."

Simon conceded that it was something which initially was concerning him. Yet, he argued that conversations with Jennifer had convinced him that there are several ways of dealing with politics. His way would be to be totally open and honest, adding:

"Just like I've been with you."

He stopped for a second and added:

"Obviously, I know that there has to be a big difference between organization politics and Politics with a capital P."

Ariel smiled, a big fatherly-like smile. He simply said:

"That's exactly what I expected you would figure out. But you see, Simon, you needed to figure it out by yourself. Just thinking about the job has made you begin to grow into it. Well, I will need to talk to Jesse.

He paused and continued:

"Hmmm, I mean the Prime Minister, next week. He is gone this week. Some sort of announcement will come in the next couple of weeks."

"Many thanks, Ariel. I cannot tell you how much I feel indebted to you."

"You know, superb direct reports make their bosses look good. Never forget that."

Simon hesitated, but still added:

"How is you wife doing?"

"Thanks for asking, Simon. She seems to have recovered, but her blood pressure is still running a bit high. I am told that this is not too much to worry about, but why is it then that I still worry?"

■ ■ ■ ■ ■

Simon was back in his office when Mark called:

"Sorry to bother you, boss, but I'd like to brief you."

"On what, Mark?"

"The upshot of the *Sea Crescent*."

"Come whenever you are ready. I'm here."

"I'll be there in five minutes."

"Sounds great. Coffee, tea or water?"

"Water will be great. Thanks."

Mark was indeed in Simon's office less than five minutes later. With him was his boss, David Heller, who was being groomed by Simon eventually to take over from him, as and when it would be required.

Mark started with a simple statement:

"I've no idea what the Palestinians will do in terms of revenge or attempted reprisals, but their whole undersea threat operation is in shambles."

Seeing that Simon was not surprised, he went on:

"I think we have retrieved all the submarine drones and related stuff."

"That's great, how many in total?"

"Thanks, Simon. Well, we have seven assemblies, including the two that were on the small boat that unloaded them from the *Sea Crescent*, and the one we had removed earlier off the coast of Haifa."

"Wonderful. But how do we know we've got them all?"

Mark had expected the question. In many ways it was obvious. Yet, it was a very difficult one. The basic truth was that they did not know, he replied:

"I've heard you say it before: "You don't know what you don't know." But here's how I reassure myself. We are pretty sure that we picked up anything they deployed after we first lucked into seeing their drop off Haifa. We don't know if there were things earlier."

He was going to continue, when Simon interrupted:

"I see where you're going: if they had dropped others before, they would have tried to do something when we circulated the disinformation about something going wrong. . . . Right?"

"Absolutely. Now, to be fair, they have taught me lessons over the last several weeks."

"How so, Mark?"

"Well, they outfoxed us in a couple of instances, and when they did not succeed, we were helped in part by sheer luck."

Simon asked Mark what he meant. Mark simply replied that at the time the *Sea Crescent* was unloading the assemblies on the two fast boats, they only managed to sink the first small boat because they were lucky the *INS Dragon* had decided to locate itself in front rather than behind the action."

Simon smiled and replied looking at both Mark and David:

"There quite a bit of truth to that. But let's remember a key principle: the more we practice and think, the luckier we get. . . . Know who said that?"

"Nope!"

"Well, truth is nobody really does. It's been credited to golfers

Gary Player or Jerry Barber, but it seems that a number of variants were in use before these guys were ever born. So, who knows?"

"Great party trick, Simon!"

■ ■ ■ ■ ■

Retrieving the underwater drones, transmitters and missiles which were sunk when the *INS Dragon* torpedo hit the small Palestinian black craft proved to be quite a bit more complex and time consuming than originally expected. Yet, *Mossad* knew they had to retrieve them as quickly as possible. Initially, Mark was concerned that the Palestinians still controlled the transmitters. If it was so, they believed that Hezbollah could try to fire one or even all of the missiles. Yet, David poured some cold water over that assumption. He argued that the deployment sequence involved three and not two steps. They first dropped the submarine drone, then the transmitter and then a helicopter would come along to complete the instructions. Thus, in David's view at least, the risk was minimum that Hezbollah could fire the missiles. Simon brought everyone down to earth:

"David is totally correct."

He paused a few seconds to set his conclusion up and continued:

"But, he assumes that Hezbollah would follow the normal procedure. Yet, as we know, the *Sea Crescent*, at some point realized that the situation had changed. Hezbollah agreed to a different procedure than previously, transshipping everything to the fast boats. We do not know whether the connection between the transmitters and the drone could have been set while still on board the *Sea Crescent*. Clearly, if they only expected to finalize the set up once onshore, they will not have that opportunity. But I would still suggest that everything be done with a great deal of caution."

Mossad and the Defense Ministry sent the same team which originally had recovered the first submarine drone. A deep-sea rescue platform was tethered to a submarine, as both sailed underwater to the precise coordinates where the Palestinian boats were sunk. They expected to find the transmitters floating near the surface and drones with their missiles on the sea floor.

They rapidly were able to locate the drones and found them resting within three thousand feet of water very much close to the area they had expected. They loaded them into the submarine via the airlock and two technicians were immediately put to work to ensure that any communication with the transmitter would fail. This was not a very hard or dangerous operation: the communication between the transmitter and the drones required "translation" of the air wave by the transmitter into sonar signals. They thus simply needed to ensure that the drones and missiles could not receive sonar signals.

Though they found the drones relatively easily, finding the transmitters was quite different: that is where the difficulty turned out to be. The currents that the sea experiences are different at different depths. So, they could not assume that the drift they measured for the deep-sea equipment would be the same for the transmitters. Further, these transmitters were not going to be very deep, probably not more than a few feet. The submarine therefore needed to sail closer to the surface, which made it more readily identifiable by any spy ship in the vicinity. The submarine eventually located them both using her radar, trained to a depth of between three and ten feet. A couple of divers loaded the transmitters into the submarine, where their radio connections were immediately shut down. The submarine returned to the area where the deep-sea platform had been temporarily "parked" and tethered it to the submarine. The whole unit returned to Haifa where the missiles were permanently disconnected from their current control systems.

■ ■ ■ ■ ■

The volley of rockets launched from Southern Lebanon thankfully did not do any real damage. They were intercepted by the Iron Dome.

Yet, the Israeli government wanted to retaliate in a way that would demonstrate to Hezbollah that these fireworks were futile. Ariel called Simon to brief him.

"Simon, the War Cabinet is bent on retaliating for the rockets that flew into Haifa and its surroundings. Probably with a couple of airstrikes."

"Well, boss, I sure will not second guess anyone, but I wonder if there isn't a better and even more subtle way."

"You have my full attention, my friend."

Simon went on to argue that they could use one of the submarine drones with its Iranian missiles to retaliate. He added:

"Remember, when we first captured and replaced the first underwater drone, we had reprogrammed the targets of the two missiles."

"I do. Go on."

"Well, we could discreetly put that submarine drone back in the general vicinity of where we found it and instruct it to fire. We would hit the training camps we had selected, and Hezbollah would not understand. We could even use two such drones, which makes four missiles, and set them up so that one of them does not explode but effectively falls in the right area, with its Iranian markings."

"I like your original idea better. I think the variation you suggested next is too transparent. They must suspect that we have their missiles and submarine drones, or at least that we control them. I'm sure they've tried to activate them and that they did not respond. So, I think it's best to keep them guessing. Retaliate with two missiles but do nothing beyond."

Simon conceded that Ariel's judgment was definitely the best. They would achieve their goal and Hezbollah could not know for sure what happened. He agreed that they might conclude that the missiles that hit came from Israel. They might even guess that they might be the Iranian missiles. Yet, they would not have any proof and would therefore be kept guessing.

∎ ∎ ∎ ∎ ∎

Ariel called the Prime Minister:

"Jesse, I've got a couple of things to discuss with you. . . ."

"Could we meet tomorrow in Jerusalem?"

"Sure. I'll use a helicopter to get there and back. What time?"

"Is 11:00 convenient?"

"See you then."

∎ ∎ ∎ ∎ ∎

Ariel walked into Jesse's office, which was located in Jerusalem, in the Government center on the same hill as the *Knesset*, dominating a part of Jerusalem's skyline.

"Ariel? How are you doing, my friend?"

"Well, I'm doing fine, but I've got a couple of serious things to discuss."

They both walked to the sitting area which Jesse always used with his senior cabinet officers or guests. Ariel accepted the offer of a glass of cold water, though he added:

"No ice cube, please."

He sat down to Jesse's right. He started with the simplest issue. He discussed the idea which Simon had offered for retaliating against Hezbollah, giving him all the credit and without mentioning that he, himself, had made the decision on the more discreet approach. Jesse smiled and added:

"Quite a smart guy, this Simon Rabinovitch."

"I do agree."

Ariel paused a second to drink from his water glass. Then looking Jesse straight in the eye, he said:

"Jesse, my second issue is less simple. Yet, I hope you will agree with me."

"Go ahead, Ariel. I cannot remember when we last disagreed on something important."

Ariel nodded, shocking Jesse with his next sentence:

"Jesse, I have decided it is time for me to retire."

Jesse could not believe his ears. He straightened up in his chair, scratching his head. He asked Ariel to repeat, which he did without glee but with much determination. Jesse asked:

"But why? My friend, why?"

Ariel swore him to discretion and upon receiving Jesse's assurances, he told him the story of his wife's stroke and of the consequent desire he had formed to spend more time with her and their children and grandchildren. Jesse was doubly surprised, as Ariel had not told him of the problem when it occurred. Just as he had with Simon, Ariel explained that the speed of her recovery and its almost complete nature had him decide that there was no point making an issue of it. Jesse jokingly, but looking severe, said:

"Well, it might have prepared me for this discussion, my friend. Anyway, before we discuss anything else, is there something you or Golda need? Would you prefer an extended leave of absence to take care of her and then come back?"

"Jesse, this is very kind of you. Thank you. But you know that I am reaching minimum retirement age anyway. So why prolong the agony? On Golda's front, everything seems in order; so thank you for the offer, but no thank you."

Ariel could see that Jesse was about to ask another question. He guessed that it was about succession. He elected to broach the issue first rather than in answer to a question. So, he did not let Jesse ask and simply said:

"By the way, I have a strong proposal to make, with respect to my succession."

"How do you know that this was going to be my next question?"

Ariel joked that he always thought that Jesse was a great manager and that this had to be the next question a great manager would ask.

Jesse had a short laugh. Regaining a serious facial expression after Ariel had named Simon as his recommended successor, Jesse asked:

"I know he is a great guy, but is he ready?"

Ariel nodded. He gave himself a few seconds to convey the seriousness of the situation. He then argued that nobody is ever perfectly ready until they have been on the job and have proven able to adapt to the new responsibilities. He then said that Simon, in his view, had the skills and the character needed. He would need some coaching at the beginning, particularly with respect to activities that were external to the agency, adding:

"He knows us inside out. I have no problem thinking of him doing any of the things he needs to do within *Mossad* to get it to deliver. His one weakness, and, by the way it is only a weakness because he has not needed the skill so far, is in terms of relating with the outside."

"You mean the Cabinet?"

"Yes. And you."

"Or my successor. . . . Not a problem. I remember a few presentations he gave to the War Cabinet. He was impressive. Come to think of it, you know? The fact that he did not try to collect brownie points with politicians, ostensibly in due course to get the nod to succeed you; I see it as good; no, as excellent. I'm sure he would enjoy the promotion, but he did not feel he had to maneuver behind your back. He trusted you and the agency. I like these kinds of guys. By the way, are you sure it's not something you actually taught him?"

"To be fair, Jesse; you must know that he did not jump at the opportunity. He was gratified by the offer, but he had reservations. He finally resolved them, and that made me then absolutely convinced I had the right person."

"How is that?"

"He was asking the right questions. He had a lucid sense of his own limitations. He was trying to find a solution."

"Were you surprised?"

Ariel smiled but did not reply. Jesse went on to ask what Ariel's time frame was. Ariel replied that he was not in an absolute hurry, but that he did not want to linger on for too long:

"I don't like the lame duck bit."

"Well, let me put the wheels in motion. By the way, we'll need to promote him in the military to the rank of general. Any issue there?"

"Don't think so; he's already a colonel."

CHAPTER.24

SINGAPORE, TEL AVIV, ISRAEL, WASHINGTON DC, USA, AND THE AUSTRIAN ALPS

Rachel Acker was excited as she walked into Yeo Yap Min's office in Singapore at the headquarters of the Military Security Department at the MINDEF Building on Gombak Drive. Gombak Drive is the name of the road which veers off Upper Bukit Timah, a large Singaporean thoroughfare, to enter a restricted military zone within the Hillview District of the City-Republic. She went through several security checks, not counting the one-hour interview when she was asked multiple questions about herself and her job. Speaking to Yap Min as she met him at the door of the conference room where their meeting was going to be, she had said:

"I don't think anyone has asked me so many questions . . . Ever!"

"I'm not surprised. Would you believe that I had pre-cleared you? The questions they asked were really the absolute minimum. We are very careful here."

She had asked for the meeting to discuss both what she had found so far and to ask for some additional information. Yap Min had suggested they should meet at his office, as this would be the easiest way for him to find documents if he could not recall the precise answer she was asking. Yap Min also told Rachel on the phone that her situation was exceptionally special:

"You are being recommended by someone who has done us many favors in the past. He vouches for your honesty. I must warn you that any indication, now or in the future, that the trust we placed in you was misplaced would lead to serious consequences."

Rachel had replied:

"You can trust me on this assignment. I know the limits and when in doubt, I'll stop short of the red line."

Their conversation went around for a while with Yap Min forced to reply that he really had no knowledge. Rachel was digging around the past of both Michael Lennon and his wife, Liok Sew Lin. Yap Min was not able to give her all the information she wanted on Sew Lin, if only because he felt that several questions were too personal. He was only able to repeat the basic story, most of which she knew, that the Liok family, though now quite wealthy, had at some point in time run into financial difficulty when the real estate market in the Republic slumped and they found themselves having to carry too large a land bank purchased with loans. The government helped them by giving them development contracts for a public housing estate. He was able to confirm that Sew Lin had helped the Singapore government identify a few of the individuals who were trying to recruit local and foreign students at NUS as spies for China.

Rachel asked whether Sew Lin had identified many such Chinese agents. Yap Min surprised her with his response:

"Not that many, but she did point out eight people, over a five-year period, which is way more than we could tolerate. In fact, hold a minute. I think I still have a list of these people."

He was going through the many files which resided on his official server and exclaimed:

"I knew it. I knew I had it."

He paused and called his assistant:

"Pauline, I'm printing something on your printer. Can you please bring it to me when it's done? Pauline walked into the room, quickly deposited a single sheet of paper with what looked like eight lines all in English and exited with a smile. Turning to Rachel, Yap Min said:

"Before I give it to you, let me redact that one name. That individual was a private citizen. There was enough circumstantial evidence to ask him to leave Singapore and thus for him to make it on the list. Still, I don't want to assume him guilty. The other seven worked in one way or another at the Chinese Embassy and they were all declared persona non grata and asked to return to China."

He added:

"Naturally, this is confidential. Hock Chai told me that you were working on a very discreet assignment and asked me to cooperate. Yet, I do not want ever to hear that someone knew where the list came from."

"You can trust me. I will not even copy it. Once back in the U.S., I will deliver it to Joel Miller."

"Joel Miller?"

"Yes, my contact for the Israeli Embassy in Washington."

"I see. Thank you."

Rachel turned specifically to Michael Lennon. Yap Min was only able to confirm that he had graduated and worked at the National University of Singapore, adding:

"Did not look like deserving much work on our part. He was liked by his students, though he quickly went back to Australia. I'm not sure why, because I would argue that our department is stronger than that of the University of Notre Dame in Australia. But maybe, it was a question of returning home. Maybe, he was simply homesick."

He paused and recalled:

"Wait a minute; I do remember something. His wife said that she had picked up on Hang Le Zhao, the last guy on the list I gave you. She had picked up on him because he was being too friendly with

Michael, or something like that. She eventually flagged him to us. In fact, we did not expel him, Hang, until he tried to recruit someone else. I'm not sure that means anything, but it may be worth looking into."

Rachel stood up and profusely thanked Yeo Yap Min. As she was leaving his office, her instinct was telling her that she might have stumbled on something significant. At the time, she was focused on the list, thinking:

Would be nice if we could find one of these people in the U.S.

■ ■ ■ ■ ■

Upon returning to Washington, Rachel immediately called Joel Miller to report on her findings. At the top of her agenda was the fact that she had a list of seven Chinese agents that had been identified more than ten years ago and then expelled from Singapore. She added that the large majority of them had been discovered by Liok Sew Lin, Michael Lennon's wife. Joel thanked Rachel profusely and told her that he would be back to her quite shortly.

■ ■ ■ ■ ■

Joel's call to Mark led Mark to conference Simon in. Simon added that he wanted Jack and Countess Renate on the call as well. They reviewed the findings and were all very excited. Countess Renate noted:

"Wouldn't it be great if we could find traces of one or more of these people today?"

Simon asked:

"Jack, do you have access to files in which one or several of the names would show up?"

"Well, Simon. It all depends upon what these people are or were doing. We could find them in immigration records if they came as visitors without a formal visa, but that is a very tedious effort. I don't need to tell you how many passports are scanned at the borders of the U.S. each and every day."

"Plus I assume that anyone could have changed their names, even if it is a minor orthographic alteration."

"Absolutely, Mark. Particularly easy with names originally spelled in something other than our alphabet. But let me offer a hope. Joel reported that the people on the list had been in Singapore in some sort of official diplomatic capacity. I am sure it would be a lot faster to check whether any of them asked for a diplomatic visa."

"Sounds great Jack. Can I leave this in your hands?"

"Sure Simon."

Simon replied:

"Thanks. Countess Renate, do you have contacts who could also check on these various names?"

"Yes and no. We have people who would be able to check in various places. But I have no universal answer. I might be able to identify someone for instance say in France and not be able to do the same in Greece."

"Can you still look into that?"

"Sure, no problem. What are you going to do, Simon?"

"Well, we're going to look through all our files, but I have to say that I have little or no hope with respect to Israel. However, certain of our diplomatic missions may have a record of one or the other name."

Simon paused for a few seconds and exclaimed:

"I think we should pay a visit to Mrs. Lennon."

Joel was surprised by Simon's suggestion. He had to ask:

"Why, do you suspect her?"

"You know, Joel, as we always say: 'You never know what you don't know.' Yet, I would be stunned if she was a suspect. After all, she's the one who was identifying these Chinese agents. It would take a highly distorted mind to dream up a scenario where she would uncover Chinese agents in Singapore to accrue some extra credibility which would allow her to be a deep-undercover Chinese spy."

Countess Renate interrupted:

"Well, Simon, your mind is indeed distorted. Yet, I'll tell you that I would not exclude that possibility. Remember, until we discover who these seven people were, your hypothesis could very well be right. What if each of these individuals was precisely sent for the purpose of being caught? Diplomatic rules argue that, unless they did something really reprehensible, they would be expulsed, but not prosecuted or punished in Singapore."

Jack opined:

"Excellent point, Countess Renate. You know, Simon, I'm very tempted by the story so far. It seems quite complex, but the general *modus operandi* is perfectly in keeping with what I would expect of a spy agency."

"OK, Jack, but, if that's true, what do you make of this and how does it fit?"

Jack outlined his own scenario:

"Well, we know that Michael taught in Singapore and then moved back to Australia. Let us assume that he is innocent. His return to Australia could be explained by the desire to build a career in a country where he would not be an expatriate. By the way, we know he and Sew Lin have a son. Could we figure out when he was born? He might simply have wanted for his son to be educated in Australia."

Countess Renate Interrupted:

"I can have Shi Tsu check on that. He probably already knows."

Jack continued with his story:

"So, here we have Michael first teaching in a secondary campus of Notre Dame University and doing an excellent job. He's invited to come to the main campus as a full professor."

Countess Renate had to ask, just to be sure she was following:

"You're still guessing, Jack; correct?"

"Absolutely. Just guessing. In Fremantle, he makes a great

contribution. He finds out about some of the work of Professors Lord and Xi and contacts them in one way or another."

"Why?"

"Well, Countess, to tell them that he is very interested in their research and has even come up with a couple of novel ideas."

Simon interrupted:

"Brilliant, Jack. Brilliant. Let me see if we're one the same wavelength. We're still assuming that Sew Lin, Michael's wife, has been deep undercover."

"May or may not, Simon. For all I know she might have shared a few tidbits with her masters and not have been caught."

"Totally plausible, Jack. But anyway, dormant or active, she realizes that the move to the U.S. in general and MIT in particular could be a wonderful opportunity for her and her country, by which I mean China rather than Singapore. For all I know, she might have been the one that suggested to Michael that he should contact the two professors at MIT."

"Excellent point, Simon. So, to finish the story, she is now in the U.S. and smack in the middle of a major technical breakthrough. She finds ways of being plugged into her husband's work and the rest is history."

Countess Renate interrupted:

"Wonderful story, gentlemen. There's just one flaw from my point of view: why would she spy in the first place? Her family is wealthy. She does not need the money."

Simon nodded and replied:

"Quite true, Countess. But money may not be the sole motivation. Ideology could be one, though, frankly I doubt it too given her background."

"That's the point, Simon."

"What, Countess?"

"Do we have any indication anywhere that she would have a

reason to prefer China over Singapore?"

Simon had to reply:

"In truth, no. The one thing we should probably look for is a form of entrapment."

Jack chimed in:

"Entrapment?"

"Yes, Jack. By this, I mean blackmail. We've got to find out if there is anything that happened in her past that someone knows, and that she would rather not see revealed."

They all agreed that their next steps ought to be to dig a bit deeper into Michael and Sew Lin, but Simon emphasized:

"I think we need to have one-on-one conversations with both of them, separately."

"Who should do that?"

"Great question, Jack. Countess, any suggestion?"

"I think I should first talk to Shi Tsu with respect to Michael. Then, Mark probably ought to pick up from there. Jack, do you agree that it has to remain unofficial at this point?"

"Absolutely, Countess. We have next to nothing. But may I suggest that we wait until we have had our first pass around the list which Rachel brought? I'm obviously not counting on it, but we could get lucky. We won't get too many bites at the cherry."

"Jack, by this I suspect you mean a non-confrontational conversation with Michael."

"Correct. Simon."

"Now with respect to Sew Lin, even if we wait a short while, who should have the conversation?"

"Well, Mark, my instinct tells me that Rachel should be the one. She should do a great job. Plus, she's a woman and that might make the relationship easier to establish."

"Agree with that, Jack. Although, back to your point, let's give ourselves a short week to see what the list tells us, if anything."

CHAPTER.25

Sew Lin Lennon had agreed to meet Rachel Acker when she asked for some of her time. In fact, she had invited her to come have tea at the house which they owned in Cambridge, MA, on Craigie Street in West Cambridge, reputedly the ritziest area in Cambridge. Though she had never heard Shi Tsu's wife describe the way the Lennons lived, Rachel had a firsthand opportunity to witness overseas Chinese opulence. The house was quite large with a very large garden. From the street, it simply looked nice, though a couple of sitting lion stone sculptures on either side of the driveway suggested that it was not quite like its neighbors. Inside, Asian furniture dominated, with vibrant colors. Little in the decoration suggested any form of understatement.

Yet, Sew Lin herself was charming as she opened the front door and took Rachel to the living room with two large sofas on either side of a low coffee table. To its left, there was a beautiful fireplace, with a mantelpiece that seemed carved from precious hardwood. On the sofas, Rachel could see four throw pillows, ostensibly made of silk and with red, yellow and green Chinese embroidery on them. On the coffee table, tea was served and awaiting Rachel.

Rachel was totally honest describing herself as a private investigator who was hired to learn more about what she called the "indirect protagonist" in the BCAL case. In reply to Sew Lin's question as to what she really needed to know, Rachel simply said:

"The truth is that I know very little. So, I'm not even sure what I need to know. However, I will say that what I want to know is simply how each of the four partners came to the point where they worked together and how that fit with their prior lives."

Sew Lin joked:

"You want to write my biography?"

But smiling broadly, she immediately added:

"Don't be offended. I am just like you, Rachel. I am not very sure what the issue is. Michael has told me that someone has leaked some of the secrets of the invention which led to the formation of BACL. He seemed to feel that it's a real problem, though he tried to reassure me, arguing that it should not decrease the value of his stake in the company. Now, between you and me, that does not bother me; we have more than what we need, and I do not see what I'd do with much more."

Rachel noted her reply. She wondered whether it was meant to reinforce the fact that they were wealthy and was to be credited back to some form of ostentation, or much more simply a true statement. She asked:

"Can you help me understand what happened to the two of you ever since you met? How did you get from Singapore to Boston?"

"First of all, it is not us two, but us four. Michael and I have two children. The first, John, was born just before we left Singapore, but he does not remember his early life there. He was too young when we moved back to Australia. The second, Ann, was born while we lived in Broome, a port and beach city on the Northwest coast of Western Australia."

"Congratulations."

"Thanks. Both now have memories of Singapore, but these were gained through our annual trips. I wanted them to know my family and, in particular, the family of my older brother. The Liok family has done a number of good things there and I wanted the children to be proud of their heritage, just as they are rightly proud of the Lennons."

"How did you get to meet Michael?"

"A classic blind date organized by a friend of mine. Not unusual in Singapore. We went out with another couple, that friend and her date. We had some good food and a few drinks. That's when I learned that Michael had spent a few years travelling and, let's be honest, goofing off in Bali and Thailand."

With a wide charming smile, she added:

"I guess in America you call this 'sowing his wild oats.'"

Rachel asked:

"Why was he in Singapore?"

Sew Lin explained that he told her that he had decided that he needed "to grow up" as she put it. He was in the Republic as a tourist as he could not work nor study quite yet. Looking at Rachel, she added:

"He was just on a tourist visa. He had applied for a student visa and was planning to continue his research work and earn a PhD in fluid mechanics."

Rachel insisted:

"Wasn't that a big change?"

"It was. But he has always told me that he simply got tired of the easy life. My own view, frankly, is that he was running out of money, probably because his parents did not want to subsidize a nomad's life of partying and debauchery. They were happy, I guess, to let him goof off like many of his mates for a while, but then, at some point, he had to come down to earth. He does not like to discuss the transition and I am not one to prod unless it is important."

"Makes sense. Did you ever ask his parents?"

"Never had an opportunity. Very early in our marriage, we surely had other things on our minds. I didn't think of the question then to be frank. You know, you are in love. Also, I tend to think I would have been more inquisitive if it has been the other way: kind of going from good to 'bad.' Anyway, early on, we would meet with them twice a year or so, but those were short stays for either of us. Then, I spent a bit more time with his mother at his father's funeral, but that's not the time when you ask these kinds of questions. And by the time we could have discussed it, they were no longer with us."

"I'm sorry. Any foul play?"

"You would have to ask the question, Rachel, wouldn't you?"

She smiled modestly at her own joke revealing perfect teeth and continued:

"No, his father was quite a bit older than his mother. He passed away in his mid-seventies. His mother died of a heart attack in her early sixties, a couple of years later. Have always thought she missed him too much."

"That's never fun. So, back to Michael at the start of his Singapore stay. He eventually received his visa to study in Singapore, I guess . . ."

"He did and immediately started working on his PhD, though I had to push him a bit."

Seeing the quizzical look on Rachel's face, she explained:

"He wanted to take just one or two classes. You know, when you stop studying and get into the real world, fake or not I should add, it's at times hard to adjust to being a student again."

She paused and added:

"Anyway, he did adjust and graduated with such praises, particularly for the research he did for his thesis, that he was offered a job as a research assistant."

"Very impressive."

"Well, I should rephrase it. He had gotten a job as a research assistant and teacher as most post graduate students do about eighteen months before defending his thesis. And he got to keep it."

"So what did he do?"

"He had kind of made a reputation for himself in an arcane corner of fluid dynamics and kept developing it."

"What was it?"

"Hydrodynamics, or the study of liquids in motion. I think he was looking at differential viscosity. But don't ask me what that is."

"I won't. Beats me too. So, why did he leave Singapore? Why did you leave Singapore?"

"Well, there were a few reasons. The main one was that being a research assistant was not a career for Michael. We had to accept that his field was a bit too narrow for Singapore and we concluded that there would be more opportunities in Australia."

"Was that all?"

"Well, let me turn around and ask you a question. . . . Are you aware of my activities during the last five years I lived in Singapore?"

"I'm not sure I know the whole thing. The one thing that they shared with me was that you were helping the government identify spy recruiters among the students."

"Good. That's all I needed to know. Well, at the time, particularly early on, Michael was being pursued by one such individual. Initially, I could not prove that he was a Chinese recruiter, but the guy's behavior was odd, to say the least."

"How so?"

Sew Lin went on to explain how Michael's Chinese friend, Hang, would be asking questions that were becoming quite pointed. She mentioned that, at the outset, Michael had a great time with him because he was quite nice and had money. That allowed Michael to live a bit better than on his meager student budget, particularly in terms of going out. She added that they were not married at that time, and with a smile said:

"And in Singapore, there are things which you don't do until you're married."

Rachel smiled back and nodded that she understood. Sew Lin continued her story saying that Michael's friend was asking bibliographic questions, explaining:

"He was asking for the main reference publications in Michael's field and Michael was happy to oblige."

"Was the fellow a student?"

"No, he worked at the Chinese Embassy."

"Did that surprise you?"

"Well, up to a point, yes. But in the end not really. Michael kept telling me that the questions were innocuous. And remember, the use of the Internet was embryonic at best then. No such thing as Google or Siri to answer all your questions. So, I tended to think of the guy as someone maybe a bit lazy. He had found someone who could spare him time in the library."

"But at one point it changed, right?"

"Yes. The questions became narrower and much more specific. He was even asking for information which Michael one day simply did not think he could provide without running afoul of the university rules."

"Did he think he was asked to be a spy?"

"Michael and I had never discussed that in those terms. But the turning point was shortly after he refused to provide something that his friend badly wanted. The fellow called him at home, and then again in the middle of the night. He was threatening him."

"With what?"

"Well, he is the one who in effect stated that some of what Michael had done was spying for him and for the benefit of China. He threatened to expose him."

"Oh My."

"Indeed. Now, by the way, that gave me whatever I needed to expose him—Michael's friend. The government caught him trying to recruit someone else and he was asked to leave soon after that. Anyway, back to our move. We had had our first child a few months earlier. So, I pushed for us to leave."

"Why? There was no longer any risk from the Chinese side, was there?"

"Well, I'm not so sure. You know, I've seen quite a few of these student-spies or even diplomat-spies. Who knows whether or not there would be someone taking over from Hang?"

"Hang?"

"The Chinese diplomat."

"Sure, how dumb of me."

"No worries. I came up with the idea of him applying for professor or assistant professor jobs at the leading universities in Australia. That's when the position in Broome came up. Imagine that: wonderful climate, relatively low cost of living, the northwest coast of Australia which would be no more than four hours or so from Singapore. It seemed like a godsend. With the help of my family's money, we found it easy to create a wonderful life for ourselves."

"Many thanks. That's quite interesting. Any further news of his friend? What was his full name by the way?"

"I'm not 100% sure. I only remember his last name distinctly. Right now, I can't think of his other names. I could probably check my files if that's crucial."

She raised her eyes and looked at Rachel, who simply replied:

"Not right now, thank you. Any further news from him?"

"No, he disappeared from the radar. I don't think Michael has heard from him since."

Rachel thanked Sew Lin and asked if they could take a short pause. Sew Lin offered to refresh Rachel's cup of tea, while Rachel excused herself to use the restroom.

Rachel shifted the conversation to the move to the U.S. She asked when they moved from Broome to the U.S. Sew Lin corrected her, pointing to the fact that Michael had in the meantime been promoted to full professor at the university's headquarters in Fremantle. Rachel wondered:

"Is that why you moved from Broome?"

"Absolutely. We were getting closer to Michael's family, and we were still not terribly far from mine. Unfortunately, that's when, within a couple of years, we had lost both of his parents."

"Is that what made you want to move?"

"Not really. Michael has a brother with a nice wife and three children. We saw quite a bit of them. Wonderful people, great fun."

Now, she added with a bright smile and some pride in her voice that Michael's career had been progressing quite nicely:

"He had really started to make a name for himself. He was noticed once, at a conference in the U.S., by Frank Lord, you know, the head of the Department at MIT. He invited Michael to visit him, which Michael did a couple of times solo, and once with me and the children as it was at the time of school holidays in Australia. Eventually, it led to an unexpected offer for Michael to join MIT as a full professor. This was an opportunity which he could not turn down."

She explained that, at the time, they were unsure as to whether the move was permanent or would be followed by some return to Australia, adding:

"He was quite careful not to burn any bridge at the Notre Dame University of Australia. In fact, technically, he is still today on an extended leave of absence. He could return at any time."

"Would you like that?"

"Not sure. I miss Australia and Singapore, but I have to concede that life in the Greater Boston area is quite pleasant."

She paused and added:

"Except for the winters. I could do with less snow."

Rachel could see that Sew Lin was getting a bit weary with the questions and, on her end, she had started to run out of topics, although there was still one crucial area that had to be explored. She asked how things were at MIT and whether Michael was giving any sign of not being happy. Sew Lin appeared a bit surprised, saying:

"Things are great. And, with the move to the new company . . . , how could they be better."

"Has Michael talked of their great invention?"

Sew lin replied with some pride:

"Well, of course, he has. But I must confess that I am not a real techie. My focus has always been business administration in general and finances in particular. So, quite quickly, his stuff started flying straight through to Rodney Marsh . . ."

"Excuse me . . . What do you mean?"

"Oh. Sorry, Rachel. Rod Marsh was an Australian cricketer. He played for the national team as the wicket keeper, you know, the guy who stands behind the wicket."

"Don't know much about cricket . . . In America, you know?"

"Well, anyway, the phrase "straight through to Rodney Marsh" refers to when the ball is thrown so well that the batsman lets it go straight to the wicket keeper rather than attempt to hit it. It's an Australian way of saying "Went over his head" or in this case my head."

"Now, that makes sense. You learn something new every day. So, you really never knew much of the invention, but must have appreciated his success."

With somewhat of a surprised look on her face, Sew Lin replied:

"Any good wife would. I even went as far as reading a couple of published pieces but had a really tough time finishing them."

"And no sign of Hang or whatever was his friend's name."

"None and quite frankly, I am not surprised. As I said earlier, I know that he was expelled from Singapore. You have to assume that he is on the blacklist for any diplomatic position in the developed world, though time passes and memories fade."

Rachel stood up and thanked Sew Lin profusely. She apologized for having taken too much of her time. Sew Lin smiled and said that she hoped everything could quickly be clarified and was therefore prepared to help as much as she could, adding, almost in a fatalistic tone:

"I hope we can put this behind us. Let's find whoever the spy is and let's all of us resume our life. It's been a bit stressful, and I can see the stress in Michael. He does not need it, as he already has higher-than-normal blood pressure."

■ ■ ■ ■ ■

Rachel reported her findings to Countess Renate, Joel, Simon, Jack and Mark. They were all quite complimentary. Countess Renate asked whether it would be possible to check some of her insights with Xi Shi Tsu, who should be able to fill in many blanks. Jack jumped on the question:

"Countess, please do not take this the wrong way. But I would prefer if we could keep the four partners in a state where they do not know all we know about them and their colleagues."

"Jack are you still suspecting Shi Tsu?"

"Well, in truth, I have to, Countess. Clearly, you vouch for him and that is worth a lot. But, what if?"

He could not finish before Countess Renate interrupted:

"I understand, Jack. You've got to keep an open mind. I'd do the same thing."

Simon returned to Rachel's report and asked her what her intuition told her. Rachel was a bit surprised by the question. She thought for a few seconds and then responded:

"Well, Simon, you know that in this job you have to keep an open mind. You're supposed to let the facts drive you to the right conclusion. Right?"

"Sorry. I understand. Yet, where is your mind at this point and is it subject to change?"

Rachel replied that she had been quite favorably impressed by Sew Lin. She said that she found her quite forthcoming and never embarrassed, adding:

"If there was anything that embarrassed her, it had to be that I took more than two hours of her time."

Returning to her flow, she argued that there was something odd in Michael's behavior, but she could not put her finger on it. She conceded that she understood the cultural trait which brings many Australian university graduates to postpone their entry in the workforce. She noted that Thailand in particular had a terrible reputation for the use of drugs and for sexual promiscuity. At the same time, she said that she was surprised that Michael would appear to be switching from one lifestyle to another that quickly, adding:

"I'd like to know more on that sudden shift. Sew Lin's suspicion that he was running out of money makes sense. But could there be something else we are missing? Also, the relationship with his Chinese friend seems odd. I get the idea of having someone to drink with. I get that the Chinese guy was probably cultivating him as a spy. But how could he not realize what was going on . . . that he was being used? He's a smart guy, right?"

"What are you saying, Rachel?"

"Well, I don't know how we could find out, but I fear we're missing something on him. I wonder whether something happened to him, Michael, while in Bali or in Thailand. Something which made him change. A nasty love affair which saw him dumped? A close brush with the law? Remember, Southeast Asia is quite tough on drug addicts and drug traffickers? Did he come close to a drug trafficker? Do you have any way of investigating?"

They all looked at each other, though they were not sitting in the same space, but sharing a video conference application. Rachel had come up with what could be a perfectly logical hypothesis, but they all instinctively realized that the only way they could find out more would be if Michael had been arrested for some offense. Jack added:

"Unless he was arrested for something, in which case there might be some record, I don't know how we could find out."

"Wait, Jack, the time frame tells us that if he spent any time in jail it had to be quite short, correct?"

Jack thought for a second and added:

"Right. Also, I think there's more: we all know how careful the Singaporeans are with granting any visa. Would anyone think they would have given a student visa to someone who had some arrestation or jail time record?"

Countess Renate let go of a short laugh and said:

"I think we need to ask. But I agree; I find the idea of jail time a bit preposterous. So, my guess is that we probably need either to uncover some critical evidence, possibly during their stay in Australia, or to conclude that Michael Lennon and his wife are in the clear."

Simon agreed with Countess Renate's judgment, though he rushed to add:

"Insufficient evidence to prove guilt at this point is about as far as I could go now."

CHAPTER.26

Jack had called a meeting from his own office to discuss with Countess Renate, Simon, Mark and Joel the results of their search for the names of Chinese individuals expelled from Singapore as per the list provided by Yeo Yap Min. Countess Renate suggested that Wong Hai Chock should join the meeting from Singapore. Jack was initially surprised:

"Countess, I have nothing against Hai Chock, but why do you think we need him?"

"Two reasons, Jack. First, he is from Singapore and can liaise with Yap Min much more easily than any one of us. Second, he has the download of all the emails on the BACL server, remember?"

Simon interrupted:

"Let's look at this from the opposite point of view: Jack any reason not to have him?"

"Not really. So, OK, Fine. Countess, can you conference him into this call?"

"Sure."

Within a minute or so, Hai Chock had joined the call. One could easily tell that it was late in Singapore, as Hai Chock was definitely looking as if he was winding down his day. Countess Renate carried out the necessary introductions. Jack started by reminding everyone that Yeo Yap Min had provided Rachel with a list of seven names of suspected Chinese spies or spy-recruiters who had been expelled from Singapore in part because of the work of Sew Lin Lennon. He added:

"I've sent the list of names to all of you. Remember something I've just learned: a Chinese name typically has three characters. The first character is the family name, the middle one is a name for all the children of the same generation and the last character is the specific first name of the individual. Occasionally, they invert the order of the second and third names but that's rare."

Everyone on the list smiled and nodded, as the comment by Jack was not really needed: they all knew how the naming conventions worked in Chinese, though, in fact, most did not know of the existence of the "generation name." Jack did not notice anything and went on:

"The good news is that through the work of all of the members of this group we have been able to trace five of these people. In fact, three of those are currently in the U.S. as Chinese diplomats, one is in Bern, Switzerland, and the last one in London, also as diplomats. The bad news is that we found no trace of the last two, and, as you can see, Hang Le Zhao is one of these two."

Simon asked:

"Is that such a surprise? In fact, I am delighted that we were able to trace five of them . . . I know this does not help for this particular mission, but why would these people not change their names anyway?"

Hai Chock immediately reacted; he looked quite excited:

"Does anyone have a copy of the original list, with the names written in Chinese rather than in English?"

"What's on your mind?"

"Well, Countess, remember that, in Chinese, a character can be pronounced and thus spelled in English in more than one way . . ."

Jack interrupted:

"Hai Chock, you just earned more than your keep. Great comment. Let me look in the files."

Hai Chock suggested that a simple solution would be for him to call Yap Min in the morning and ask for the list. I am sure he has it in English and in Chinese. Jack replied:

"Great idea. Can we regroup tomorrow evening your time?"

■ ■ ■ ■ ■

As planned, the group got back together the following evening. Hai Chock brandished the sheet of paper with the seven names in both English and Chinese characters. He added:

"Here you go. By the way, I can come up with at least one or two phonetic variations for each of the names . . ."

Simon piped in:

"For example, Hai Chock, what about Hang Le Zhao? What could be the variations you could think of?"

"Well, Simon, all three characters have at least two meanings and one has three: Hang can also be read as Xing. Similarly, Le can be read as Liao, and Zhao can be read as Zhe or Zhuo. So, you can imagine the permutations."

"Great. Let me ask you the reverse question: Is it possible that the names for which we have found matches could turn out to correspond to other people?"

"Unfortunately, that is also true. You'd have to do some deeper analysis."

Jack concluded:

"I can't debate this. But I don't know it is crucial at this point. Do you agree, Simon?"

"Yes. No problem. Is that OK with you as well, Countess?"

"Absolutely."

Simon concluded:

"So, Hai Chock has given us permutations for Hang's name. I guess we should look for Hang Liao Zhao, Hang Le Zhe, Hang Le Zhuo, Xing Le Zhe, Xing Liao Yin and all the others. Do we agree?"

■ ■ ■ ■ ■

"Simon, Jack here."

"What's up?

"You won't believe it, but there is a Xing Liao Zhe in Washington, DC."

"Really?"

"Yes, sir. He is a military attaché at the Chinese Embassy."

"Well, well, well. We know what we need to do now, don't we?"

■ ■ ■ ■ ■

Rachel called Sew Lin back. She asked if they could get together for a few minutes. Sew Lin offered her home as a meeting place.

"Sew Lin, do you recognize this person?"

"That's Hang, whatever his full name was? Where did you find it?"

"In the diplomatic immigration files. This gentleman is not Hang, but Xing Liao Zhe and he works as a military attaché at the Chinese Embassy in Washington."

Sew Lin sat down in the sofa and started crying. Rachel came closer and sat in the armchair next to the sofa. She asked:

"What's wrong?"

In between sobs, Sew Lin said that she was scared to death. As a Chinese speaker herself, she noted that Xing and Hang could be written with the same Chinese character. She explained that it could well mean that Xing followed them to keep threatening her husband changing his name to avoid any trace that he might have picked up through his being declared *persona non grata* in Singapore. Yet, in less than a minute, she was back to her usual self, charming and calm:

"But Michael did not say anything. Maybe it's just a coincidence."

Rachel simply said in as comforting a voice as she could:

"I wouldn't worry at this point. Would you still like me to talk to the FBI to seek some protection for you and Michael?"

∎ ∎ ∎ ∎ ∎

"Hai Chock?"

"Yes, Countess?"

"I'm sure you still have the email files from the BACL server; correct?"

"Absolutely."

"Could you please look and see if there are emails from Michael or Sew Lin Lennon to Xing Liao Zhe, or vice versa?"

"Call you back in a half hour."

Within less than a half hour, Hai Chock was back on the phone to Countess Renate:

"Bingo. Quite a few. Who else has the whole file?"

"I sent it to Jack Turnbull a few weeks ago."

"Great. I much prefer for them to go look into these emails. Thanks. Bye."

∎ ∎ ∎ ∎ ∎

Rachel had been asked to interview Shi Tsu, his wife, Xi Chun Hua, as well as Ng Ho Lim. She was accompanied by Mark, although she had originally said she preferred to operate alone. However, Simon was intransigent, arguing that the risk of having her briefed on everything was certainly too great. He therefore needed someone who had the whole story to attend. They eventually compromised and allowed Rachel to meet with Chun Hua by herself, while Mark attended the other two conversations.

Rachel reported that the interview with Ho Lim had been a bit frustrating, because there were ostensibly a number of pieces that seemed to be missing. She knew that he had confessed to having started his job as a spy and then changed his mind. He had been placed under surveillance by the FBI, for his protection. He was able to continue to work effectively, though he principally used video conferencing to communicate with his colleagues. Yet, he did need from time to time to go to the office; there was no way some of the equipment he used for test could be relocated to his "office away from the office." When he had to go to the actual office, he was always accompanied by a couple of guardian angels whose job it was to make sure that nothing happened to him. The idea of relocating him to Tel Aviv for some time had been discussed, but very quickly rejected as too impractical.

The problem, in Rachel's mind, is that there was much too little to prove that Ho Lim had actually switched his allegiance. Surveillance by his guardian angels and electronically definitely did not pick up any contact, in person, by telephone or through cyberspace. While on the surface that would have seemed to be sufficient, Rachel, correctly argued that it was not:

"If the whole point of his switch was to become a double agent, wouldn't you expect him to lay low for some time. He should go dormant until the current issue is settled."

She went even further, in a direction which no one, not even Simon, had anticipated:

"What if he was the one charged with the execution of anyone who betrays his or her allegiance to China?"

The issue immediately caused a flurry of activity in *Mossad* and the FBI. Questions arose from everywhere: "What if Rachel was right?" "How can we protect the other partners and their wives or families?" "What if his mission included sabotage?"

■ ■ ■ ■ ■

The twin interviews with Shi Tsu and his wife were considerably less challenging. The strong support granted to Shi Tsu by Countess Renate was ostensibly a major factor. Rachel had the perfect opportunity to contrast the way Xi Chun Hua had organized their private lives and that which was chosen by Sew Lin Lennon. Though their house, in the same general area as the Lennons, was quite nice and probably equally expensive, the inside of the house decorated by Chun Hua was a tasteful mix of oriental and old New England styles. Knowledgeable individuals might figure out that numerous pieces of furniture or decorative elements were in fact of very high quality and quite old; yet the average guest would most likely not notice. It was almost as if Chun Hua had done everything so that her house was comfortable, nicely decorated but simultaneously totally inconspicuous and unobtrusive.

After obtaining the appropriate warrant, Jack had asked a friend to look into the laundry business. Everything added up. There was indeed here or there the odd skirmish, but those are usual in these kinds of businesses. However, if there was a link to organized crime, it was exceptionally well hidden.

Rachel found all answers totally plausible, helped in no small way by the long time which the family had spent in the U.S. in general and the Boston area in particular. Everything seemed to connect appropriately with everything else. Mark could only concur. Shi Tsu was ostensibly quite a brilliant man and Mark did not start the game of trying to trip him. But he was able to ask enough questions on his relationship with Frank Lord to conclude that Shi Tsu was the most modest of the two but could well be the smartest. Rachel had been able to look into his history, as well as those of Frank and Michael, at MIT; nothing other than reports of early escapades with younger lady students for Frank did come up.

■ ■ ■ ■ ■

Countess Renate conferenced Jack and Simon to give them the

update from Hai Chock. They were amazed that she was able to find out everything so quickly. Simon spoke up:

"Jack, can you have someone look through what you have?"

"Sure. I will need a warrant, but that should not be terribly hard. I'm also going to ask for a warrant to see any email on any home server he has."

■ ■ ■ ■ ■

"Michael, we need to talk."

The meeting he was having, in person, with Simon had been suggested so that Simon could form his own opinions. In fact, his goal was to confront Michael with some of the information the team had developed. Simon knew that there was nothing that would stand up in a court of law, but he was trying to decide whether Michael was a true spy, or someone who did something stupid that was forcing him to skirt the law.

"Michael, we have looked at the four partners and their spouses in our bid to uncover where the leak might be coming from. Is there anything that you can help us with?"

Michael looked down and was ostensibly deep in thoughts. Yet, he did not reply to Simon's first question. Simon pushed a bit further:

"Michael, are you under some undue pressure?"

Suddenly, Michael surprised Simon. He blurted out:

"I need protection. I need protection. Can you help me?"

"We'll see. Protection against what?"

"Someone knows something about my past and has been threatening me."

"Michael, how about this? You tell me in total confidence what the problem is, and I'll see how I can help you."

"I'd love to, but how can I be sure?"

"I do not represent any U.S. entity. You know that."

"Hope I will never live to regret it!"

EPILOGUE

TEL AVIV, ISRAEL

Unfortunately, the story which I just felt I needed to tell did not finish too well.

Firstly, I did not retire. It's probably quite ironic, but the moment I had made the decision to retire and arranged my succession in order to spend more time with my wife, Golda, and our children and grandchildren, she experienced a massive stroke, which, this time, sadly ended her life. I am still heartbroken, though it was quite comforting to see so many of my colleagues at her funeral the day after she died; some of you may not know that, in our culture, we bury the dead as soon as possible. While the many politicians who were there, as well as a number of individuals from *Mossad*, were certainly most welcome and a great help, the greatest help came from the presence of both Simon and his wife Jennifer. They knew that Simon was in line to have my job, I had told him and the Prime Minister himself, had offered the job, which he had accepted. He had been told that the wheels had been put in motion for him to be promoted to the rank of Brigadier General, the first of two levels in the General Officers ranks in Israel, leaving aside the *Rav Aluf,* (the only member of the armed forces with the title of Lieutenant General).

Simon and I subsequently had a conversation during which he convinced me that I should stay in my position for the time being. He specifically argued that it would surely keep my mind occupied and would allow him to understudy me more directly. I was amazed that he would be prepared to step, however momentarily, away from the two promotions. Yet, it made it even more obvious to me, if it was ever necessary, that Simon was the right man. My long-term belief that the more someone wants a higher job the more likely they are to not be qualified enough was resonating in my brain.

The Prime Minister agreed to name Simon Deputy Director of *Mossad*, while retaining his earlier responsibilities, on the condition that he should appoint someone as Deputy Director of his group, Disruption, as well. David Heller did get the nod and I feel quite gratified that the untimely and sad demise of my late wife will have at least had one great positive influence: it will have allowed us to orchestrate with much greater care succession at the top of our agency.

■ ■ ■ ■ ■

As I am sure will surprise no one, our formal complaint against China and Iran at the United Nations, more specifically at the Security Council, went absolutely nowhere. Yet, we had the satisfaction of showing to the world the transshipments of weapons by both the Chinese and the Iranians on a boat that was known to belong to Hezbollah. Despite these videos, which I should add were quite clear, the Security Council could not overcome the expected veto from China, which was joined by Russia. Thankfully, the other permanent members voted with us, as did Ireland and Norway among the non-permanent members. All other non-permanent members abstained, but, in many ways, who could blame them? They knew that China's veto was inevitable. Why then take the risk of upsetting China when there was nothing for them to gain.

■ ■ ■ ■ ■

We were able to verify that we had indeed picked up all the submarine drones. We cannot but feel grateful that we were so lucky to pick up the first Palestinian drop. We could have just as easily only stumbled on the scheme with the last drop off; imagine. We would have missed the whole sequence of events and would have had to live under quite unpleasant a menace. We have had to suffer further unprovoked attacks by Palestinian forces both north, in Lebanon, and south, in Gaza. Each time, we used one of the captured submarine drones and a couple of Iranian missiles to retaliate. In the end, I am pretty sure that the Palestinians of Hezbollah figured out that we were the ones firing the missiles. However, to this day, I am equally sure that they do not know from where we were firing. I keep enjoying the irony of the fact that we were shooting at Hezbollah targets in Southern Lebanon, and in one case at a Hamas target in Gaza, using missiles provided to us by their greatest international supporter.

Yet, I remain convinced that, however difficult on the political front, we will need to find a way to deal with the fact that the vast majority of Palestinians are potential friends of Israel. I know that of those who work in our country, of the nearly 20% Arabs who are Israeli citizens, very few are ready to follow the terrorists. At the same time, how difficult must it be for each of these individuals to look as if they support Israel: terrorism is a disease which relies on totalitarian means to secure the allegiance of people. We, Israel, need to do a better job in the education of all our citizens, whether they are Jews or not. We must find ways to work more closely with the Arab or Muslim part of our population: we should find a way to enlist them to our general cause. Then and only then will there be a reason for them to take the risk to support us against the terrorists.

■ ■ ■ ■ ■

I must also report that we have not been able, at least so far, to get anything done on the drug trafficking front. It is frustrating to see that the drug trade, in our region, as well as sadly worldwide is often used to support other illegal activities. Cutting off that source of funding for Hezbollah or any other group like them, would absolutely be a great victory. Yet, we have no jurisdiction in the ports of the Red Sea or the Gulf of Aden where we know that transshipments take place. We informed whomever we felt we should. But catching a boat carrying drugs on the Red Sea or in the Gulf of Aden is literally equivalent to finding the proverbial needle in a haystack.

■ ■ ■ ■ ■

Together with Countess Renate's Shadow Experts and the U.S. authorities, we were able to identify the source of the leaks which made it possible for China to develop the transmitters that allowed communications across the air/water barrier. He confessed to Simon.

In turns out that the real spy was Michael Lennon. Jack and Mary Lord were totally exonerated as we already know, as were Xi Shi Tsu, his wife and Ng Ho Lim on whom, at some point, some amount of suspicion has existed. Michael Lennon's story is a lot more complex than any of us thought. It so happens that a part of it was also news to his wife, who though looking for Chinese recruiters while she was still in Singapore had not caught up with the fact that her own husband was being drawn into the spy-web.

After earning his first university degree in Australia, Michael, as we all had believed, did travel within Southeast Asia, as quite a number of his compatriots did. The attraction of Bali in Indonesia, and Phuket and Pattaya in Thailand was always hard to resist. In particular, the somewhat loose morals in many beach towns in Thailand was a permanent magnet for young males. That several, non-professional, local women enjoyed partying and more with these good-looking foreigners certainly made that magnet ever more powerful.

We discovered, however, that, like many of his compatriots, Michael ended up running out of money. However, in contrast to the usual practice of young Australians to look for the odd job locally or return to Australia to earn some money and qualify for unemployment subsidies after a short while, Michael went in the wrong direction. He agreed to help and in effect participate in the drug trade. Yet, he was lucky. First, he was not intrigued, nor did he fall victim to Thailand's efforts to curb drug use. More importantly, he was never asked to participate in the shipment of drugs to either Indonesia, Malaysia or Singapore: this could have cost him his life, as drug traffickers are routinely executed when convicted in these three countries. His mission involved distributing drugs within Thailand, and even more narrowly within the expatriate community of Thailand.

Yet, one day, the proverbial "shot" came awfully close to him. Though he was not involved in the particular deal, one of the carriers from whom he received drugs got caught. Like Michael, he was supposed to stay within Thailand. Michael knew him well; they had shared a room at one point. However, he did not clean up his luggage sufficiently when he travelled for a short weekend to Penang, an island and idyllic tourist resort off the Northwest coast of Malaysia. He was caught there with more drugs than tolerable in his possession. He was quickly tried, convicted, sentenced to death and hanged. That it created a minor diplomatic rift between Malaysia and Australia was through newspaper stories a constant reminder to Michael of how close he had been.

He effectively decided, virtually right then and there, he told us, to stop all of his drug-related activities. He used his last few financial reserves, mostly Thai Bahts, to fly to Singapore. That is also when he decided to start work on his PhD at the National University of Singapore. He told us that his parents made that a condition of resuming some financial help. They were happy to see him doing "finally something intelligent." There, after a short while, he met

Sew Lin who eventually was going to be his wife, though they dated conservatively for a few months. The individual who introduced them turned out to be just a very nice friend of a friend, as is often the case.

The story could have finished at that point, but destiny did not want it that way. While at university, he met a fellow student who eventually introduced him to a friend of his who, he was told, was a junior consular attaché in the Chinese Embassy; his name was Hang Le Zhao. Now, Hang was charming and seemed to have materially deeper pockets than Michael, a useful trait for a young man who did not dislike some partying. Having noted that Michael did enjoy the odd beer, to be followed by several others before getting to harder liquor, Hang invited him for drinks a few times. On one of these occasions, Hang was very careful to appear to drink with him but avoided matching Michael beer for beer or shot for shot. Eventually, what had to happen happened: Michael was drunk and reminisced about his past. He confessed to his relationship with the individual who was caught and executed.

The next morning, having realized the stupidity of what he did the prior evening, he called Hang and asked him to keep the story totally secret. He was indeed afraid that Hang might reveal his past to the Singaporean authorities. While he would certainly not have been tried or worse convicted as a drug trafficker, his ability to keep studying in Singapore might have compromised. Plus, he was dating a beautiful Singaporean girl, but was not far enough along for the relationship to be officialized in any way. Add to that the risk that she would dump him if she found out, and the picture was a complete mess. Hang said he understood and promised to stay mum on the topic. He did ask him once or twice for the odd information on the work he was doing, but it all seemed innocuous. The questions became a bit more pointed when, after having earned his PhD, he took a job as a research assistant at NUS. He was surprised, but not terribly worried.

He did tell the story to his wife, but never revealed the part about the past exploits in the drug trade or the drunken talk that started the whole thing. Sew Lin was working with the Singapore Government to identify and root out Chinese spy recruiters. Michael could have made her task easier had he confessed at the time that he was being blackmailed. Yet, he fatefully withheld that information from her, He only mentioned that it looked as if his Chinese friend, Hang, was asking odd questions and even in a couple of instances putting some pressure on him. She did not push to find out why someone like Hang could pressure Michael; I bet that she was worried that he had done something terribly wrong in his post-Australian days and, at that point, did not really need to know. She made a note to ask later, but in fact never did.

When things heated up for Michael, and the spying angle became visible, she was the one that declared that they had to move away from Singapore. They had just had their first child. The excuse was perfect for Michael to seek a job in Australia and to start his teaching career. Sew Lin mentioned to Yeo Yap Min that Hang Le Zhao was suspect in her eyes. After a relatively short inquiry by Yap Min's office, Hang was expelled from Singapore. Somehow, I am told the Chinese Embassy did not raise major objections. My guess is that they were used to these activities and viewed the expulsions as the cost of "doing spy business in Singapore."

Eventually, Hang contacted Michael anew when he had been hired by MIT, and was in the U.S. He said that he might need some more information and told him to call him Xing. Yet, he threatened him and swore him to secrecy saying that he would immediately make the appropriate information public if Michael told his wife his new name or that he was now a military attaché in Washington. I cannot understand why Michael gave in to that blackmail. He had not disclosed his drug-related activity to anyone, but, then again, why should he have? He was never arrested. He was even never questioned. He was asked whether he used drugs and had taken drug tests; yet he could truthfully say that he did not use drugs and the tests always come out negative. One has to assume that it was all due to the burden of the guilt he felt at the eventual execution of someone he knew and worked with.

Despite the obvious reservations, Michael decided he was stuck and started passing some information to Hang, though it was pretty innocuous. He was surprised that certain questions were so precise and openly wondered how the Chinese could possibly know such details. Yet, he complied, though most of what he did was to identify actual published sources and pass these on. At best, he was serving as a research assistant to the Chinese. Unfortunately, as always is the case, some small insight leads to requests for deeper and broader insights, and when Adrian Lee returned to China and his successor Ng Ho Lim arrived, the requests started coming for blueprints. He tried to resist and rebel, but a surprising phone call to his home in the middle of the night made him reconsider.

The sad part in the story is that it did not take much to get Michael Lennon to talk. The moment he saw that we had most of the information we needed, he came out, offered a full confession and asked whether he could be granted protection. I am told he seemed almost relieved when he realized he was "caught." At this point, I do not know how these negotiations are going and whether he will find himself expelled from the U.S., convicted and jailed in the U.S. or accepted and effectively pardoned. My own view is that, if I could make sure he is sincere, he could well make a wonderful double agent. One thing is for sure: his last two "secret" communications with Xing passed along totally misleading information concocted with the help of his partners.

As for Xing Liao Zhao, alias Hang Le Zhao, he was expelled from the U.S. Unfortunately, and sadly, I am confident that he will someday resurface somewhere else to ply his well-worn trade.

Signed: A.L.